The European Union in Inter

Series Editors:
Sebastian Oberthür is a Pr

European Studies, Vrije Universiteit Brussels, Belgium. **Knud Erik Jørgensen** is a Professor in the Department of Political Science and Government, Aarhus University, Denmark. **Alex Warleigh-Lack*** is Executive Director of the Centre for Research on the European Matrix (CRONEM) and Professor of EU Politics at the University of Surrey, UK. **Sandra Lavenex** is Professor of International Politics at the University of Lucerne, Switzerland and Visiting Professor at the College of Europe in Natolin (Warsaw). **Philomena Murray** is Jean Monnet Professor in the School of Social and Political Sciences at the University of Melbourne, Australia.

Editorial board:
Stephanie Anderson; Ummu Salma Bava; Grainne de Burca; Maurizio Carbone; Roy H. Ginsberg; Amelia Hadfield; Stephan Keukeleire; Andrés Malamud; Sophie Meunier; Michael H. Smith; Ramses Wessel and Reuben Wong.

Thanks to consecutive rounds of enlargement and the stepwise broadening and deepening of internal integration, the EU now undeniably plays a key role in international politics, law and economics. At the same time, changes in the international system continue to pose new challenges to the EU. The range of policies implied by the EU's international 'actorness' grows with every summit, and the EU regularly 'imports' and increasingly 'exports' various policies.

Against this backdrop, this book series aims to be a central resource for the growing community of scholars and policy-makers interested in understanding the interface between the EU and international affairs. It will provide in-depth, cutting-edge contributions to research on the EU in international affairs by highlighting new developments, insights, challenges and opportunities. It will encompass analyses of the EU's international role, as mediated by its own Member States, in international institutions and in its strategic bilateral and regional partnerships. It will further examine the ongoing profusion of EU internal policies with external implications and the ways in which these are both driven by and feed back into international developments. Grounded in political science (and its various sub-disciplines, including International Relations and International Political Economy), law, sociology and history, the series reflects an inter-disciplinary commitment.

Titles include:

Laura Allison
THE EU, ASEAN AND INTERREGIONALISM
Regionalism Support and Norm Diffusion between the EU and ASEAN

Frauke Austermann
EUROPEAN UNION DELEGATIONS IN EU FOREIGN POLICY
A Diplomatic Service of Different Speeds

Dimitrios Bourantonis, Spyros Blavoukos and Clara Portela (*editors*)
THE EU AND THE NON-PROLIFERATION OF NUCLEAR WEAPONS

Joachim Koops and Gjovalin Macaj
THE EU AS A DIPLOMATIC ACTOR

Alexander Mattelaer
THE POLITICO-MILITARY DYNAMICS OF EUROPEAN CRISIS RESPONSE OPERATIONS
Planning, Friction, Strategy

Louise G. van Schaik
EU EFFECTIVENESS AND UNITY IN MULTILATERAL NEGOTIATIONS
More than the Sum of Its Parts?

Luis Simon
GEOPOLITICAL CHANGE, GRAND STRATEGY AND EUROPEAN SECURITY
The EU-Nato Conundrum

*Alex Warleigh-Lack, is currently on leave as an editor of the series

Institute for
European Studies
Vrije Universiteit Brussel

The European Union in International Affairs series.
Series standing order ISBN 978–1137–00500–7 (cased)
Series standing order ISBN 978–1137–00501–4 (paperback)

You can receive future titles in this series as they are published by placing a standing order. Please contact your bookseller or, in case of difficulty, write to us at the address below with your name and address, the title of the series and the ISBNs quoted above.

Customer Services Department, Macmillan Distribution Ltd, Houndmills, Basingstoke, Hampshire RG21 6XS, England

---

The EU, ASEAN and Interregionalism

Regionalism Support and Norm Diffusion between the EU and ASEAN

Laura Allison
Research Fellow, Public Policy and Global Affairs Programme,
Nanyang Technological University, Singapore

palgrave
macmillan

Softcover reprint of the hardcover 1st edition 2015 978-1-137-49479-5

First published 2015 by
PALGRAVE MACMILLAN

Palgrave Macmillan in the UK is an imprint of Macmillan Publishers Limited, registered in England, company number 785998, of Houndsmills, Basingstoke, Hampshire, RG21 6XS

Palgrave Macmillan in the US is a division of St Martin's Press LLC, 175 Fifth Avenue, New York, NY 10010.

Palgrave is the global academic imprint of the above companies and has companies and representatives throughout the world.

ISBN 978-1-349-50484-8 ISBN 978-1-137-49480-1 (eBook)
DOI 10.1057/9781137494801

A catalogue record for this book is available from the British Library.

Library of Congress Cataloging-in-Publication Data
Allison, Laura, 1980–
The EU, ASEAN and interregionalism : regionalism support and norm diffusion between the EU and ASEAN / Laura Allison.
pages cm.—(The European Union in international affairs)
1. Regionalism—European Union countries. 2. Interregionalism—European Union countries. 3. Regionalism—Southeast Asia. 4. Interregionalism—Southeast Asia. 5. European Union. 6. ASEAN. 7. European Union countries—Foreign relations—Southeast Asia. 8. Southeast Asia—Foreign relations—European Union countries. I. Title.
JN34.5.A48 2015
341.242'20959—dc23 2014036819

Typeset by MPS Limited, Chennai, India.

Contents

List of Figures and Tables

Figures

Table

Acknowledgements

I would not have been able to complete this book without the help of those around me. I am deeply grateful to Professor Philomena Murray and Dr Pradeep Taneja, both at the University of Melbourne, for their support and advice. Their comments and suggestions helped me tremendously.

Also, I would like to express my gratitude to the interview and survey participants who took the time to meet me for an interview or respond to the survey. Their information and insights proved invaluable and I appreciate the interest they took in my research.

During the research phase I presented this work at numerous international conferences where I received valuable and constructive comments and suggestions. These conferences have contributed greatly to this book and I am very grateful for such opportunities.

I would like to acknowledge my appreciation of the financial support I received from the Australian Government and the University of Melbourne during the research stages of this project, without which this project would not have been possible.

I would like to thank the editors at Palgrave Macmillan for their assistance and patience and would also like to thank the anonymous reviewers of my book who provided valuable feedback on my research.

I am also very thankful to my family. I would like to thank my parents, John and Jacqueline, my sister, Alexandra, and my brother, Ben, for their understanding, patience and encouragement. My thanks also go to my extended family, some of whom are sadly no longer here, who showed great confidence in me and offered much support. I would also like to say thank you to my fiancé, Andreas. I am deeply grateful for his love and understanding and I am very thankful for the support and patience he has showed.

Code for Interview and Survey Responses

Throughout the book, interview and survey responses will be coded as follows:

Interview respondents will be numbered I1, I2, I3.

Survey respondents will be numbered S1, S2, S3.

To indicate the position of the respondent, the following abbreviations will be used:

AO	ASEAN Official	EOA	EU Official in Southeast Asia
AA	Academic in Southeast Asia	OA	Academic in Oceania
EO	EU Official	EAA	Academic in East Asia
EA	Academic in the EU		

For the purposes of this book, and based on the locations of interview and survey respondents, Southeast Asia refers to the member states of ASEAN – Brunei Darussalam, Cambodia, Indonesia, Lao PDR, Malaysia, Myanmar, the Philippines, Singapore, Thailand and Vietnam. Oceania refers to Australia and New Zealand. East Asia refers to Japan, China and South Korea.

List of Acronyms and Abbreviations

AADMER	ASEAN Agreement on Disaster Management and Emergency Response
AATIP	ASEAN Air Transport Integration Project
ABMI	ASEAN Bond Market Initiative
ACC	ASEAN Coordinating Council
ACD	ASEAN Cosmetics Directive
ACDD	ASEAN Customs Declaration Document
ACIA	ASEAN Comprehensive Investment Agreement
ACP	African, Caribbean and Pacific Group of States
ACT	ASEAN Consultation to Solve Trade and Investment Issues
ACTLN	ASEAN Cosmetic Testing Laboratory Network
ACTS	ASEAN Customs Transit System
ACWC	ASEAN Commission on the Promotion and Protection of the Rights of Women and Children
AEC	ASEAN Economic Community
AEM-EU	ASEAN Economic Ministers and EU Trade Commissioner Meetings
AEMM	ASEAN-EU Ministerial Meetings
AFAS	ASEAN Framework Agreement on Services
AFC	Asian Financial Crisis
AFTA	ASEAN Free Trade Agreement
AHTN	ASEAN Harmonised Trade Nomenclature
AIA	ASEAN Investment Area
AICHR	ASEAN Intergovernmental Commission on Human Rights
AICO	ASEAN Industrial Cooperation
AIPA	ASEAN Inter-Parliamentary General Assembly

AIPMC	ASEAN Inter-Parliamentary Myanmar Caucus
AMM	ASEAN Ministerial Meeting
AcMM	Aceh Monitoring Mission
AMRO	ASEAN +3 Macroeconomic Research Office
APA	ASEAN People's Assembly
APAEC	ASEAN Plan of Action for Energy Cooperation
APAST	ASEAN Plan of Action on Science and Technology
APEC	Asia-Pacific Economic Cooperation
APRIS	ASEAN-EU Programme for Regional Integration Support
APT	ASEAN +3
APTA	ASEAN Preferential Trading Arrangement
ARF	ASEAN Regional Forum
ARISE	ASEAN Regional Integration Support by the EU
ASC	ASEAN Security Community
ASCC	ASEAN Socio-Cultural Community
ASEAN	Association of Southeast Asian Nations
ASEAN ISIS	ASEAN Institute of Strategic and International Studies
ASEF	Asia Europe Foundation
ASEM	Asia-Europe Meeting
ASP	ASEAN Surveillance Process
ATIGA	ASEAN Trade in Goods Agreement
BRICS	Brazil, Russia, India, China, South Africa
CAP	Common Agricultural Policy
CEN	European Committee for Standards
CENELEC	European Committee for Electrical Standards
CEPT	Common Effective Preferential Tariff
CFSP	Common Foreign and Security Policy
CITES	Convention on International Trade in Wild Flora and Fauna
CLMV	Cambodia, Lao PDR, Myanmar, Vietnam
CMI	Chiang Mai Initiative
CMIM	Chiang Mai Initiative Multilateralisation

COASI	The Asia-Oceania Working Party
COHOM	The Human Rights Working Group
COREPER	*Comité des représentants permanents* (Committee of Permanent Representatives)
CPR	Committee of Permanent Representatives
CSIS	Centre for Strategic and International Studies
CSO	civil society organisation
DG	Directorate General
EAS	East Asia Summit
EASCAB	EU-ASEAN Statistical Capacity Building Programme
EC	European Commission
ECAP III	ASEAN Project on the Protection of Intellectual Property Rights
ECHO	European Commission Humanitarian Office
ECHR	European Convention on Human Rights
ECI	European Citizens' Initiative
ECJ	European Court of Justice
ECSC	European Coal and Steel Community
EDSM	Enhanced ASEAN Dispute Settlement Mechanism
EEAS	European External Action Service
EEC	European Economic Community
EESC	European Economic and Social Committee
EIDHR	European Instrument for Democracy and Human Rights
EMU	Economic and Monetary Union
EP	European Parliament
EPC	European Political Cooperation
EPG	Eminent Persons Group
ERP	European Recovery Plan
ERT	European Roundtable of Industrialists
EU	European Union
FDI	Foreign direct investment
FRA	Fundamental Rights Agency

FTA	Free trade agreement
GAM	Gerakan Aceh Merdeka, Free Aceh Movement
GATT	General Agreement on Tariffs and Trade
GDP	Gross domestic product
GFC	Global Financial Crisis
GMP	Good Manufacturing Practice
GSP	Generalised System of Preferences
HLP	High Level Panel
IAI	Initiative for ASEAN Integration
ICT	Information and Communication Technology
IMF	International Monetary Fund
INTERFET	International Force for East Timor
JCC	ASEAN-EU Joint Cooperation Committee
Lao PDR	Lao People's Democratic Republic
LAWASIA	Law Association for Asia and the Pacific
MFN	Most favoured nation
MILF	Moro Islamic Liberation Front
NAFTA	North American Free Trade Agreement
NATO	North Atlantic Treaty Organisation
NGO	non-governmental organisation
NHRC	National Human Rights Commission
NLD	National League for Democracy
NTB	non-tariff barrier
OSCE	Organization for Security and Co-operation in Europe
PMC +1	ASEAN Post Ministerial Conference with the EU
QMV	qualified majority voting
READI	Regional EU-ASEAN Dialogue Instrument
SAARC	South Asian Association for Regional Cooperation
SEA	Single European Act
SEOM	Senior Economic Officials Meeting
SEOM-EU	ASEAN-EU Senior Economic Officials Consultation Meeting

SLIM	Simpler Legislation for the Internal Market
SPDC	State Peace and Development Council
STEER	Singapore-Thailand Enhanced Economic Relationship
TAC	Treaty of Amity and Cooperation
TEEC	Treaty Establishing the European Economic Community
TEU	Treaty on European Union
TFEU	Treaty on the Functioning of the European Union
TOR	Terms of Reference
TREATI	Trans-Regional EU-ASEAN Trade Initiative
UK	United Kingdom
UKABC	UK-ASEAN Business Council
UN	United Nations
UNFF	United Nations Forum on Forestry
UNUCRIS	United Nations University Institute on Comparative Regionalism Studies
US	United States
USD	United States Dollar
VAP	Vientiane Action Plan
WTO	World Trade Organization
ZOPFAN	Zone of Peace, Freedom and Neutrality

The idea at the heart of the European project is a simple one: create institutions and rules within which countries can conduct their business more effectively than through bullying and war-mongering – and other countries will seek to do the same. The success of European integration has stimulated the creation of many other regional projects, such as ASEAN and Mercosur. In my view, the EU's creation of a rules-based framework that is respected worldwide makes Europe a global actor.

Olli Rehn[1]

1 Ambitions of Actorness

> There is now a relationship between (the) European Union (EU) and South East Asia that is mature enough that we can be ambitious and it is time to move forward ... We support the centrality in the integration process of the Association of Southeast Asian Nations (ASEAN) and the wider region and for the EU that's a guarantee that these relations will remain open and inclusive.
>
> Catherine Ashton, former European Union High Representative for Foreign Affairs and Security Policy, opening of the EU-ASEAN post-ministerial conference, 2012.

> Today's Euro-crisis has dented the belief that regional integration is the way to go.
>
> Survey Respondent 16, EU delegation official in Southeast Asia, 2012.

The European Union's (EU's) ambition to be an international actor by promoting its regionalism experience to the Association of Southeast Asian Nations (ASEAN) is currently encountering significant challenges. Its ability to be an influential actor in international affairs, and particularly the notion that regional integration provides prosperity and security, have been queried by citizens and political parties within the EU's member states and also by many beyond its borders (Longo and Murray, 2011). This questioning of the advantages, and indeed the consequences, of European integration is largely a result of ongoing financial and economic crises presently inflicting the region. These crises have demonstrated that the EU has not been immune to economic and financial shocks and that systems of governance within the organisation must continue to evolve in order to manage such moments of crisis and potentially prevent similar occurrences in the future. The current debt crises in a number of EU member states demonstrate that, despite the EU's high level of economic integration, the fragility of individual member states' economies impacts on the functioning, solidarity and reliability of the EU and its ability to provide for its citizens.

Nevertheless, recent statements by EU officials have defended regionalism, despite the current challenges, and have reiterated the contribution regionalism can make to ensuring peace, stability and prosperity amongst European states (Barroso, 2012a). In addition, the European Commission and the Council of the EU continue to argue for the development of regional integration in other regions of the world, such as Southeast Asia, and include the promotion and support of regional integration in their foreign policies and statements. José Manuel Barroso, former President of the European Commission, expressed the importance the EU places on the continuous integration of ASEAN at a press conference following the 9th Asia-Europe Meeting (ASEM) Summit.

> Our region-to-region relations will be further facilitated if the regional integration process in Asia, through ASEAN, makes further strides. Open regionalism is indeed a basis for effective multilateralism. (Barroso, 2012a: 1)

A dichotomy currently exists between the EU's ability to include the promotion of regionalism beyond Europe into its external policies and the present challenges facing the EU. Gaens *et al.* (2012) have stated that the Global Financial Crisis (GFC) and subsequent debt crises in Europe have affected the EU's self-confidence. Whilst Gaens *et al.* (2012: 96) state that 'the debt crisis has discredited both the European integration model, in general, and monetary union, in particular', this has not weakened the EU's narrative of espousing regionalism as beneficial for other regions, as evident in the policy documents and guidelines released by the European Commission and Council of the EU (European Commission, 2003; Council of the EU, 2012a). Indeed, amidst turmoil within the EU, the message which continues to be sent out to the EU's interlocutors is that the integration experience of the EU was not only valuable to European nation states after World War II but is also of benefit to other regions with vastly different historical, political and economic contexts, such as ASEAN.

The crisis within Europe has presented another challenge to the EU's ability to promote regionalism beyond the European region. In addition to reassessing the value of European integration and the relevance of such an undertaking, concerns have also been raised by academics and ASEAN officials regarding the resources, both moral and material, which the EU can pledge to support the development of other regional organisations such as ASEAN (I1 AO, 2011; I3 AA, 2011). However, such apprehensions have not been realised because, in the context of the EU's current crisis, the EU has become even more determined to promote regionalism to ASEAN. This is evident by the fact that the programmes and funding which the EU has invested in to fulfil this aim have not ceased or been downscaled.

In the face of crisis, the EU has not wavered from its position of supporting ASEAN's regional integration development yet as I will illustrate, its actorness in this regard has been limited. In addition to its internal crisis, the EU is also encountering a maturing ASEAN which is increasingly affirming its own role as a regional organisation and defending the political, economic and institutional norms to which it adheres and which do not always align with those of the EU, or those promoted by the EU to ASEAN. As this book shows, a determined and resolute ASEAN has affected the EU's ability to exert its actorness on its own terms and through its own policy choices in Southeast Asia.

The concept of actorness, as analysed in-depth in Chapter 2, involves determining if an actor such as the EU has the capacity to transform an environment (Lucarelli, 2007). Actorness is only realised, however, if the actor and its interlocutors both perceive it to have the responsibility and ability to do so, and once this is determined, the actor utilises its resources effectively to ensure that its aims are achieved (Lucarelli, 2007; Wunderlich, 2012).

Actorness is the focus of this book for several reasons. Firstly, when considering similar and overlapping concepts related to foreign policy such as presence, influence and power, actorness is the most comprehensive and precise concept. As will be discussed in Chapter 2, presence and influence have been included as components of actorness and therefore contribute to its analytical framework. Niemann and Bretherton (2013: 266) explain that presence is 'a passive concept that is manifested both directly, through the unintended external consequences of internal policies and indirectly, through the subtle processes of structural power associated with perceptions of the EU's reputation'. Allen and Smith (1990) focus on presence as opposed to actorness, however in this book, similar to Wunderlich (2012), I include presence as a criterion for actorness, enabling the analysis to be broadened to include the role of both actors under examination, the EU and ASEAN, and the expectations and perceptions of these actors, as emphasised by Allen and Smith (1990).

Secondly, in keeping with Jupille and Caporaso's definition of actorness, the 'capacity to act' (1998: 214) and Sjöstedt's definition whereby actorness refers to functioning 'actively and deliberately in relation to other actors in the international system' (1977: 16), presence is distinct from, and a contributing factor to, actorness. I consider influence, on the other hand, to focus too heavily on the recipient of actorness as opposed to the agent to be deemed the central framework for analysis in this book. In addition, Groen and Niemann (2012) consider influence not to be a component of actorness, but rather that actorness can enable influence to occur. How ASEAN is influenced by the EU is certainly a consideration within this book, yet of primary concern are the perceptions and reactions to the EU's attempts to be an international actor with regard to its relations with ASEAN, enabling actorness to be the primary and preferred concept.

Finally, power focuses more on the agent than the recipient of any power exertions. Also, it often presupposes an asymmetrical relationship between two actors before the nature of the relationship has been ascertained. Power can be a useful frame of analysis to examine actors in the international arena; however, in this book, I also aim to incorporate a significant amount of analysis of the recipient of the EU's external policies, ASEAN, and therefore have preferred actorness as my frame of assessment. Niemann and Bretherton (2013) have argued for literature on EU external action to step back from the 'what type of EU power' debates which have been the focus of much analysis in recent years. The civilian and normative power concepts which have emerged in relation to the EU have, according to Niemann and Bretherton (2013), often been built on the assumption that the EU possesses enough actorness to exert these forms of power. As the many studies which have attempted to apply the concept of normative power to the EU have often produced disappointing findings regarding the EU's normativity, Niemann and Bretherton (2013) suggest that EU actorness should first be analysed before conceptualisations and investigations related to power be carried out.

Summarily, actorness is the chosen concept for analysis in this book as it is considered central to the realisation of foreign policy aims and external relations of the EU. This is because it enables an examination of the EU's ability to act, its presence and the perceptions of the EU in Southeast Asia.

In the context of EU-ASEAN relations, the EU's actorness has not matched its level of determination. This is primarily because ASEAN judiciously appraises whether EU integration norms are relevant to ASEAN and therefore determines the EU's capacity to be an actor. The data collected for this book through interviews and surveys has revealed that ASEAN is content with and thankful for the support it receives from the EU with regard to the development of regionalism yet is increasingly asserting its own independence and determination to refer to the EU only when it fulfils ASEAN's own economic and political interests. The EU may continue to be the most integrated regional organisation, and a *sui generis* international actor, yet the capacity for it to be an actor of consequence is becoming increasingly contingent upon the perceptions of evolving regional *sui generis* actors such as ASEAN and their perceptions of the EU integration experience as relevant to their own.

A reconceptualisation of EU external action

My aim in this book is to determine the EU's actorness as a consequence of its promotion of regionalism to ASEAN. Scholars who have conducted research on the EU as an international actor with the ability to influence international affairs have commonly asserted that the EU is a certain type of power (Duchêne, 1972; Manners, 2002; 2006a; Meunier and Nicolaïdis, 2006; Aggestam, 2008; Wood, 2009; Damro, 2012). The EU's power has previously been determined by what the EU is, does, or should do. Consequently, conceptions of the EU as a power have often been based on the normative ideals which the EU espouses, or the policy aspirations it projects. To date, a number of these conceptualisations, whilst contributing to the development of a research agenda which examines the EU's influence beyond its borders, have been markedly introspective in their approach. These studies have often failed to include the perceptions of the EU's external interlocutors or the impact the EU has had externally as an actor. I therefore challenge some of the established processes of conceptualising the EU as an actor and contest the use of power as the basis of such conceptualisations throughout this book.

I do so by arguing that the views of the EU's external interlocutors and the impact the EU has had externally must be incorporated into studies of EU actorness. I draw upon aspects of the framework put forward by Allen and Smith (1990) in which they incorporate an evaluation of the EU's presence, and the varying dimensions of presence, as a way to assess the foreign policy role of the EU. Similar to Allen and Smith (1990), I emphasise the fact that EU foreign policy is multidimensional in nature and my findings, even after 20 years since their seminal publication, echo the claim that the EU continues to be a 'flexible' actor which 'expresses a collective yet pluralistic identity' (Allen and Smith, 1990: 23). This is based on the fact that the EU is not a political entity in the same sense as a nation state. Allen and Smith's claim in 1990 that 'while Western Europe is clearly consequential in the international arena ... its status and impact are inherently ambiguous' (Allen and Smith, 1990: 19) remains relevant and a worthwhile starting point for investigation as the EU's range and type of interlocutors expand and change.

ASEAN has been chosen as the subject of investigation with regard to the status and impact of the EU's actorness as it is the most active regional institution in Asia and the institution which is at the centre of regionalism efforts in the broader Asia-Pacific region. ASEAN is therefore a useful subject of examination in the context of EU actorness and its interregional partnerships. The inclusion of an analysis of EU impact in the context of EU-ASEAN relations has thus far been overlooked in some previous studies, though not all. For example, Wong (2012) analyses ASEAN's perception of the EU as either a model or reference point for ASEAN integration. Indeed, it is also important to examine where EU actorness has been affected by the EU's inability to act and instances where it has not been able to achieve what it initially aimed to accomplish. Some previous studies have focused heavily on the EU's ideals and achievements, without taking into consideration moments of policy failure and crisis (Manners, 2002; 2006a).

I contend that it is crucial to incorporate the analysis of internal and external perceptions of EU policies and actions in order to gain a comprehensive assessment of EU actorness. This allows for an analysis of reactions to policy achievements and failures as viewed by those working within the EU and external actors which interact with the EU. Furthermore, the increasing economic and political importance of the Southeast Asian region and the renewed and increasingly stronger relations between the EU and Asia in recent years have been well-noted (Christiansen *et al.*, 2013), making it timely to undertake an in-depth analysis of EU-ASEAN relations.

Conceptualisations based on labels referring to power do not provide an accurate framework with which to understand the EU's ability to contribute to, or shape, international affairs. The main reason for this is that the exertion of power does not always adequately reflect the dynamics of the relationship between the EU and its interlocutors. Moreover, in previous studies, the term 'power' has often been associated with the EU's normative and ethical ideals and aspirations (Diez, 2005; Manners, 2006a; Aggestam, 2008; Forsberg, 2011). I argue that conflating normative values of the EU with power exertion has created an ambiguous and distorted image of EU actorness. It also does not provide an accurate account of what the EU has done or achieved based on the objective examination of empirical evidence.

To remedy the introspectiveness of previous research, I examine the EU's promotion of its regionalism experience to ASEAN. Such a study allows for an evaluation of EU actorness based on empirical analysis and the examination of external perceptions. So as to move beyond conceptualisations based on power, I draw upon previous scholarly work on processes of norm diffusion (Manners, 2002; Acharya, 2004; 2011a). To date, scholars have not given sufficient attention to the connection between EU actorness and norm diffusion. Norm diffusion can provide a framework for assessing EU influence externally without pre-determining that its relations with external actors must centre on a conception of EU power. This is under the condition, however, that the frameworks used do not only favour EU norms and also take into consideration the norm recipient.

This book broadens the pre-existing research agenda on norm diffusion which to date has primarily covered processes of Europeanisation and also normative change within regions (Acharya, 2004; Börzel and Risse, 2012; Jetschke and Lenz, 2013) by building upon studies which have examined either the role of the norm entrepreneur (Manners, 2002) or the norm recipient (Acharya, 2004; 2011a). It is firmly grounded in the belief that actions of both the norm entrepreneur and the norm recipient must be taken into account in order to establish an accurate determination of actorness. It therefore takes the innovative approach of simultaneously evaluating the role of the norm entrepreneur, in this case the EU, and the perceptions of the targeted norm recipient, ASEAN, in the process of the EU's promotion of its norms of regionalism so as to provide a more comprehensive assessment. It is also original in simultaneously utilising the norm diffusion framework presented by Manners (2002) to examine the norm entrepreneur role of the EU and the frameworks for norm localisation and subsidiarity developed by Acharya (2004; 2011a) to analyse the role of ASEAN as a norm recipient.

Through a study of EU-ASEAN relations I find that the EU's actorness is not consistent. Across a range of policy areas and contexts actorness manifests in different ways and to varying degrees. By separating the study of the EU's regionalism experience into three areas – economic integration, institutionalisation and political norms – the potential for varying results within each aspect of regionalism has been possible to determine. As I show in this book, the EU's actorness does indeed vary across the different areas of regionalism, indicating that such an approach is of value to future studies on actorness, comparative regionalism and norm diffusion. If the EU is conceptualised less as a homogenous international actor and more focus is given to the variations of actorness across policy areas, as has been done by some scholars such as Langan (2012) and Smith (2012), a more accurate and nuanced assessment of the EU as an international actor would be possible.

In this book I present the hypothesis that *the EU has set itself up as a norms diffuser in its engagement with ASEAN. This diffusion is contingent upon ASEAN's receptiveness. It is therefore ASEAN which has the determining role in the realisation of the EU's regionalism promotion policies.*

The questions which guide this study are:

- Why does the EU consider itself to have the ability and responsibility to promote and diffuse its norms of regionalism to ASEAN?
- How do those within the EU and ASEAN regard the EU as an actor?
- How does the EU attempt to promote its norms or regionalism to ASEAN?
- To what extent has the EU been successful in exporting its norms of regionalism to ASEAN?

These questions form the basis for the structure of the book, which is explained in further detail in the book overview section of this chapter.

Central to this study is an understanding of the key definitions pertaining to regionalism and regional integration. The term regionalism in this book aligns with the comprehensive definition given by Hurrell (1995) who states that regionalism encompasses regional awareness and identity, regionalisation, regional interstate cooperation, state-promoted regional integration and regional cohesion. Regional awareness refers to the rhetoric and language which contributes to definitions and redefinitions of regional identity. Regionalisation involves 'the growth of societal integration within a region and to the often undirected processes of social and economic interaction' (Eliassen and Arnesen, 2007: 206) and is often distinguished from regionalism in its referral to the processes of regionalism as opposed to the policies and outcomes of integration initiatives (Söderbaum, 2007).

Regional interstate cooperation can be both formal, with emphasis on institutionalisation and legal frameworks, or a looser arrangement whereby interstate cooperation involves regular but informal meetings. As Eliassen and Arnesen (2007) point out, institutionalisation is not the guarantor of effectiveness or political importance and there is therefore no single formula for successful or positive regional cooperation. The legal and institutional relationships within which economic transactions take place fall under the definition of regional integration. Finally, regional cohesion is the dynamic whereby the interplay between the above-mentioned aspects of regionalism results in a 'cohesive and consolidated regional unit' (Eliassen and Arnesen, 2007: 207). As the most comprehensive of the aforesaid terms, unless otherwise specified, regionalism is the most commonly used term throughout this book.

Higgott's (2007) four approaches to regionalism are also pertinent to this book as they offer a framework with which to interpret differing forms of regionalism and different paths to regional integration and cooperation. The first approach presented by Higgott (2007) is *de facto* regionalism, which is informal, market-led regionalism that leads to greater economic integration. This is described as a rationalist-economic approach to regionalism. The second approach is *de jure* regionalism. This approach has a legal-political orientation and is formal, rule-governed, state-led regionalism with a high level of institutionalisation. Thirdly, instrumental regionalism refers to regionalism which is initially informal and interest-led. It results from a collective interest in pursuing a common policy in a certain policy area, which is often projected towards, or in response to, a third party. This approach is based on realist assumptions. Finally, a socio-cultural approach, cognitive regionalism, is also initially informal and is built upon shared cultural, historical and emotional connections which distinguish 'insiders' from 'outsiders' (Higgott, 2007: 88).

This presentation of four approaches to regionalism allows us to move beyond European conceptualisations of integration. For example, Haas's (1958) oft-quoted definition of European integration is informative, and the neofunctional premise on the shift of loyalties to a new centre does often stretch across numerous contexts. Haas described European integration as a phenomenon whereby actors 'in several distinct national settings are persuaded to shift their loyalties, expectations and political activities towards a new centre, whose institutions possess or demand jurisdiction over the pre-existing national states' (Haas, 1958: 16). Whilst Haas had no intention for this definition to be applied beyond the context of Europe, its emphasis on legality and institutionalisation limits its ability to be utilised elsewhere. Higgott's (2007) set of approaches to regionalism demonstrates that in the emergence of regionalisms around the world, the possibility for variation can be as great as the contextual differences from which they arise.

Throughout the following chapters, discussions on the EU's attempts at promoting regionalism, and also the similarities and differences between European and Southeast Asian regionalism benefit from an awareness of these approaches. They enable a contextualisation of divergent forms of regionalism and are a useful reminder that integration research has moved beyond the EU being an exemplar of regionalism.

Research methods

The originality of this book is primarily based on its reconceptualisation of the EU as an international actor and the methods through which this reconceptualisation is achieved. To date, there has been a significant lack of research on how the EU engages with Southeast Asian regionalism and the effects of, and reactions to, its promotion of regionalism to ASEAN. There is, therefore, a need to reconceptualise the EU as an international actor and, in order to do this, both internal and external perceptions must be taken into account.

The research undertaken for this study responds to this argument by collecting and analysing data based on interviews and a survey. The uniqueness of this research project is also based on the fact that an assessment of EU actorness has been undertaken using qualitative data based on in-depth interviews and surveys conducted with officials and scholars working in, and on, the EU and ASEAN. Whilst scholarly literature and official documents related to the EU and ASEAN provide a valuable basis from which to begin this study, they must be complemented by interviews and surveys conducted with elites and academics working in related fields. This is because such data provides the insight, depth and contemporaneity that cannot be obtained from other sources.

Interviews and surveys are considered the most appropriate methods of data collection as they also allow for authoritative and first-hand insights from individuals working or studying in the area of EU-ASEAN relations. For this project, it was vital to collect data from Europe and Southeast Asia in order to determine whether the EU's policy towards ASEAN is received as intended and produces the results expected from it in both Europe and Southeast Asia.

The project is therefore primarily a case study, which involves 'a research strategy which focuses on understanding the dynamics present within (a) single setting(s)' (Eisenhardt, 1989: 534). The case under examination is EU-ASEAN relations with a focus on the EU promoting norms of regionalism to ASEAN. Patton (2002: 448) has explained that no matter the case study, the researcher must always 'connect data on the lowest level unit of analysis as possible' and also that 'the analyst's first and foremost responsibility consists of doing justice to each individual case. All else depends on that'. Interviews and surveys, therefore, were the appropriate choice for data collection as they enabled empirical research to be undertaken at the individual level, from which broader interpretations, patterns, themes and perceptions could be ascertained.

In addition, Patton's (2002) claim that a well-structured case study should be holistic and context sensitive has driven the design of this research project. Using this holistic approach I have sought to understand the perception of the EU's promotion of regionalism to ASEAN by analysing the parts, which in sum, contribute to the greater whole (Patton, 2002) and provide an overview of EU actorness in the context of its relations with ASEAN. I have done this by collecting data from a range of individuals connected to the EU and ASEAN; by incorporating three main data sources – interviews, a survey and secondary data sources such as academic and official literature; and by examining three separate policy areas in which the EU advances its norms – economic integration, institutionalisation and political norms.

The second important component of a solid case study design, context sensitivity, has also been incorporated into this project. To ensure an understanding of the context in which a phenomenon takes place, this book, especially in Chapter 3, contextualises the EU-ASEAN relationship before embarking upon the perception analysis of the EU's promotion of its norms of regionalism.

Although research and literature on interregionalism and EU-ASEAN relations more specifically are increasing (Gilson, 2005; Doidge, 2007; Reiterer, 2009; Rössler, 2009; Camroux, 2010; Wong, 2012), interviews and surveys covering this area have not been carried out extensively. The interviews and survey conducted for this project provide the basis for establishing a clear understanding and analysis of the impact the EU has on Southeast Asian regionalism. To date, only a small number of comprehensive studies which involve respondents from Europe and Southeast Asia have been administered (Chaban and Holland, 2008; Murray, 2008; Bersick 2010; Chaban and Holland, 2010).

An analysis of these elite perceptions of EU policy was the most relevant and effective way to assess the EU's promotion of regionalism, both from an EU and Southeast Asian perspective. I carried out detailed interviews so as to gauge opinions of individuals working in governmental institutions in Europe and Southeast Asia. Academics working in these two regions were also interviewed. In Europe, interviews were carried out with five officials working in the 'Asia and the Pacific' section of the European External Action Service (EEAS). An academic at the United Nations University Institute on Comparative Regionalism Studies (UNUCRIS) was also interviewed. In Southeast Asia, interviews were conducted with an individual from the ASEAN Secretariat and a former Secretary-General of ASEAN, a member of the EEAS at the Delegation of the EU to Indonesia and Brunei Darussalam in Indonesia, and an academic at the EU Centre and an EEAS official at the Delegation of the EU to Singapore, both located in Singapore. This wide range of locations and institutions allowed for a comprehensive set of responses in both Europe and Southeast Asia, providing a solid basis from which to determine similarities and differences in opinion between individuals in these two regions.

The final number of in-depth qualitative interview participants was 11. Six interviews were conducted in Europe and five in Southeast Asia. The interviews were conducted in the second half of 2011. Interviews were approximately one hour in length, and were done on a one-on-one basis. The questions were designed to elicit qualitative data responses from the interviewees. As much as possible, the same questions were asked to all respondents to facilitate comparative data analysis. The interview questions for this research project included open-ended questions, follow-up questions and probes to elicit further, in-depth information where necessary, as suggested by Rubin and Rubin (2005).

The interview questions were designed to meet two main objectives and were guided by the central research aims and questions. Firstly, it was important to have questions that could be asked in both the European and Asian contexts. It was understood that although the same questions were asked in both regions, depending on the experiences and knowledge of the respondent, the answers would be interpreted differently, eliciting nuanced responses. This was crucial to the project as a major component of this study is to determine if the way in which the EU projects itself at the international level is in fact the way that it is perceived by others. In this sense, these interviews have been essential in developing this understanding. The second objective relates to a central research question: how do those within the EU and ASEAN regard the EU as an actor? In order to answer this question, this project has addressed the role and conceptualisation of the EU as an international actor, its policies towards ASEAN and its efforts to promote regionalism to ASEAN. The interviews reflected these main areas of research, creating a comprehensive set of data to analyse.

In addition to the interviews, a survey was administered in Europe and the Asia-Pacific. The survey has played a crucial role in providing an overview of opinions in these two regions. As the survey could include more respondents than the interviews, it provided the opportunity to determine any overarching trends or views within the topic of research (Marshall and Rossman, 1995). In some cases, the survey allowed for more detailed questions to be asked than in the interviews and through the use of multiple-choice questions it allowed for statistical data analysis to be undertaken. In the survey, a mixture of multiple-choice and open-ended questions were asked, giving respondents the opportunity to give extended answers where appropriate.

In Europe, survey respondents included officials working in the EEAS, the European Institute for Asia Affairs, the European Policy Centre, the European Institute for Security Studies and a range of European universities. In Southeast Asia and the Asia-Pacific, surveys were sent, *inter alia*, to officials working at the ASEAN Secretariat, officials working at EU Delegations throughout Southeast Asia, individuals at the Asia-Europe Foundation (ASEF) and a range of Southeast Asian and Asian-Pacific universities. Similar to the interviews, the survey questions were designed to elicit qualitative data in both Europe and Asia. To encompass the widest range of elite perceptions as possible, the survey questionnaires were sent to individuals working in governmental institutions, academic institutions and non-governmental organisations. In total, 81 questionnaires were sent out and 34 were returned, giving a response rate of 42%. Among the respondents, 28% were academics based in Europe, 12% were EEAS officials based in Southeast Asia, 12% were think tank members from Europe, 9% were academics based in the Oceanic region, 9% were academics based in Southeast Asia, 9% were academics based in East Asia, 6% were EEAS officials based in Europe, 6% were anonymous academics, 3% were Council of the EU officials in Brussels, 3% were academics in North America and 3% were anonymous.[1]

To complement the primary sources of data collection, secondary sources were also utilised and mainly involved the collection of academic materials such as journal articles, conference papers and books. They also included official government documents such as policy papers and speeches released by the EU and ASEAN. Research also involved an analysis of legal documents such as the Lisbon Treaty and the ASEAN Charter. Other secondary sources which were used were newspaper articles and Internet materials, especially those from the websites of the EU and ASEAN.

The triangulation performed through the collection of data from a range of primary and secondary sources has enabled the robustness and consistency of the findings to be verified (Eisenhardt, 1989; Patton, 2002). In addition, as there are currently only a limited number of experts and practitioners involved in EU-ASEAN relations, the triangulation method assisted in collecting comprehensive data from a narrow field of sources. The collection of data from numerous sources has been crucial because as Denzin (1978: 28) explains, 'no single method ever adequately solves the problem of rival causal factors. Because each method reveals different aspects of empirical reality, multiple methods of observations must be employed'.

Book overview

This book proceeds in six chapters. Firstly, Chapter 2, 'Seeking to Reconceptualise the EU as a "Power"', develops the argument that the previous conceptualisations of the EU as an actor have failed to include analyses of external perceptions adequately and have focused on conceptualisations of the EU as a power which do not provide for an accurate description of EU actorness. I do this by examining and critiquing the relevant scholarly literature on EU actorness and EU power, arguing that many previous studies have been insular and introspective and have not been based on empirical investigations which involve both internal and external actors. With regard to power specifically, Chapter 2 engages with a number of definitions of power and applies Galtung's (1973) definition to substantiate the claim that power is the incorrect framework with which to assess EU actorness. I argue that norm diffusion is a more appropriate tool for assessment, and therefore present an analysis of existing norm diffusion frameworks and a reconceptualisation of the concept (Manners, 2002; Acharya, 2004; 2011a).

In this chapter I draw together the conceptual and theoretical frameworks critiqued in Chapter 2 to create a set of criteria for the EU's actorness with regard to its promotion of regionalism to ASEAN. These criteria are used in Chapters 4–6 to determine the EU's actorness.

In Chapter 3, 'Drivers of Interregionalism: EU-ASEAN Engagement', I answer the question which asks why the EU considers itself to have the ability and responsibility to promote and diffuse its norms of regionalism to ASEAN. By analysing the motivations for EU-ASEAN engagement I establish the reasons why the EU pursues the policy of promoting its norms of regionalism. The impetus for EU-ASEAN engagement comes from economic and political motivations, with economic impetus in particular arising from the shared objective to retain access to each other's markets. With regard to political motivations, goals of legitimacy and relevance have a strong impact on the interregional relationship. In this section, modes of interregionalism, such as the ASEM and the EU's desire to be a member of the East Asia Summit (EAS) are analysed. External expectations of the EU and ASEAN, as well as the internal decision-making processes and interests of their respective member states are all examined as factors affecting the interregional relationship. The chapter concludes with the argument that these various motivations for the EU and ASEAN to be interlocutors affect the coherence of the connection between the two organisations. This chapter, together with Chapter 2, provides the overarching theoretical and contextual framework from which the analysis of the EU's promotion of its regionalism experience can be undertaken, which is the purpose of Chapters 4–6. The following three chapters answer the three remaining research questions, which ask what type of actor the EU is regarded as internally, within the EU, and externally by ASEAN; how the EU attempts to export its norms of regionalism to ASEAN; and, to what extent the EU has been able to diffuse its norms of regionalism to ASEAN.

Chapter 4, 'The EU, ASEAN and Economic Integration', examines how the EU exports its norms of economic integration, which has principally been through the ASEAN-EU Programme for Regional Integration Support (APRIS) and the current ASEAN Regional Integration Support by the EU (ARISE) programme. Based on interview and survey responses, this chapter finds that ASEAN continues to refer to the EU for support in this area, albeit under its own conditions. This has allowed the EU to be a strong actor in the realm of economic integration within Southeast Asia.

In this chapter, I argue that the EU's attempt to promote its norms of economic integration is the most successful of the three areas of regionalism promotion covered in this book. The EU's relevance to the development of ASEAN's economic community and its ability to be viewed as an international actor with valuable lessons of economic integration for the Southeast Asian region are heavily influenced by the EU's distinctiveness. The challenge for the EU is to ensure that its economic integration experience is applicable to ASEAN and also to understand the ASEAN context sufficiently to promote and support norms which are valuable to ASEAN. Interview and survey responses referred to these challenges and data collected referred to the frustrations of EU officials concerning the pace of implementation of EU initiatives and the development of ASEAN economic integration. ASEAN officials, on the other hand, referred to a lack of understanding of ASEAN and ASEAN's needs and core norms by EU officials and institutions as one of the main reasons for the lack of implementation and slow progress.

Chapter 5, 'The EU, ASEAN and Institutionalisation', argues that the EU's promotion of institutionalisation to ASEAN has only had a moderate impact. I argue in this chapter that the distinctiveness of the EU is a factor determining the receptiveness level of ASEAN and the degree to which ASEAN finds the EU's institutionalisation relevant. Institutionalisation in this chapter refers to the organisational structure, decision-making processes and legal frameworks underpinning the EU and ASEAN. Furthermore, this chapter analyses aspects of ASEAN's institutionalisation which reflect structures within the EU, such as its Committee of Permanent Representatives (CPR), ASEAN's pillar system, and contents of the ASEAN Charter.

I contend in this chapter that the EU's promotion of its institutionalisation norms has not been as significant as ASEAN's active scrutiny of EU structures as meaningful sources of inspiration. This has resulted in the creation of institutions and processes which can be seemingly attributed to the EU experience yet are distinct to ASEAN. Using a theoretical framework based on historical institutionalism, I show that the EU and ASEAN have followed divergent institutional paths, despite ASEAN referring to the EU for inspiration, largely due to their historical differences. I argue that the EU's international actorness has been limited with regard to its promotion of institutionalisation. This is because ASEAN is seen to be the determining factor of whether any promotion will take place, and also of what the results of such promotion will be. The EU's actorness in this regard is also limited by a continued expectation and understanding gap between the institutional norms the EU aims to promote and the level and style of institutionalisation desired by ASEAN. This gap is discernable in the perception differences of EU and ASEAN officials illustrated by interview and survey responses regarding the design, contents, aims and results of the EU's support to ASEAN integration.

Chapter 6, 'The EU, ASEAN and Political Norms', examines the EU's promotion of human rights to ASEAN. Although the promotion and protection of human rights are core political norms expounded by the EU and central in determining the nature of the EU's foreign policies, the promotion of economic integration has taken precedence over political norm promotion. Similar to Chapters 4 and 5, the EU's distinctiveness affects its ability to promote human rights as a political norm. This is because as human rights promotion and protection are not necessarily norms specific to the EU, the EU's relevance in respect of these norms is not strong enough for it to have a robust norm entrepreneurship role. This chapter maintains that with regard to the promotion of human rights to ASEAN, the EU cannot be considered an international actor. This is based on its inability to significantly transform ASEAN's political norms to reflect those that the EU attempts to promote. I explain in this chapter that ASEAN has begun to include human rights into its political agenda, examples being the inclusion of statements on human rights in the ASEAN Charter and the creation of the ASEAN Intergovernmental Commission on Human Rights (AICHR). Nevertheless, there is little evidence to suggest that this has been a result of norm promotion by the EU. Such developments within ASEAN can be better explained by the internal pressure ASEAN member states have been placing on ASEAN to address human rights concerns and the efforts of the wider international community and organisations such as the United Nations (UN).

The concluding chapter examines the key findings and main arguments of this book, and explains how they substantiate the hypothesis and answer the central research questions. Based on the perception analysis conducted for this study, I contend that previous conceptions of the EU as a certain type of power have been incomplete and inaccurate. This is principally due to the fact that because earlier studies have been relatively insular in their approach and focus, the determining factor of actorness has been overlooked. This defining element is the perception of the EU's interlocutors. This is because a main finding of this study is that the perception of the EU by ASEAN officials has determined the extent to which the EU's support is accepted and its initiatives are implemented. By examining the EU's promotion of its norms of economic integration and institutionalisation, and its political norms of human rights protection and promotion, this book demonstrates that the EU's actorness is not consistent across the three areas examined. This study also demonstrates that ASEAN affords the highest amount of relevance to the EU's economic integration experience, and it is therefore the EU's promotion of economic norms which contribute the most to the EU's international actorness.

Finally, the conclusion presents suggestions for further research which have been raised during the course of this study. There are, for example, opportunities to analyse other instances of norm promotion and diffusion between the EU and ASEAN; for instance, the promotion of security norms or political norms other than human rights. In addition, the conceptual analysis and framework established in this study could also be applied to other interregional dynamics beyond the EU and ASEAN.

2
Seeking to Reconceptualise the EU as a 'Power'

> The EU still has a long way to go first of all within the EU itself before being able to play a leading role in its external relations. Moreover, the international system is becoming even more decentred within a fluid multipolar configuration that would most likely make it hard for any one international actor to take the lead in establishing itself as a kind of benign hegemon.
>
> Survey Respondent 29, Academic within the EU, 2012.

> More than ever our citizens and the new world order need an active and influential Europe. This is not just for us, for the rest of the world it is important that we succeed. ... together we have the power, and the scale to shape the world into a fairer, rules based and human rights abiding place.
>
> José Manuel Barroso, former European Union Commission President, State of the Union Address to the European Parliament, 2012.

EU capabilities and perceptions of EU actorness

Both EU official documents and academic literature have made reference to the EU's ambitions to be a visible and consequential actor that actively pursues foreign policies in the interest of the EU. This book aims to reconceptualise the EU as an international actor by drawing on frameworks of norm diffusion and utilising a set of criteria for the assessment of international actorness based on previous scholarly research. In this chapter I examine and critically assess the literature on international actorness to establish the set of criteria questions I use to determine the EU's actorness regarding its policy of promoting regionalism to ASEAN. I also analyse norm diffusion frameworks and devise an analytical framework with which to assess the processes of norm diffusion occurring as a consequence of the EU's promotion of regionalism to ASEAN.

José Manuel Barroso stated in his 2012 State of the Union address to the European Parliament (EP) that in reaction to the current crises of the EU, there is a need to 'stop trying to answer the questions of the future with the tools of the past' (Barroso, 2012b: 1). The EU has experienced, and will experience, significant change as a consequence of the turmoil from which it is emerging. Therefore, the 'tools of the past' which have been employed to assess actorness must be reconfigured and reappraised to sufficiently analyse these changes. The EU's current 'crisis of confidence' (Barroso, 2012b), not to mention its financial and economic crises, are affecting its ability to be an actor and the perceptions of what its role in the world is and should be.

Interview and survey responses have demonstrated a wide array of reactions to the EU's current capabilities as an actor, and an actor which has the ability to promote its regionalism experience to ASEAN. Responses have differed in levels of optimism and confidence. Demonstrating this diversity, one survey respondent stated that, 'the EU is of increasingly failed irrelevance and of little import to Southeast Asia. Its utility resides in a model of regionalism to be avoided by Southeast Asia' (S9 OA, 2012). Another, when asked if the EU had a leading role to play in the world, stated, 'I think a lot depends on how the EU comes out of the currency crisis that hasn't gone away yet. At the moment its leadership potential looks somewhat blunted, but IF it survives and comes out stronger then yes it could' (S2 EA, 2012).

Scholars have also examined and reacted to the EU's capabilities as an international actor. In addition to early works by Cosgrove and Twitchett (1970) and Galtung (1973), in 1977, Sjöstedt provided one of the first comprehensive frameworks for assessing the EU as a global actor and predicted how the then European Community would evolve as an actor. His determination that the EU 'seems to be some sort of half-developed international actor' (Sjöstedt, 1977: 112), whilst somewhat vague, raised important questions to propel further studies of EU actorness and the challenges related to doing so. Sjöstedt (1977: 127) himself admits that 'what an international actor really is' is difficult to ascertain. In his framework he suggests that actorness requires a 'delimitation from other actors and the capacity for autonomous action' (Niemann and Bretherton, 2013: 265).

Niemann and Bretherton (2013) suggest that the first aspect of his definition was not able to capture sufficiently the different levels of political authority which were present in the European Community at the time. They suggested that some aspects of Sjöstedt's conceptualisation remained grounded in concepts related to state actorness and therefore could not be easily applied to the European Community. Subsequent work on EU actorness has attempted to remedy this fact by focusing on the EU's *sui generis* nature which distinguishes the EU from other actors in the global arena. A new phase of research has now started to move beyond a focus on the EU as a *sui generis* actor to assess its actorness in relation to others (Niemann and Bretherton, 2013). The second component of Sjöstedt's definition regarding autonomy has become central to work on actorness alongside concepts such as impact, presence and perception analysis.

More recently, Moravcsik (2009) has made an optimistic claim that the EU is a 'quiet superpower'. In contrast to realist claims that European power would have diminished after the Cold War, and that transatlantic and intra-European cooperation would flounder with the absence of a common threat, Moravcsik argues that a liberal interpretation is more accurate and explanatory. This is because the liberal claim that actions are positive-sum and based on variable social interests has proved true for the EU's global role post-Cold War. According to Moravcsik (2009: 403), none of the realist predictions have materialised and the EU's per capita income, institutional advantages and converging ... national interests between European countries and other great powers, and especially its 'civilian power' capabilities, which are discussed in further detail below, ensure Europe's rising power. He reminds us that Europe is the world's second superpower after the US, the pre-eminent global 'civilian superpower' and the world's second military power (Moravcsik, 2009). Circumvention of the potential conflict of interests among EU member states and how EU actorness differs from that of great powers which are states notwithstanding, Moravcsik presents a sanguine account of the EU's role in the context of its internal economic and political turmoil.

Sjöstedt (1977), Moravcsik (2009) and numerous more scholars (Duchêne, 1972; Hill, 1983; Pelinka, 2011) show the breadth of attempts to elucidate EU actorness and also the levels of optimism concerning the EU's capabilities. As Rosamond points out, 'one of the longest-standing problems in the study of EU external relations concerns the conceptualisation of the EU as an actor' (Rosamond, 2005: 464). Following on from these scholars, this chapter continues the research on the EU's global role. Similar to previous analysis, it examines how EU perceptions are analysed against its ambitions to have a global role and attempts to reconceptualise frameworks for the assessment of EU power and actorness.

The EU as an international actor: Types of power and their critiques

Lucarelli (2007) has argued that there is an insufficient amount of research pertaining to the external image of the EU. She argues that an evaluation of the EU as an international actor requires three main areas of appraisal: the ability of EU international action to 'transform the "target environment"', the external perception of the EU and the domestic perception of the EU. According to Lucarelli (2007), these three areas of analysis are imperative for the complete construction and realisation of the EU as a political actor. This is mainly due to the fact that these three aspects are intrinsically linked; they all affect each other and ultimately affect the nature of the EU, the decisions it makes and the actions it takes. Nevertheless, due to the fact that previous research has often focused on the credibility, legitimacy and success of the EU project as opposed to the effectiveness of EU external action, a comprehensive approach to EU foreign policy that takes in all of the above factors has been largely overlooked.

In addition to Lucarelli's criteria for the assessment of the EU as an international actor, Wunderlich (2012) also provides criteria for regional actorness which are employed in this book to establish the necessary elements of international actorness. The criteria consist of 'internal self-understanding and self image, recognition and presence and institutionalisation and decision-making structures' (Wunderlich, 2012: 6). I judge whether the EU is an international actor with regard to its relations with ASEAN and its policy of regionalism promotion against these criteria, with EU perceptions of its own actorness examined. In addition, ASEAN's recognition of the EU as an international actor is also assessed, as is the EU's presence within ASEAN and Southeast Asia. Presence, as defined by Allen and Smith (1991), includes the ability and legitimacy of an actor to use its resources, as well as perceptions of the actor. I also examine the EU's institutionalisation and decision-making processes regarding its policy of regionalism promotion to ASEAN as determinants of the EU's actorness.

In order to formulate his definition, Wunderlich (2012) built upon existing frameworks of assessment for actorness. For example, Wunderlich refers to Hettne's (2011) criteria for 'actorship', which involves an analysis of 'regionness', the internal structure and identity of a regional entity; 'presence' – defined as the size and economic and military strength of an actor; and 'actorness', which, according to Hettne (2011), refers to the ability to act in international affairs. Doidge (2007) argues that regional actorness requires action triggers which include the goals and interests of an actor, policy structures and processes which determine an actor's capacity to take decisions and form policies, and performance structures which include the resources available to act upon and implement the decisions made and policies created.

An assessment of the actorness of regional organisations requires a set of criteria which assesses both the normative and structural constitution of the organisation. This is because dichotomies between norms and interests, strategic and ethical behaviours and aims, means and results can only be assessed simultaneously if actorness criteria include normative and structural considerations. This includes an actor's institutions, member state interests and roles, decision-making processes and internal and external perceptions of whether the regional organisation is considered to be an actor of consequence which has the validity and capability to influence the development of regional organisations such as ASEAN. Wunderlich's (2012) definition of regional actorness and the criteria presented by Lucarelli (2007) are useful and comprehensive frameworks for the analysis of the EU's international actorness. These are complemented by the criteria put forward by Hettne (2011) and Doidge (2007), which provide more detailed points of assessment yet still fall under Wunderlich's and Lucarelli's more comprehensive frameworks. Therefore, based on the elements of assessment inherent in Wunderlich's (2012) and Lucarelli's (2007) definitions, I have devised a set of questions which relate to the EU's promotion of regionalism to ASEAN. These questions are:

Internal self-understanding and self-image

- Does the EU consider itself to have the capacity and responsibility to promote its regionalism experience?

Recognition

- Has ASEAN viewed the EU as relevant with regard to its regionalism experience?

Presence

- Has the EU been able to utilise its resources to promote its regionalism experience?

Institutionalisation and decision-making structures

- Have the EU's institutional structures and decision-making processes been adequate in facilitating the EU's promotion of regionalism?

Impact on the 'target environment'

- Has the EU been able to transform the 'target environment'?

Domestic perception, external perception

- Have approaches and results been deemed successful, internally and externally?

I will use these questions to assess the EU's actorness with regard to the promotion of the three areas of regionalism analysed in this book – economic integration, institutionalisation and political norms.

Previously, in most cases, the EU's actorness has been conceptualised by determining the nature of the EU's power and how this power is exerted externally (Duchêne, 1972; Wood, 2009; Manners, 2002; Manners, 2006a; Aggestam, 2008; Damro, 2012; Meunier and Nicolaïdis, 2006). The number of terms that have been used to describe the EU's external role has caused the area of study to fall victim to a scholarly debate that at times becomes more about semantics than the key concepts at stake. Not only has there been a plethora of EU conceptions based on power but clear definitions of these conceptions and consensus on what type of power the EU is also require further clarification. Sjursen states that 'existing conceptions of the EU as a "civilian"/" normative"/"civilizing" power lack precision and are "normatively based"' (Sjursen, 2006a: 235). The debate concerning the types of power an actor exerts has largely revolved around the presence or absence of military power. A more nuanced approach to the power of actors is required, and an overview of the relevant literature assists in clarifying this major distinction.

An early conception of EU power, civilian power, is defined as power that an actor exerts through non-military means (Duchêne, 1972; Wood, 2009). Hard power, in contrast, refers to power that uses coercion and force. For Duchêne, the EU was considered to be a civilian power in that it focused on economic and political means as opposed to military instruments. The exercise of civilian power relies on persuasion, negotiation and attraction as opposed to coercion (Hill, 1990). It has been suggested that framing the EU as a civilian power was an exercise in trying to establish a distinct role for the EU in international affairs (Orbie, 2006).

However, Duchêne's conceptualisation of the EU as a civilian power was not free from criticism and debate. Galtung (1973) and Bull (1982) were also major contributors to the conceptualisation of the EU as an international actor. In contrast to Duchêne, Galtung regarded the EU as becoming more of a civilian superpower rather than a civilian actor at the international level. Bull, in contrast to both Duchêne and Galtung, dismissed the concept of civilian power and, taking a more realist perspective, placed importance on the military capabilities of the EU, even though he admitted that military integration was impractical (Orbie, 2006).

Similarly, soft power refers to power that does not utilise military force. Nye (2009a) created this term as a way to counter the narrow view of power that was dominant prior to the 1990s which focused heavily on the concept of power being associated with material possessions and instruments. Soft power extended power to include more ideological, economic and political concepts. Specifically, Nye (2009b) referred to soft power tools as culture, values and policies, stating that it is 'the ability to obtain preferred outcomes through attraction rather than coercion or payments' (Nye, 2009b: 2). Both a benefit and prerequisite of soft power is legitimacy (Center for Strategic and International Studies, 2007). For others to respond to the use of soft power an actor needs to be viewed as legitimate. Simultaneously, the more an actor exerts soft power the more its legitimacy is accepted by others. This is due to the nature of soft power and its reliance on the use of norms, values, culture and policy decisions (Center for Strategic and International Studies, 2007).

The concept of legitimacy is especially pertinent to this book, and is discussed in greater depth in Chapter 3, as the promotion of regionalism is reliant upon means which can be categorised as soft power tools, such as the exchange of ideas and practices and the offering of advice. Jokela and Gaens (2012) define legitimacy as including input legitimacy – democratic control and accountability, output legitimacy – performance and the achievement of aims and purposes, and identity – a shared understanding of common norms and values. If these aspects of legitimacy are taken into consideration, the EU's soft power credentials are currently under strain. As to input legitimacy, Longo and Murray (2011) explain that the current debt crises in Europe are emphasising the disconnection its citizens feel to the EU and the lack of opportunities for citizen participation. Also, with regard to output legitimacy, Longo and Murray (2011) explain that there is a growing sense among those in the EU that closer integration may not be providing its citizens with the core EU aims of prosperity and stability. This dissatisfaction also affects the third aspect of legitimacy, a common identity based on shared norms and values, due to the fact that the EU's norms and values related to citizen protection and prosperity are currently being questioned. It is the EU's 'power of attraction' for other regions, rather than the 'power of coercion' (Nye, 2009a), which is a determinant of the EU's capability to promote its norms of regionalism to ASEAN. As this is closely related to the EU's legitimacy, the current conditions in Europe have the potential to affect and determine the extent to which the EU's power of attraction is received by external actors such as ASEAN.

The concept of normative power became prevalent in the 1990s as a response to a lack of 'normative theorising and to promote normative approaches to the EU' (Manners, 2006a: 184). Not only does normative power provide an explanation for a type of power that involves norms and values, it is also considered to be an approach that can be used to analyse what the EU is and does (Manners, 2006a). For Manners, the essence of normative power Europe lies in the fact that the political form of the EU is different from any other political body in the current international system and, that as a consequence, its nature causes it to act in a normative way (Manners, 2002). Normative power involves the use of norms to influence others, and rather than military or economic force, power is exerted through the spread of ideas and opinions through imitation and attraction (Manners, 2006a; Diez, 2005). In other words, normative power is the power to change what is considered normal and acceptable in world politics through the diffusion of norms (Manners, 2006a). In the case of the EU, normative values include the promotion of democracy, human rights, civil freedoms and the rule of law (Wood, 2009).

Manners also provides a framework for the assessment of normative action (Manners, 2008). He presents a three-part analysis that consists of virtue ethics, deontological ethics and consequentialist ethics. Virtue ethics are ethics which emphasise the importance of moral character or virtuous actions. In this way, virtue ethics require an actor to 'live by example', it also demands that an actor, in this case the EU, exercise its normative power consistently and coherently, which involves promoting norms that it adheres to, and more importantly, not promoting norms that it does not uphold. This also requires an actor not to promote its specific norms, but rather norms that are universally held to be legitimate (Manners, 2008: 56).

Deontological ethics emphasise the importance of normative power means. According to deontological ethics, an actor cannot be a valid normative power if it acts in an illegitimate way. This form of ethics places a lot of importance on rights, duties and laws and the way in which normative ends are pursued and achieved. This is what Manners refers to as 'being reasonable' in international politics (Manners, 2008).

The third form of ethics, consequentialist ethics, appraise normative power based on the impact and results of action. With regard to consequentialist ethics, Manners suggests that the EU 'should do least harm' in its external actions (Manners, 2008: 59). Two main factors which contribute to the EU doing least harm are the encouragement of local ownership and the practice of positive conditionality (Manners, 2008). In sum, virtue ethics, deontological ethics and consequentialist ethics refer to a consideration of principles, actions and impacts in order to assess the positive and legitimate use of normative power.

In the context of the EU's promotion of regionalism to ASEAN, however, the analyses in the following chapters challenge the concept of the EU as a normative power based on Manners's framework as discussed above. This is for two main reasons. Firstly, Manners's definition of normative power is heavily based upon the premise that the EU has the ability to change what is normal and accepted in another context, especially with regard to political norms. However, regarding ASEAN, the findings of this study indicate that it is in fact technical norms related to economic integration rather than political norms which have had the greater impact on ASEAN. Secondly, regarding virtue ethics, it has been norms which are specific to the EU, rather than universal norms, which the EU has had greater success in diffusing. Chapter 6 explains that in many cases, the EU has not acted consistently with regard to political norms such as human rights norms which it declares are fundamental to its political narrative, primarily because economic interests tend to override adherence to political norms. Whilst deontological and consequentialist ethics are not challenged with regard to the EU's promotion of regionalism to ASEAN, the aforementioned findings demonstrate that its conceptualisation as a normative power is challenged and not necessarily appropriate.

Diez, in contrast to Manners, gives a slightly different interpretation of normative power as he does not see it as being completely different from military or hard power. This is due to the fact that Diez believes that military means may be used to support the diffusion of non-military values (Diez, 2005). Manners, on the other hand, views the use of military power and the development of military capabilities as having the ability to undermine the EU's normative power and to simply project the tensions between states to a larger scale (Manners,

2006a). Sjursen (2006a) also makes a point that differs from Manners, stating that a lack of military instruments does not necessarily lead to normative power as civilian methods of power exertion can potentially be aggressive or forceful. An area of normative power that Sjursen (2006a) and Manners (2006b) agree on is that it is cosmopolitan in nature. For Sjursen (2006a), normative power is seen as a way to simultaneously strengthen international law and also cosmopolitan law by recognising and supporting the rights of individuals as well as the rights of states.

Diez (2005) discusses normative power in relation to identity, claiming that discourse surrounding normative power, and normative power Europe in particular, assists in the construction of the EU's identity as well as the identity of others in relation to the EU. Discourse on EU normative power, for Diez (2005), enables the EU to develop its identity and to distinguish itself from other actors. This can be seen in contrast to Manners's premise that the EU is a distinct actor because of its normative nature and use of normative power (2002). Diez, on the other hand, does not consider the EU to be distinct, recognising that there are other normative actors in the world. An example is the US, which is regarded as a normative power, but one that utilises military power in a different way to the EU (Diez 2005). Aggestam (2008) also questions the distinctiveness of the EU stating that although the EU is a distinct polity, whether this creates a distinct foreign policy is another matter.

Merlingen (2007: 449) presents two different sides of EU normative power. On the one hand, normative power projects by the EU look to 'limit the degradation and humiliation of individuals, but on the other, they also subject local orders to Europe's normativizing universalist pretensions'. He also observes the two sides of power; in one respect it 'humanizes and improves the life of populations, but it also creates patterns of arbitrary domination between internationals and locals' (Merlingen, 2007). Especially in the context of the Southeast Asian region, the conceptualisation of the EU as a normative power which enables patterns of dominance as described by Merlingen (2007) is not necessarily something to which the EU should, or wants to, aspire. As a result of the colonial histories whereby a large number of ASEAN states were colonised by European states, a narrative of normative power is neither accurate nor beneficial to the EU. As a survey respondent stated, 'I have been very often told by ASEAN state or non-state actors that the 'arrogant' and patronising attitude of the EU harms the interregional dialogue a lot and the willingness of ASEAN to rely on the EU proposals'

(S29 EA, 2012). The response from this survey participant indicates that there is the perception within Southeast Asia that the EU is potentially condescending and overbearing. Merlingen's (2007) concerns regarding normative power are especially pertinent in the ASEAN context, and I therefore pursue a different path of conceptualisation which does not rely on the EU as a normative power in order to avoid moralistic and normatively burdened analyses.

Also related to the exercise of normative power is the issue of pursuing a normative or strategic agenda. Contention arises as to whether the adherence to and promotion of norms and values can be reconciled with the desire to fulfil strategic interests (Hyde-Price, 2006; Youngs, 2004; Mayer, 2008). Such a *problématique* is especially significant to this study as it seeks to examine how the EU engages with ASEAN by promoting its norms of regionalism. This is due to the fact that the EU's norms of economic integration, institutionalisation and political norms cannot always be easily categorised into the pursuit of fulfilling strategic interests or the adherence to the EU's norms and values. This also becomes evident when the EU's promotion of political norms does not necessarily complement the EU's economic and trade interests with ASEAN, as is examined in Chapter 6. Views vary from the assertion that strategic or economic interests are concealed within a normative agenda yet play a determining role in external action to the admission that normative ideals and interests are constant aspects of foreign policy (Youngs, 2004).

Zielonka (2008: 475) believes that strategic interests are definitely at play, stating that the EU 'looks and acts like an empire because it tries to assert political and economic control over various peripheral actors through formal annexations or various forms of economic and political domination'. The method of legitimation that the EU employs, according to Zielonka, is one that assumes that its own norms are right and that it possesses the most efficient model of economic and political integration (Zielonka, 2008). Diez (2005) adds to the complexity of the issue by observing that it is even difficult to understand the difference between norms and interests. Due to the fact that what is considered normative or strategic is not based on empirics but rather on political choices and subjective analysis, it is often difficult to clearly identify what is normative and what is based on self-interest. Moreover, Diez (2005) makes the observation that it would be illogical to consider a normative agenda that does not also contain strategic interests.

Forsberg (2011) continues the debate on normative power, and whilst asserting that normative power has continued utility, there remains obscurity, dispute and differing interpretations of the concept. He states that, 'the question of whether the EU actually is a normative power has been difficult to answer because the parameters have not been properly specified and participants in the debate tend to talk past each other' (Forsberg, 2011: 8). The range of definitions and variations of normative power as presented in this chapter thus far attest to this fact. The debate continues and a most recent contribution has been made by Langan (2012: 1) who includes normative power in his discussion of the EU's relations with the African, Caribbean and Pacific (ACP) countries. He defines normative power as the EU's utilisation of moral norms in the public legitimisation and self-rationalisation of geopolitical interest and commercial gains with its external 'partners'.

Langan links the EU's economic and trade interests with its normative agenda by scrutinising what he refers to as a 'moral economy perspective' to the EU's external relations. By doing so, he recognises the interplay between the EU's moral and normative imperatives and its material interests and gains as a result of its engagement with external actors. Such a framework as presented by Langan is of pertinence to this book in the regard that it acknowledges the interplay between normative and strategic actions and priorities and the impact this has on actorness. In the following chapters of this book, it is made apparent that such an interaction influences the perceptions of the EU's external action and its capacity to engage with dialogue partners such as ASEAN.

The concept of ethical power has emerged as a way to address and frame the increasingly complex nature of EU power. Ethical power encompasses civilian, military, social and material power (Aggestam, 2008). Rather than focusing on what the EU is, as does normative power, ethical power looks at the ethical dilemmas behind the use of military or civilian measures (Aggestam, 2008). As opposed to merely describing or understanding the use of power, ethical power looks to justify the decisions made and action taken when exercising power, paying special attention to the intentions and purposes of external action (Aggestam, 2008). In the context of the EU, ethical power recognises that normative power no longer covers all aspects of EU power exertion, including the use of military instruments. It also acknowledges the interests and strategic decisions made by the EU as well as its normative agenda.

Also, when considering the EU specifically, ethical power gives a different account of EU external action than normative power. Whereas normative power accounts of EU action claim that the EU exerts power in order to shape what is normal in international politics, ethical power debates make the observation that normative developments at the international level have had the effect of allowing the EU to have a more defined and forceful role in the world (Aggestam, 2008). Unlike normative and civilian power, ethical power recognises that there is also an important, internal dimension to the external role of the EU. Normative and civilian power concepts place a large amount of emphasis on the external aspects of the EU, albeit from an internal perspective, yet ethical power considers both the domestic and international levels when analysing EU action (Aggestam, 2008).

Hyde-Price (2008) discusses ethical power in relation to the EU but does not believe that strong ethical discourse in relation to the EU's foreign policy is a beneficial approach. He claims that a strong ethical agenda can easily lead to hypocrisy when tensions arise between upholding an ethical agenda and meeting strategic or political aims. In addition, Hyde-Price (2008) claims that it is very challenging for the EU to pursue an ethical agenda due to the current state of international relations, which for Hyde-Price is extremely realist in nature, comprising a competitive, anarchical, self-help system that is organised into the Westphalian structure of states. A final concern regarding ethical power is the risk of what Hyde-Price (2008: 35) refers to as a 'moralistic crusade'. As ethics can be seen as very contextually specific, when one considers their values, norms and ethics to be universal, the risk of appearing superior or patronising increases dramatically. Similar to Merlingen's (2007) concerns regarding normative power, Hyde-Price's (2008) apprehensions about moralistic patronisation are also a relevant claim in the context of EU–ASEAN relations.

In addition to the concerns regarding ethical power and the belief that it can lead to a sense of moral superiority, or at least appear this way to third parties (Mayer, 2008; Hyde-Price, 2008), there is also the risk of the EU placing itself in the centre of world politics even though it does not hold such a central position (Mayer, 2008). Mayer (2008) even suggests that normative and ethical power may only be possible when one has considerable relative power. According to Mayer (2008), if an actor is faced with a major threat, or does not possess a relatively powerful position in the world order, then normative and ethical behaviour may be abandoned in favour of more traditional forms of hard power. Mayer (2008: 62) suggests that the EU's external action should be framed as 'Europe's global responsibilities' as opposed to an over-emphasis on ethical and moral discourse to avoid the image of moral superiority and to give a more accurate reflection of EU action. In addition, according to Mayer (2008), the promotion of norms and values, which is seen as an integral part of normative and ethical power, should be replaced by offers of global responsibility through open dialogue.

Finally, whilst for some the EU is considered an effective ethical power, for Mayer, there are requirements that must be met before the EU can be termed as such. These include the need to

> Enhance capacities where needed to meet existing global responsibilities alone and in concert with other institutions; reduce expectations through a more realistic assessment of the EU's abilities, being guided by responsible modesty and awareness of the Union's own priorities and limits rather than by ambitious exaggeration; (and) develop a new and credible discourse within Europe and outside on the EU's responsibility in a non-European world. (Mayer, 2008: 77)

Another conceptualisation based on a certain form of power has been smart power. The concept has mainly emerged in relation to American foreign policy but has also become an important concept for the EU. The concept is attributed to Joseph Nye, who recognised that soft power, although necessary, was not sufficient for effective foreign policy (2009a). Instead, there is a perceived need to combine both hard and soft power in order to achieve foreign policy aims. With reference to the US, smart power has been described as 'an approach that underscores the necessity of a strong military, but also invests heavily in alliances, partnerships and institutions of all levels to expand American influence and establish legitimacy of American action' (Centre for Strategic and International Studies, 2007: 7).

In the European context, in scholarly discourse, Smith (2011) has presented arguments for a more holistic approach to EU power externally. Smith argues that the EU now has a range of different forms of power, which include both soft and hard power instruments, which it strategically employs towards external actors.[1] Smith does not refer to smart power explicitly but the concept of a comprehensive use of power instruments finds echo in Nye's notion of smart power. Whilst the EU's role in Southeast Asia has not focused on hard power instruments and it is claimed that the EU has a marginal security role in the region (Jetschke and Portela, 2013), EU officials have referred to a concept of smart power for the EU. Benita Ferrero-Waldner[2] in her speech on 24 September 2007, for example, made the claim that the EU's soft power is not enough to face the current threats to the EU. Thus, she proposed a new form of power, smart power, as a way for the EU to take an assertive role on the international scene. Ferrero-Waldner (2007) rejected the notion that the EU is purely a soft power due to the fact that it has, for at least the last ten years, been building a military dimension and establishing and utilising crisis management tools. This is accepted by Ferrero-Waldner as necessary for the EU and she explains that the current challenge is to 'ensure coherence between the civilian and military sides; and to use our soft, attractive power more strategically (2007: 3). In concluding her speech, Ferrero-Waldner clearly stated that the type of power that the EU should aim for is smart power, a power that successfully combines elements of hard and soft power.

Hugh Richardson[3] also referred to smart power in his speech, 'Smartening the EU's Soft Power' of 16 May 2008. Similar to Ferrero-Waldner, Richardson also claimed that soft power is no longer an adequate tool for the EU. He stated that the EU must keep its normative values but create a form of power that strengthens them and gives them more force and utility (Richardson, 2008). The ways in which the EU can develop its smart power are through an enhanced crisis management role and through addressing climate change and energy security (Ferrero-Waldner, 2007; Richardson, 2008).

A third advocate for the utilisation of smart power is Olli Rehn, the former EU Commissioner for Enlargement and current Commissioner for Economic and Monetary Affairs and the Euro and Vice-President of the Commission. Rehn, in his speech of 2008, reflected the points made by Ferrero-Waldner (2007) and Richardson (2008), and also made the observation that the EU needs to make its external policies more coherent and effective by using a complete range of policy instruments and resources (Rehn, 2008b).

Finally, recent discussions on the EU's international actorness in terms of power have scrutinised the EU's power with relation to perceptions of the EU as a single market and its position as a trade or market power (Damro, 2012; Meunier and Nicolaïdis, 2006). Damro, for example, in order to conceptualise the EU as a market power, begins by assessing the EU's identity, as does Manners (2002) in his conceptualisation of the EU as a normative power. In contrast to Manners, Damro (2012: 683) asserts that the EU is most often perceived as an integrated market and the EU's identity as such allows it to exercise its power 'through the externalisation of economic and social market related polices and regulatory measures'. Damro (2012: 685) argues that the EU is 'a power that can and does use its market and regulatory strengths to externalise internal polices'.

This power is based on the EU's identity as an integrated market, and the EU's externalisation processes involve encouraging other actors to comply with EU levels of regulation or behave similarly or complementarily to the EU's market policies and regulatory measures (Damro, 2012). In addition to influencing external actors to conform to EU market integration norms, there is also the process of ensuring that these actors conform to the policies which the EU is attempting to externalise. This dynamic is the intentional process through which the EU exerts itself as a market power, yet Damro explains that there are also unintentional processes which are largely based upon the EU's power position as a comparatively large market which provide incentives for external actors to coordinate their regulations based on the perception of the EU as a functioning and successful integrated market.

The findings of this study find resonance with Damro's conception of EU power more than any of the other conceptions presented above. The fact that the EU's actorness is manifest most strongly with regard to its promotion of economic norms of regional integration can be associated with Damro's conceptualisation. However, I argue that the EU's success in diffusing these norms is not so much related to its power but more connected to ASEAN's perception of the EU experience as relevant to ASEAN, and I therefore diverge from his conceptualisation in this respect.

The breadth of conceptions of EU power and the contentious nature of attempts to label the EU as a certain type of power reveal the difficulty of attaching concepts of power to the EU's external action. Therefore, such notions, and especially those related to normative pretensions, are replaced by those which allow for a more neutral analysis of the EU's actorness with regard to its relations with ASEAN in this study.

Power frameworks

Whether the EU is a civilian, soft, normative, ethical, smart or market power has often taken precedence over the importance of the central concept of power and its effects. Therefore, this section engages with, and critiques, definitions of power, which then provides a clear framework for an analysis of EU actorness with regard to the EU's relations with ASEAN and its policy of promoting its regionalism experience to ASEAN.

The majority of scholarly research on power has presented definitions which involve three types of power (Poggi, 2006; Manners, 2013). These definitions have been variations of the same overarching concept, which has included power exertion involving aggressive, military or coercive behaviours; rewarding or encouraging behaviours; or attractive or ideational behaviours. For example, Etzioni (1961) argues that power involves coercion, utilitarian power and normative power. Additionally, Boulding's (1989: 23–29) framework of power consists of 'destructive power' or the 'power of threat', 'productive power' or the 'power of exchange' and 'integrative power' or the 'power of love'. Poggi (2001: 134–149) also presents a trio of power sources – 'political power', 'economic power' and 'ideological' or 'normative' power.

Similarly, Galtung (1973) presents three types of power. I engage with Galtung's framework in this study as it provides a detailed overview of the dynamics required in a relationship for power exertion to occur. For the purposes of this study, Galtung's definition of power provides a meaningful basis of analysis. Its similarities to other scholarly work on power, however, suggest that a number of frameworks would be applicable and provide similar analytical outcomes. Galtung's three types of power are ideological, remunerative and punitive power. Ideological power refers to the power of ideas, remunerative to the power of having goods to offer and punitive to the power of what Galtung refers to as having 'bads' to offer, for example, destruction, force and violence. These three aspects of power can also been seen in terms of cultural (ideological), trade and economic (remunerative) and military (punitive) power (Galtung, 1973).

For one actor to have the ability to exert power over another, Galtung (1973) prescribes a number of criteria. In the case of ideological power, some form of submissiveness is required in the receiver for this power to have any effect. For remunerative power, there is a need for dependence; the receiver must require something from the actor exerting the power in order for the power transfer to take place. Finally, fear is the factor that is necessary in order for punitive power to be exercised (Galtung, 1973). Recognising the features that need to be present for the exercise and transfer of power also enables Galtung to identify which aspects restrict the use of power. Rather than being influenced by another actor due to submissiveness, dependence or fear, one can become largely autonomous with the opposite of these three factors. Self-respect, instead of submissiveness, enables one to be free from ideological power. Self-sufficiency as a replacement of dependency makes remunerative power redundant, and fearlessness frees one from punitive power (Galtung, 1973).

In addition to this, Galtung also presents three sources of power, stating that there is 'power deriving from something one is; power deriving from something one has', and 'power deriving from a position in a structure' (Galtung, 1973: 36). When discussing the power of states,

Galtung (1973) combines the power that derives from something one is and has and refers to it as resource power. The power that a state derives from its position in a structure is termed 'structural or relational power' (Galtung, 1973).

A further point made by Galtung (1973) that is relevant to the discussion on EU power is the importance of dominance as the main element in power transference. Galtung states that dependence is the means through which dominance can be attained. In the context of interactions between global actors, dominance can refer to the situation where

> The Centre supplies something that the Periphery (1) thinks is indispensable, and (2) thinks it cannot be obtained elsewhere. And this is highly related to identification: the Periphery thinks these things are indispensable because it has been taught to think so, because it has adopted and adapted to the culture of the Centre. (Galtung, 1973: 45–46)

Finally, the opposite of dominance is equality, and the two structures interact and arise as a reaction to each other and to avoid each other (Galtung, 1973).

As a result of an in-depth analysis of the concept of power using Galtung's framework, it becomes clear that the term 'power', when used in reference to the EU's external role, is not always the correct expression. Most importantly, it demonstrates that EU power is often framed in a way that obscures an understanding of EU external action. Moreover, using the term 'power' in conjunction with other terms such as 'normative' and 'ethical' is potentially contradictory, or at minimum gives an oxymoronic message (Sjursen, 2006b). For example, when considering the EU's relations with ASEAN, the use of the term 'power' is incorrect.

Using Galtung's power theory, it is difficult to find the necessary elements of submissiveness, dependence or fear that allow the EU to exercise power in the region. In fact, the growing economic and political strength of ASEAN may cause the EU to be more dependent on the Southeast Asian region rather than the other way around. The fact that the EU has a trade deficit in goods with Southeast Asia is just one example of this. Another example, which is discussed in further detail in Chapter 3, is the fact that an invitation from ASEAN to the EU to become a member of the EAS is yet to be offered. This is despite the EU's expression of interest in becoming a member of the summit. Furthermore, with respect to the EU's resource power, the amount of such power is contested in ASEAN as there is no consensus on whether the EU is a relevant actor to either engage with or learn from in the context of regional integration. Even Galtung's concept of transference from the centre to the periphery is problematic as what constitutes the centre or the periphery with respect to the EU and ASEAN is also unclear. Therefore, the use of the term 'power' with reference to the EU's relations with ASEAN is not an appropriate reflection of the nature of the relationship between the two actors.

In addition to the misuse of the term 'power', the discourse on EU power as opposed to influence reflects the internal emphasis of the literature. The Center for Strategic and International Studies (2007: 6) makes reference to the distinction between power and influence by stating that, 'there is no other global power, and yet American hard power does not always translate into influence.' In this sense, the term 'power' often creates a bias towards focusing on the process of the exercise of power as opposed to the impact, or influence, that power has. Regarding the EU, the result is often an excessive emphasis on what type of power the EU is rather than its interactions with other actors and the effects it has on them.

Studies of EU external action: An expanded research agenda and processes of norm diffusion

Scholars have noted the lack of research on the impact of EU external action. Questions raised by Hill (1990: 34) more than two decades ago still require further investigation and ongoing revision. Such questions include

> How far do the policies which states collectively embark upon, particularly in the political sphere, matter to outsiders? If they do, then who are the other states or groups who are most affected and why? What is the nature of any influence which might be exerted, and how far is it the result of deliberate, coordinated policy, or alternatively, the mere product of reputation, history and private enterprise?

Moreover, Hill refers to the importance of considering all levels of interaction with relation to EU foreign policy, '...what can we say about the broad pattern of interaction, not just between member states and the European collective machinery, but between states, the European collective, and the global order as a whole' (Hill, 1990: 34).

An example of the internal perspective of EU power discourse is present in the construction of Manners's evaluation of the EU as a normative power. For example, the diffusion factors of contagion, informational diffusion, procedural diffusion, transference, overt diffusion and the cultural filter which Manners (2002) presents focus heavily on the actor exercising normative power, in this case, the EU. Although reasonable, these factors do not pay attention to the processes involved for this diffusion to be received. The reactions to such diffusion efforts are largely disregarded, and the receiver of such power is viewed as relatively passive. In Manners's 2008 article, he makes the statement that, 'it is one thing to say that the EU is a normative power by virtue of its hybrid polity consisting of supranational and international forms of governance; it is another to argue that the EU acts in a normative (i.e. ethically good) way' (Manners, 2008: 45). What is absent is reference to the fact that the EU is a normative power as a consequence of the results of its actions and as a result of other actors viewing the EU as a normative power. Granted, Manners does go on to mention that, 'normative power in general, and the EU's normative power in particular, is sustainable only if it is felt to be legitimate by those who practise and experience it', yet the focus on those who experience the EU's normative power still remains under-developed (Manners, 2008: 46).

As previously discussed, much research has focused on what type of power the EU is and what form of foreign policy the EU has. Although significant, much of this study has added to the insular and introspective approach to studies on the EU as an international actor. There is also a lack of self-awareness, which leads to an inability to match external expectations and perceptions of the EU with internal ones and leads to what Nicolaïdis and Howse (2002) refer to as the projection of an EU-topia as opposed to what the EU is, and is capable of doing, in reality. Another risk of an insufficient amount of self-awareness is the trap of being too Eurocentric and assuming a role as a superior global actor that smacks of 'missionary zeal' (Diez, 2005: 623). Manners (2006a) claims that there is a need for an element of 'reflexivity'. I contend that the focus should not only be on 'reflexivity' as a way to understand or better establish an EU identity or the EU itself. Rather, similar to Bicci (2006: 289) who explains that 'reflexivity' refers to 'an ongoing reflection about the action, its context, its effects on such a context and the feedback of those expected effects on the action', 'reflexivity' in the case of EU foreign policy should refer not only to the EU analysing itself but also to how others are affected by, and react to the EU, and how effective and successful the EU is at achieving its foreign policy aims.

Therefore, what remains necessary is an evaluation of whether the EU is considered an international actor of consequence by external actors. This is for a number of reasons. Aggestam (2008) discusses the tension between ethical decisions and ethical behaviour, pointing out that ethical principles do not always produce the desired outcomes. Accepting that there is not always a seamless transition between principles and behaviour, and that intentions do not always produce the expected outcomes, a focus on the efficacy of EU foreign policy demonstrates the need to assess what is appropriate and what is effective. In other words, does the EU's approach to foreign policy actually produce the necessary and desired results? This question, in order to produce a complete analysis of EU foreign policy, must be answered from an EU and external perspective. Sjursen (2006b) adds to this by stating that the assessment of EU foreign policy is lacking in two areas: the first is a need to have a more rigorous theoretical analysis of the justification of norms and how to clarify just in what way the EU is – or is not – a normative power. The second is a heightened focus on empirical analysis to which a conceptual framework can be applied.

In sum, much of the literature to date has not paid enough attention to the external impact of the EU's foreign policy decisions and actions. If this has been done, it has mainly been from an internal perspective. Diez (2005) states that the identification of an actor as a certain type of power is dependent on the impact that actor has on others. Additionally, 'whether or not a particular identity construction is regarded as problematic depends on the context in which it is viewed' (Diez, 2005: 632). In this regard, the aim of this book is to broaden this research agenda so that it encompasses the assessment of the practical and concrete effects of and reactions to EU foreign policy.

In order to do this, conceptual frameworks of norm diffusion which incorporate an analysis of external perspectives are applied to the EU's policy of regionalism promotion. The norm diffusion framework developed by Manners (2002) presents a comprehensive framework for the assessment of norm diffusion processes which focus on the norm entrepreneur, which in this study is the EU. So as to provide sufficient conceptual analysis of the norm recipient in this study, ASEAN, Acharya's (2004) norm diffusion framework centred on norm localisation and his framework on norm subsidiarity (2011a) are utilised.

As previously mentioned, Manners presents six different ways in which norms can be diffused – contagion, informational diffusion, procedural diffusion, transference, overt diffusion and the cultural filter (Manners, 2002). Contagion refers to the unintentional diffusion of norms from one actor to another. Informational diffusion, on the other hand, is the result of 'strategic communications'. Procedural diffusion is the process by which two actors institutionalise a relationship to foster dialogue and cooperation. Transference refers to the exchange of 'goods, trade, aid or technical assistance' which can include the 'exportation of community norms and standards'. Overt diffusion occurs when an actor is physically present in another state or international organisation and, finally, the cultural filter affects 'the impact of international norms and political learning in third states and organisations leading to learning, adaptation or rejection' (Manners, 2002: 244–245).

Acharya's (2004: 239) theory of norm diffusion aims to explain how 'local agents reconstruct foreign norms to ensure the norms fit with the cognitive priors and identities'. An external norm is more likely to be adopted if it does not threaten the norms that are already in place in the domestic context (Acharya, 2004). If this is the case, then norm localisation has more chance of occurring. Localisation refers to the process by which 'norm-takers build congruence between transnational norms and local beliefs and processes' (Acharya 2004: 239). Acharya (2004), rather than viewing the receivers of norms as relatively passive, considers norm-takers as both active and strategic in their adoption of external norms from other actors. Acharya (2004) states that Southeast Asian actors have been actively choosing to localise norms that increase their legitimacy, authority, credibility and power and simultaneously rejecting norms that threaten the domestic order. In addition, localised norms do not replace existing norms but rather enhance existing beliefs. A domestic norm will only be rejected in favour of an introduced norm if the domestic norm has already been challenged from within (Acharya, 2004).

In addition to an explanation of processes of norm localisation, norm displacement and norm rejection, Acharya (2011a) also provides a framework of norm subsidiarity. Whereas norm localisation focuses its attention on how a foreign norm affects the local environment, norm subsidiarity involves processes of norm acceptance, rejection and creation which occur as a consequence of an actor's external relations and its power and autonomy in relation to another external actor. Acharya (2011a: 97) defines norm subsidiarity as the phenomenon whereby 'local actors create rules with a view to preserve their autonomy from dominance, neglect, violation, or abuse by more powerful central actors'. According to Acharya (2011a: 100), norm subsidiarity occurs when actors feel the need to challenge potential 'exclusion or marginalisation from global norm-making processes' or when they are 'confronted with great power hypocrisy'. The former motivation allows weaker states to assert their own 'ideas, interests and identities' when the potential to be dominated by the norms of stronger states or actors exists (Acharya, 2011a: 100). The latter impetus for norm subsidiarity is a result of weaker states 'when they see the violation of their cherished global norms by powerful actors and when higher level institutions tasked with their defense seem unwilling or incapable of preventing their violation' (Acharya, 2011a: 100).

Acharya's (2011a: 101) explanation of norm subsidiarity presents two possible effects. The first is the 'challenging/resisting effect', whereby an actor creates norms and rules that allow the actor to enhance its independence to manage its own affairs free of intervention from any 'higher authority'. The second effect is the 'supportive/strengthening' effect, which involves actors supporting global norms that are already in existence which contribute to their autonomy.

When comparing norm localisation and norm subsidiarity, Acharya (2011a: 98) makes some distinctions. Notably, whereas localisation chiefly involves the import of foreign norms and local actors are considered 'norm-takers', subsidiarity can involve the rejection of external norms if there is fear of domination by external actors, norm creation or norm exportation, which involves the export or universalisation of a local norm. Acharya (2011a) makes the point that these processes can work in tandem and a local actor can simultaneously follow processes of localisation by assessing the import of foreign norms and also concurrently reject, create and export norms as it feels necessary.

Acharya (2011a) argues that norm subsidiarity is a dynamic which is inherent in weaker states, and occurs as a result of weaker states fearing domination by external powers. The relationship between the EU and ASEAN is not one that is determined by power dynamics, and especially those in which the EU is the dominant power. Nevertheless, norm subsidiarity is still a worthwhile process with which to analyse the interplay between the EU's efforts to promote its norms of regionalism and ASEAN's role in asserting its authority and independence by assessing which of the EU's norms are of relevance to ASEAN.

Acharya's frameworks of norm diffusion are employed in this study as they adequately provide a structure for the assessment of the extent to which processes, modes of governance and norms distinct to the EU have been localised or rejected by ASEAN. An assessment of whether ASEAN has created subsidiarity norms also provides opportunity to further understand the role that ASEAN plays in its normative development *vis-à-vis* regionalism. For in cases where EU norms have not been localised by ASEAN, norm subsidiarity allows for the asessment of what other processes have occurred and the actions which ASEAN has taken with regard to its local norms of regionalism.

Previous literature and conceptual analyses which have focused on processes of Europeanisation often have similarities to Acharya's (2004; 2011a) frameworks. The main difference has been that they have often focused on internal processes within the EU and its close geographical neighbours. Europeanisation as a concept has had varied and contested definitions. Those more suited to the internal European context have included 'the development of institutions of governance at the European level' and 'the achievement of the political unification of Europe' (Buller and Gamble, 2002: 9–10). Definitions which have the potential to have a broader application beyond Europe include Buller and Gamble's (2002: 16) definition whereby Europeanisation is 'a situation where distinct modes of European governance have transformed aspects of domestic polity' and Radaelli's (2000: 4) definition whereby Europeanisation

> Consists of processes of a) construction, b) diffusion and c) institutionalisation of formal and informal rules, procedures, policy paradigms, styles, 'ways of doing things' and shared beliefs and norms which are first defined and consolidated in the EU policy process and then incorporated in the logic of domestic (national and subnational) discourse, political structures and public policies.

Compared to Acharya's (2004, 2011a) concepts of localisation and subsidiarity, however, these definitions do not provide the same depth of analysis which allows for the questions of how and why a domestic polity is transformed to be answered. Nor do these definitions allow for a comparative analysis of why certain transformations take place and others do not. Moreover, Buller and Gamble's (2002) definition of Europeanisation, similar to studies on the EU as an international actor or a certain type of power, does not give sufficient attention to the recipients of Europeanisation and the role they play in processes of transformation.

Therefore, in this book, concepts of diffusion and norm entrepreneurship are prioritised over Europeanisation, despite the recognition that there is a certain level of overlap among these concepts. Olsen's (2007) discussion on diffusion further reveals the potential of conceptualisations based on diffusion processes to take into consideration all actors involved. Similar to Acharya (2004, 2011a), Olsen (2007) explains that diffusion processes will not always result in exact replicas of what has been diffused and are mostly transformed during the process. This is often because diffusion takes place within a 'framework of resources, capabilities, incentives and sanctions' and, in addition, diffusion has to 'attend to the resources mobilised for promoting European forms in other parts of the world, as well as the resources available for non-Europeans to resist unattractive forms' (Olsen, 2007: 85). As well as recognising the need to analyse the context in which diffusion takes place, Olsen (2007) also attempts to outline the conditions necessary for norm recipients to allow diffusion to happen.

Olsen (2007) lists properties such as the attractiveness, distinctiveness, legitimacy and functionality of European norms as determinants of whether norms are received and diffused. Of relevance to this study, Olsen (2007: 85) makes the suggestion that 'the shifting long-term European export–import balance of forms is one possible indicator of whether Europe is becoming a more or less important entity in its interaction with the rest of the world'. Such a statement links closely to the central research questions of this study which endeavour to determine how the EU's efforts to export its regionalism experience to ASEAN, and the results of such a policy, impact on perceptions of the EU as an international actor.

In order to assess how the EU's norms of regionalism have been exported to ASEAN, Manners's six processes of norm diffusion are examined throughout the book. As discussed earlier, these processes focus heavily on the norm exporter, with little attention given to the role the recipient plays in the process of norm diffusion. Although Manners (2002) alludes to the role of the recipient in the sixth process, the cultural filter, I will also utilise Acharya's (2004, 2011a) frameworks of norm diffusion, which are considered to provide a more comprehensive analysis of the role of the norm recipient. I will use the following questions based on Acharya's framework to assess the diffusion of the EU's norms of regionalism to ASEAN.

- Does the norm resonate with domestic norms?
- Do local actors see the benefit of the norm?
- Are existing norms considered inadequate?
- Is the norm seen to enhance the profile of ASEAN and its beliefs?
- Does ASEAN seek to replace a norm that has been challenged from within?
- Will the external norm increase instability?
- Have challenging/resisting behaviours been evident?
- Have supportive/strengthening behaviours been evident?

These questions and Manners's six diffusion processes are used in Chapters 4, 5 and 6 of this book to assess the processes of norm diffusion with relation to the EU's norms of economic integration, institutionalisation and its political norms.

Conclusion

This chapter has provided the conceptual and theoretical frameworks which will be used in the remainder of the book. Firstly, through an analysis of the literature on EU international actorness, it becomes apparent that a more comprehensive set of criteria to assess actorness, one which includes the normative and structural composition of the EU, is necessary. In order to do this, I created a set of criteria questions based on the frameworks of analysis presented by Lucarelli (2007) and Wunderlich (2012) which will be used in this book to assess the EU's actorness in relation to its promotion of economic integration, institutionalisation and political norms to ASEAN.

Secondly, this chapter critiqued the relevant literature on EU power and argued that framing the EU as a certain type of power does not always allow for an accurate examination of EU external action. Scholarly definitions of power (Etzioni, 1961; Boulding, 1989; Poggi, 2001; Galtung, 1973), when examined in conjunction with the EU's relations with ASEAN, demonstrate the fact that power is the incorrect term to use in this context. Therefore, rather than examining the EU's policy of norm promotion to ASEAN in terms of defining the EU as a power, I employ an approach which uses an examination of norm diffusion. Manners's (2002) six methods of norm diffusion are used throughout this book to assess the process of norm entrepreneurship by the EU. However, as Manners's (2002) norm diffusion framework does not afford sufficient attention to the norm recipient being examined in this study, namely ASEAN, Acharya's (2004, 2011a) frameworks of localisation and subsidiarity are also employed.

3
Drivers of Interregionalism: EU–ASEAN Engagement

ASEAN is too big to ignore and too sweet and weak to bully.

Interview Respondent 8, EU delegation official in Southeast Asia, 2011.

Europe has to decide, is this going to be an important part of the world for them? If so, maybe they will have to increase their presence, even though now they have so many financial problems and so many difficulties.

Interview Respondent 1, Former Secretary General of ASEAN, 2011.

The EU and ASEAN as drivers of interregionalism

The EU and ASEAN are drivers of regionalism in their own geographical and political contexts and supporters of regionalism within their own regions and elsewhere. In addition, they are both advocates of interregional dynamics and relations, to which their willingness to be dialogue partners attests. Since the establishment of an official cooperation agreement between the EU and ASEAN, with the signing of the *Cooperation Agreement between the Member Countries of ASEAN and the European Community* on 7 March 1980 (ASEAN–EU, 1980), the relationship between ASEAN and the EU has changed considerably. In 1980, the relationship primarily focused on affording each other most-favoured nation status as stated in the General Agreement on Tariffs and Trade (GATT) and development cooperation between the EU and ASEAN. The most recent Plan of Action, the *Bandar Seri Begawan Plan of Action to*

Strengthen the EU–ASEAN Enhanced Partnership (2013–2017) (ASEAN–EU, 2012a), demonstrates how the cooperation between the two regional organisations has broadened to cover political/security, economic/trade and sociocultural issues.

Nevertheless, there still remains among many the opinion that the relationship between the EU and ASEAN requires further attention and improvement (Islam, 2011; Camroux, 2012; Oegroseno, 2012). Indonesia's ambassador to the EU, Arif Hvas Oegroseno, has stated that the EU and ASEAN need to accord their partnership higher priority.

> Although ASEAN has regularly held summit meetings with such global players as China, Japan, Korea and the U.S., the EU, which also holds summit with the same states, has not viewed ASEAN as a potential strategic partner in these high-level deliberations. ASEAN is similarly guilty of not seeing the advantages of collaborating on these top-level exchanges with the EU. (Oegroseno, 2012)

Oegroseno calls for the EU to regard ASEAN as a strategic partner, and that for the Plan of Action for 2013–2017 (ASEAN–EU, 2012a) to be implemented satisfactorily, the EU must establish a delegation and appoint a head of delegation to ASEAN, as other actors such as the US, China and Japan have done (Oegroseno, 2012).

Both the EU and ASEAN are currently facing the challenge of retaining and enhancing the importance and relevance they possess in relation to each other. For the EU, one of the biggest challenges is to convince ASEAN that its regionalism project is still of merit and that its internal concerns are not hindering its ability to engage with ASEAN. Survey and interview responses have indicated concern regarding the impact the economic and financial crises in Europe have potentially had on the relationship between the EU and ASEAN. As one survey respondent commented, 'the EU is for the moment distracted by its internal problems' (S5 EOA, 2012). An interview respondent commented that, as a consequence of the crisis in Europe 'we will need to work hard to get back our self-esteem' (I11 EO, 2011). Another significant challenge is for the EU to demonstrate that it does give priority to ASEAN and the Southeast Asian region and that high-level officials within the EU contribute to the EU's presence in the region primarily by attending summits and meetings.

For ASEAN, the challenge it faces is the ability to prove that its development of regionalism, and in particular the realisation of its economic community by 2015, is moving at a sufficient pace for EU support to be continued and to avoid EU officials becoming discouraged by ASEAN's slow implementation of initiatives.

A survey respondent based in Southeast Asia stated, 'ASEAN is not yet very much integrated and therefore not easy to "grasp"' (S5 EOA, 2012). An official at the EEAS stated that, 'ASEAN does not have the same amount of ambition as the EU' and that, 'ASEAN does not have the institutions to set up what they hope to achieve' (I7 EO, 2011). Dissatisfaction with the level of regionalism development in ASEAN was prevalent among interview respondents working at the EEAS. Moreover, interview and survey data indicated that although ASEAN may be a worthwhile partner, the EU and its member states currently give other actors more priority. One survey respondent stated that there is 'an obsession with China (and to a lesser extent the other BRICS (Brazil, Russia, India, China, South Africa) within the EU and the individual member states' (S2 EA, 2012). In addition, ASEAN's endeavours to be the central driver of regional groupings within the Southeast Asian region and Asia, as discussed later in this chapter, must be balanced against according the EU the priority and importance sufficient to maintaining a constructive relationship with the EU, as Oegroseno (2012) suggests.

Moreover, the survey responses indicate that the state of the relationship between the EU and ASEAN has the potential to improve. This is evident by the fact that the current state of the relationship was considered 'fair' by the majority of the respondents, as shown in Figure 3.1 below.

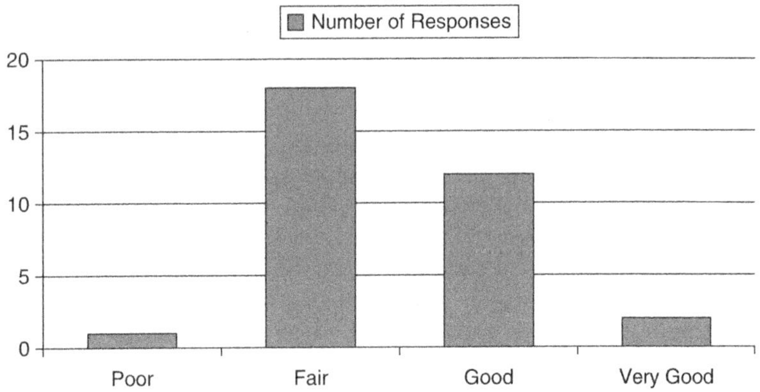

Figure 3.1 How would you describe the state of the relationship between the EU and ASEAN?

When asked about the importance of the relationship, however, the majority of respondents stated that, on a scale which included 'minor importance', 'important', 'very important' and 'vital', the relationship was 'important'. These responses are presented in Figure 3.2 below.

Similarly, the responses presented in Figure 3.3 below indicate that, according to the survey respondents, the importance of the two actors to each other will continue to increase. The majority of respondents answered 'agree' to the statements 'the importance of ASEAN to the EU will steadily increase' and 'the importance of the EU to ASEAN will steadily increase'. Despite the perception that the relationship between the two actors is important, the responses in Figures 3.1 and 3.2 and the responses to the statements 'the EU should give greater priority to its relations with ASEAN than it does currently' and 'the EU is an influential actor in the Southeast Asian region' in Figure 3.3 below are indicators that the relationship has the potential to be enhanced. This point was also reflected in comments made by survey and interview respondents, with the main perception being that the EU, in particular, does not prioritise its relationship sufficiently. A survey respondent stated that 'ASEAN is not yet regarded by the EU as a strategic partner, so the importance is attached more in words than in deeds' (S20 EAA, 2012). In addition, an interview respondent stated that, 'in Brussels, ASEAN doesn't count' (I8 EOA, 2011).

This chapter investigates the current state of the relationship between the EU and ASEAN and determines the primary motivations for their

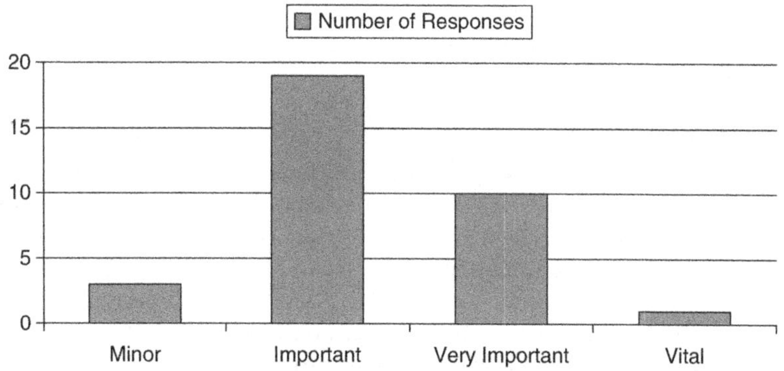

Figure 3.2 How would you rate the importance of the relationship between the EU and ASEAN?

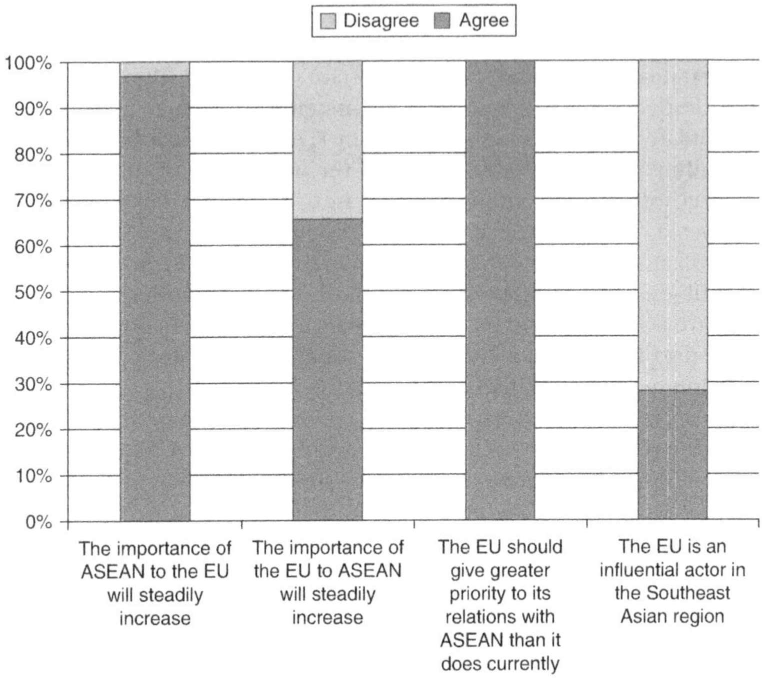

Figure 3.3 Do you agree or disagree with the following statements?

mutual interest in fostering an interregional dialogue and partnership. For both actors the motivations primarily emerge from the contribution their interregional relationship can make to fulfil their economic and political interests.

Economic motivations

The EU's desire to actively engage Southeast Asia economically has two main dimensions. The first is the desire to have access to Asian markets and to provide a market for Asian goods. The other, closely linked to this, is to ensure that the EU is not excluded from the increasingly powerful economic entity that is ASEAN, and the economies of its member states. Demonstrating this point not only with regard to economic relations but also to relations more generally is the *East Asia Policy Guidelines* of 2007. They state that the EU should strengthen its relationship with Asian regional bodies

> To enrich the expertise of Member States, the Council Secretariat and the Commission on regional foreign and security policy matters, to establish better channels through which the EU can deliver messages when it feels that its interests are at stake and to develop common analysis and approaches, allowing the EU to deploy its weight more effectively in concert with others. (Council of the EU, 2007: 4)

In the last decade, although trade has increased between the EU and ASEAN, the EU has had a stable trade in goods deficit with ASEAN, which stood at approximately 24.8 billion euro in 2011 (Europa, 2013a). With individual ASEAN states the EU has also run trade deficits except for its trade relations with Myanmar, with whom it has a surplus, and Singapore, where trade is balanced (Delegation of the EU to Singapore, 2010). In 2009 the trade deficit for trade in goods between the EU and ASEAN was at 17.9 billion euro. In 2011 the deficit stood at 24.8 billion euro (Europa, 2013a). Whilst the EU had a trade in services surplus of 3.2 billion euro in 2011 (Europa, 2013a), the persistent trade deficit in traded goods demonstrates an opportunity for the EU to increase its economic involvement with Southeast Asia and the need for it to continue to address the deficit in trade in goods between the two regions.

The European Commission's, *Towards a New Asia Strategy* (European Commission, 1994: 3) expresses the fact that engagement with Asia is based upon the acknowledgement of the economic importance of the Asian region. It states that:

> The increase of the relative weight of Asia in the world economy will considerably reinforce the political weight of this region on the international scene. To keep Europe in its major role on the world stage it is imperative to take account of the emergence of these new Asian powers.

The EU's 2003 *A New Partnership with South-East Asia* is also explicit in its recognition of the economic importance of the Southeast Asian region.

> A recent major study on long-term developments in international trade has predicted that by 2050 the centre of gravity of the world economy will have shifted to the Asia Pacific region, with ASEAN emerging as the world's largest exporter.[1] In spite of the uncertainty of such long-term predictions, it can hardly be doubted that South-East Asia will increasingly be one of the most dynamic growth engines of the world economy. (European Commission, 2003: 8)

More recently, the Council of the EU's *Guidelines on the EU's Foreign and Security Policy in East Asia* (Council of the EU, 2012a: 4) also refer to the economic importance of the Southeast Asian region, stating that it has 'major economic interests at stake' in the region. The guidelines explain that Mainland China, Hong Kong, Macao, Taiwan, Japan, ASEAN and Korea together made up more than a quarter of the EU's global trade in 2010 and that this percentage is increasing (Council of the EU, 2012a). ASEAN accounts for 5.2% of the EU's total trade, and the EU's trade with East Asia is at 27% of its total trade, which is greater than the percentage of total trans-Atlantic trade, which is at 22.7% (Council of the EU, 2012a).

In addition, Dent (2004) states that in the 1990s, three major economic centres arose – the US, Asia and the EU. However, the relationships between these three powers were not equal. Strong ties between the US and Asia were present, as were agreements between the US and the EU. Asia and the EU, however, did not have a similar level of interaction (Cameron, 2007). Recognising this, the EU sought to increase its involvement with ASEAN so as to be able to benefit from the increased economic power of Southeast Asia and to maintain an avenue for pursuing its interests in the region (Cameron, 2007). A sense of urgency was evident in the 1995 European Commission document, *Free Trade Areas: An Appraisal*, which warned against regulatory systems in Asia aligning with those of the US as a consequence of cooperation in the Asia-Pacific Economic Cooperation (APEC). According to the Commission, this would have a detrimental effect on the EU's ability to remain economically engaged with Asia.

> If the countries of East Asia were, as a result of regulatory co-operation within the Asia-Pacific Economic Cooperation (APEC), to align their regulatory systems practices to those of the United States, this would place the EU at a competitive disadvantage, at least to the extent that a large and dynamic part of the world economy developed as result of a system which diverged significantly from that of the Union. (European Commission, 1995: 7)

The creation of ASEM was also influenced by this argument. In a speech by Kristalina Georgieva (2010), the European Commissioner for International Cooperation, Humanitarian Aid and Crisis Response, the importance of ASEM was emphasised. Georgieva (2010: 2) stated that ASEM had a vital role to play as a 'space for contact, dialogue and convergence between Asia and Europe'. With regard to economic motivations more specifically, she mentioned that the EU needed to be able to accommodate the increasing financial strength of China and other Asian economies, that the EU and Asia have strong interests in working together at the G20 and that the EU should keep its markets open and not pursue protectionist approaches in order to allow global growth and protect and foster relations between Europe and Asia (Georgieva, 2010).

ASEAN's economic interest in engaging with the EU also motivates it to retain the EU as a dialogue partner. Significantly, 26% of foreign direct investment (FDI) into ASEAN comes from the EU (Chia, 2011). As a main source of impetus for ASEAN economic integration, FDI is a crucial motivator of ASEAN's interest in maintaining relations with the EU (Chia, 2011). Severino (2007a) has pointed to the fact that investments are attracted to China, and away from ASEAN, due to China's large domestic market and cheap land and labour and that China and India are becoming the more popular destinations for foreign investment. This being the case, it is also important for ASEAN to maintain its relationship with the EU and continue to provide an attractive destination for FDI so as not to lose investments to China and India.

Additionally, as Islam (2010: 18) suggests, 'Asian nations need to boost sales in Europe to maintain their impressive growth rates', and whilst the donor–recipient dynamic between the EU and ASEAN has developed into a more symmetrical relationship, EU development aid is still important for a number of developing countries within ASEAN (Islam, 2010).

Former Secretary General, Surin Pitsuwan in a press statement at the 18th ASEAN–EU Ministerial Meeting presented the statistics related to ASEAN's trade and FDI connection to the EU.

> ASEAN total trade with the EU has grown from USD 160.5 billion in 2006 to USD 202.5 billion in 2008. The EU is ASEAN's second largest trade partner (after Japan), with a total trade volume of over 169.8 billion euro in 2009. Further, the EU's share of ASEAN's total trade accounts for 11.2% of ASEAN's total trade in 2009. The total EU FDI flows to ASEAN has also grown from USD 10.6 billion in 2006 to USD 13 billion in 2008. (Pitsuwan, 2010)

More recently, Karel De Gucht, the European Commissioner for Trade in a speech at the second EU–ASEAN Business Summit pointed out that 'at €160 billion per year, Europe accounts for over 10% of ASEAN's total trade in goods. The percentage for services is even higher – at 13%

of the total' (De Gucht, 2012a: 3). De Gucht also explained that despite the economic and financial crises in Europe, the EU continues to be the world's largest trading power and whilst admitting that there was a trade in goods deficit with ASEAN, De Gucht attributed this to 'our (the EU's) significant oil and gas bill' (De Gucht, 2012a: 3).

The figures and official statements presented in this section are strong economic drivers of EU–ASEAN engagement. Especially in the case of the EU there is a sense that this economic relationship has the potential to be improved and also that the EU is in a precarious position not to be neglected by ASEAN due to the attention given to other ASEAN partners and multilateral fora which exist that do not include the EU, such as APEC. A major focus for ASEAN is to ensure that it remains an attractive destination for FDI, even with the emergence of other markets which potentially lure investments away from ASEAN.

Legitimacy, relevance and survival

EU documents regarding Southeast Asia such as *A New Partnership with South-East Asia* (European Commission, 2003), the *East Asia Policy Guidelines* (Council of the EU, 2007) and the *Guidelines on the EU's Foreign and Security Policy in East Asia* (Council of the EU, 2012a) refer to similar values, features and security issues as reasons for EU cooperation with the region.[2] Although this provides justification for the EU to pursue an active relationship with ASEAN, it is difficult to argue that this is a sufficient factor; two actors can agree to have similar values without necessarily cooperating with each other to maintain those values. This is potentially the reason why some scholars have sought to find a deeper motivation behind EU action in the Southeast Asian region.

Söderbaum, Stålgren and Van Langenhove claim that one of the EU's main foreign policy objectives is 'to establish itself as a global actor and promote a world order where regions gain increasing legitimacy as actors in international affairs' (2005: 375). Similarly, Farrell (2009: 1171) states that the EU policy of promoting regionalism has two objectives; the first is the 'preservation of a regional order' and the second is the 'enhancement of the EU's global presence'. The EU Institute for Security Studies's 2010 report, *A Strategy for EU Foreign Policy*, states that:

> ... for the Union, multilateralism is not only the preferred avenue for the conduct of international action: it is also part of its own identity and so the Union has a vital interest in an international system based on norms and rules that facilitates the survival and expansion of its own model. (EU Institute for Security Studies, 2010: 18)

Youngs (2004) discusses the effect that the EU's external image has on its internal cohesion and legitimacy. He argues that, 'talking about values externally can be seen as one factor contributing to efforts to strengthen their vitality internally' (Youngs, 2004: 419). He also explains that the nature of the EU, based on 'deliberation, socio-economic networks and co-operation through – and predicted upon – respect for individual rights' (Youngs, 2004: 419) naturally lends itself to the legitimacy of the projection of these values externally.

However, the EU's claimed ideals of promoting values such as democracy, human rights and regionalism do not always match its actions, resulting in an incoherent approach to external relations and the failure to accomplish the legitimation that the EU desires. Youngs (2004) refers to this point when he mentions the reaction that non-governmental organisations (NGOs) have had to the EU's attempts at the promotion of EU values internationally. Many NGOs have disapproved of the conditionality that the EU places on third states as it is one way in which to justify reduced aid flows to states that do not have high strategic importance (Youngs, 2004). Zielonka (2008: 480) also states that, 'while EU norms and regulations may well benefit targeted global actors, they are at root designed to protect and promote EU interests'. The issue here is the tension between strategic interests and norm promotion. When norms are promoted externally for strategic reasons, and not for their intrinsic value, the result is an unreliable and unstable external policy that can change as quickly as the political environment. This dilemma is potentially very difficult, or even impossible, to overcome; the EU cannot reject the values that are at the core of its identity and structure, nor is it feasible for it to act without consideration of its strategic interests. Therefore, what remains is the need to reassess the manner in which the EU combines the promotion of its values and the protection and pursuit of its self-interest to create the most coherent external policy as possible.[3]

At the same time as wanting to have more of a presence globally, regional bodies such as the EU also find engaging other regions beneficial as they become stronger and more organised. A potential explanation for this is presented by Hänggi and Roloff *et al.* (2006: 17) who state that, 'interregional cooperation is used as an instrument to balance the dominance of other regional groupings'. In other words, competitive instincts motivate the creation and maintenance of interregional relations. Evidence of this is the desire for the EU to promote ASEM as a response to APEC's refusal to grant the EU observer status (Hänggi and Roloff et al., 2006). In addition, the EU seeks an active role in Southeast

Asia as a way to promote its ability to be a legitimate international actor. If the EU, as a unified actor, can exert influence in another region of the world, then its utility and efficacy are reinforced. It also aims to promote regionalism in Southeast Asia, attempting to legitimise and normalise not only the active presence of the EU in international relations but also the concept of regionalism.[4] Evidence of this is the funding the EU provides for regional projects and initiatives aimed at strengthening regional institutions in Southeast Asia (Rüland, 2002), for example, the APRIS programme. As one survey respondent stated:

> In a sense, the EU's agenda (of promoting regionalism to ASEAN) is no other than 'supporting ASEAN in its effort and help to succeed'. Why? It is probably indeed the EU way of making itself seen in the world and reinforcing its position – but also to promote its values. (S5 EOA, 2012)

Additionally, the Commission's 2003 document, *A New Partnership with South-East Asia*, explicitly refers to the importance of regionalism. It states that 'a strong ASEAN is probably the best guarantee for peace and stability in the region. The EU can contribute through providing its expertise in regional integration, if asked' (European Commission, 2003). Survey and interview respondents expressed the view that the promotion of regionalism and interregionalism are also preferable as they help to simplify external relations. A survey respondent stated that the policy of promoting regionalism is based on 'a mixture of a well-meant wish to "do good" and entirely justifiable self-interest'. This respondent explained that it is 'easier to export to one integrated market than to 10 different countries' and that 'the EU will indirectly benefit from peace and stability in the ASEAN region' (S16 EOA, 2012).

Furthermore, in response to the survey question, 'why is the EU trying to promote its own model of regional integration in the Southeast Asian Region?', the four most popular responses were 'to promote its own values', 'to meet economic interests', 'to enhance security and stabilty in Southeast Asia' and 'to reinforce its position in the world'. For this question, the response rate was 88% (30 respondents), and the respondents were given the opportunity to choose as many responses as they felt were appropriate.

The results show that there is no consistent agreement on any single reason presented, which suggests great diversity among respondents. The two most prominent choices, however, received 80% and 77% of total responses, respectively. This suggests that these two explanations received the most common agreement among all survey participants. Figure 3.4 below provides the responses to the abovementioned question.

The most predominant response, 'promoting EU values', reflects survey respondent 16's comment above regarding a mixture of self-interest and the desire to 'do good' (S16 EOA, 2012). This is because promoting EU values can be interpreted as a self-interested desire to increase EU legitimacy and the legitimacy of EU values and simultaneously be interpreted as a normative and altruistic agenda – provided that there is consensus on the virtue of EU values. As the second most prevalent response in Figure 3.4 below, 'meeting economic interests', can also be interpreted as a self-interested driver of promotion policies, the survey results to this question suggest that EU self-interest is a strong motivator for the promotion of regionalism to ASEAN.

However, global legitimisation of the EU and EU norms is a sensitive area and, as a result, is stated in a less obvious manner by the EU. I deem this to be due to the fact that a conscious recognition of the self-interested pursuit of self-legitimisation can be viewed as quite arrogant and conceited and would adversely affect any attempts of a symmetrical relationship with Southeast Asia. In interviews conducted for this study respondents referred to the fact that EU officials did not want to appear overbearing and that a policy-sharing situation is preferable as 'it is counter-productive to go in with a lecturing attitude' (I7 EO, 2011).

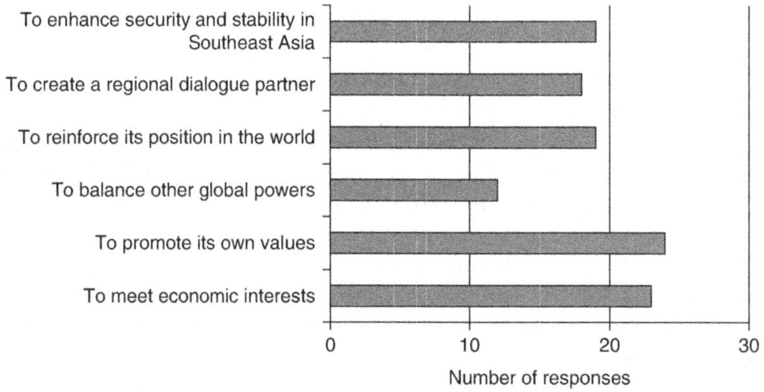

Figure 3.4 Why is the EU trying to promote its own model of regional integration in Southeast Asia?

Instead, the similarities between the two regions are emphasised – the values, norms and security issues that they share, despite the fact that perceptions of the EU's motivations are more focused on the reinforcement of EU values and economic interests.

Much international relations literature has examined which conditions lead to peace and development (Doyle, 1986; Waltz, 1979; Quackenbush and Rudy, 2009; Leftwich, 1993). Doyle's (1983) claim that a separate peace exists among liberal states in that they do not enter into conflict with each other and that tension arises mainly between non-liberal and liberal states reflects the foundational values espoused within the Lisbon Treaty. Article 2 of the Lisbon Treaty states that, 'the Union is founded on the values of respect, freedom, democracy, equality, the rule of law and respect for human rights, including the rights of persons belonging to minorities' (EU, 2009). Kant's description of the three sources for 'perpetual peace' are discussed by Doyle (1986) and include constitutional law relating to republican representation and a separation of powers; international law which allows for free speech, accommodation and respect for other liberal states, which could also include a pacific union of liberal republics through a mutual non-aggression pact or security agreement; and cosmopolitan law which enables the right to hospitality towards foreigners and promotes mutual respect and understanding. It also allows for economic cooperation and eventual interdependence and a free market mechanism whereby financial and trade connections allow states to accommodate each other with minimal state direction and control (Doyle, 1986).

Doyle's liberal democratic peace theory which draws on Kant's 'perpetual peace' framework reflects the EU's foundational values. Tang (2012), however, has analysed the conditions for peace among the states of ASEAN and has argued that neither a constructivist approach to peace within ASEAN based on a collective security arrangement nor democracy and economic interdependence linked to the theory of liberal peace is the primary source of peaceful relations in Southeast Asia. This is because Tang (2012) claims that there has been relative peace without democracy and economic interdependence for decades in Southeast Asia. Furthermore, whilst there has not been a major war between any ASEAN member states since ASEAN's inception, militarised interstate disputes have occurred, potentially exaggerating ASEAN's security role.

According to Tang (2012), it is instead the national pursuit of liberal capitalist economies which has contributed to ASEAN's peace by virtue of the fact that such economies rely on stable and open economic markets and conditions. For the developing economies of ASEAN, of initial concern was maintaining and developing trade and investment links with external partners – intraregional economic coordination only came at a later stage. ASEAN's initial role, therefore, was not to promote similar values to those of the EU but to provide a conducive environment for the development of liberal capitlalist economies. It has therefore been a 'capitalist' peace in Southeast Asia rather than a 'liberal' peace promoted by the EU which has contributed to relatively peaceful relations among the states of ASEAN (Tang, 2012: 412).

Leftwich's analysis of the argument that democratic good governance based on liberal-democratic polities facilitate peace and prosperity is also pertinent to a discussion on the EU and ASEAN. Leftwich refers to the often unspoken assumption that whilst the premise that liberal capitalist democracies lead to peaceful international relations is of Western orgin, this concept is often thought to have universal application. He therefore questions whether democracy is the 'ncessary prior or parallel condition of development, not an outcome of it' (Leftwich, 1993: 605) and assumptions which presuppose that political liberalisation is a necessary condition for greater development. He finds that 'good governance' has rarely preceded economic development, and Tang's (2012) findings regarding the ASEAN states support his arguments. Tang (2012) and Leftwich (1993) are similar in that they do not deny the positive and preferable conditions which democratic, capitalist and liberal societies and economies create. They also agree that there has been a tendency in the literature to assume that there has been one teleology which has occurred throughout all regions of the world. Whilst there is an emphasis within the EU on the values of good governance and democracy, Leftwich explains that it is not the 'combination of liberal economies and democratic politics that will determine developmental outcomes, but the manner of their interaction' (Leftwich, 1993: 615) and that the 'appeal for 'better' governance is virtuous but naïve' (Leftwich, 1993: 619). Similar to Tang's findings, Leftwich claims that it is developmental states rather than democratic ones – states which are likely to pursue market friendly strategies – which will develop into liberal states. For Leftwich (1993: 621), the 'Western insistence on markets, governance and democracy as the keys to development seem ideological and naïve'.

As ASEAN's peace and development have not solely involved the values which the EU promotes, as argued by Tang (2012) in particular and Leftwich (1993) in general, the supposition that the EU's promotion of its values is self-interested begins to present itself. However, this argument is not as stark as it may appear; it is not the case that there has been a disregard for the underlying values of EU policy such as democracy, good governance, equality and respect for human rights by ASEAN. Instead, it has been more a question of prioritising certain values over others and the timing of when these values have been included into the ASEAN agenda which is in contrast to the EU's insistence on value promotion and the liberal peace theory presented by Doyle (1986). For it is true that both the EU and ASEAN support the principles of a liberal capitalist economy, and it is also true that ASEAN has begun to include democracy, human rights and good governance as ASEAN objectives, yet historically, ensuring positive conditions for the development of ASEAN states has been the priority for ASEAN, regardless of political regime type or human rights records, as the inclusion of Myanmar and the states of Indochina as members have demonstrated.

I therefore argue that ASEAN's policy of accommodation and engagement with states within the region as opposed to an initial insistence on values related to liberal states as a condition for membership is an example of a differing approach to regionalism than the EU's. This results in the EU's promotion of its values at times being unsuitable for ASEAN. This in turn leads to the conclusion that if the perception exists that the EU aims to promote its values to ASEAN, as indicated in Figure 3.4 above, then this is for at worst self-interested, or at best, misguided purposes.

A central way in which ASEAN has sought to bolster its legitimacy and increase its acceptance as an actor both among its citzens and its partners has been to promote itself as the central actor within Southeast Asia which drives regional fora and partnerships. As one interview respondent stated:

> It (ASEAN) has managed its relations with the US, China, and all that quite well. So because of that it wants to engage the big powers. Of course, one can laugh and say well the big powers will engage ASEAN on their terms but in reality I think ASEAN has managed to at least provide some space for itself to maneuver in this sea of relations with all these various powers acting in this region. (I3 AA, 2011)

The signing of the Treaty of Amity and Cooperation (TAC) by a large number of ASEAN's partners is one example of how ASEAN has managed to negotiate with its interlocutors on its own terms. This treaty is a non-agression pact obliging its members to peaceful interaction and resolution of disputes and differences.[5] Initially, the EU was unable to sign the

TAC as it was only possible for states to do so. ASEAN changed a protocol within the TAC which then allowed organisations such as the EU to sign. Of significance is the fact that signing the TAC is a prerequisite of membership into the EAS; however, as discussed later in this chapter, the EU is yet to receive an invitation to this summit. ASEAN's success in persuading states which are not members of ASEAN to sign the TAC is a way in which ASEAN aims to reinforce its position as an actor which can negotiate with its partners in a persuasive and assertive manner.

Another example of how ASEAN has aspired to be the central actor within the broader Asian region and to engage with its neighbours as a way to strengthen its relevance and importance is its role in regional fora within Southeast Asia and East Asia (ASEAN, 2008; Wah, 2007). For example, the ASEAN +3 (APT), the ASEAN Regional Forum (ARF) and the ASEAN Post-Ministerial Meeting Plus One demonstrate the centrality of ASEAN in the broader Asian region. Acharya (2009: 498) argues that it is more accurate to refer to ASEAN as a 'hub' rather than a leader of such regional organisations. Acharya (2009) asserts that one of ASEAN's motivations to be a 'hub' is not to be marginalised by emerging organisations within the region such as APEC, and in the case of the EAS and the East Asian Community, ASEAN is 'leading by default' due to the fact that states such as Japan and China are 'neutralised by their mutual rivalry' (Acharya, 2009: 499). Nevertheless, despite Acharya's claims of ASEAN's lack of leadership in these organisations, the ASEAN Charter (ASEAN, 2008) makes explicit reference to ASEAN's desire to be the driver and central actor of regional groupings and arrangements. Article 1(15) states that a purpose of ASEAN is 'to maintain the centrality and proactive role of ASEAN as the primary driving force in its relations and cooperation with its external partners in a regional architecture that is open, transparent and inclusive' (ASEAN, 2008: 5). Others, such as Islam (2010) and the Council of the EU (2010) have also observed the centrality of ASEAN in regional frameworks such as ASEM and the ARF.

ASEAN's drive to be a 'hub' for regional organisations, if not a central actor and leader of these regional frameworks, is another way ASEAN aims to bolster its credibility, relevance, utility and legitimacy. Similar to its encouragement of its interlocutors to support and commit themselves to the principles of the TAC, and indeed similar to the EU's promotion of regionalism to ASEAN and other parts of the world, ASEAN's determination to have a central role in regional frameworks is, at least in part, driven by its desire to strengthen and justify the norms of cooperation and interaction upon which it is based and the principles of multilateralism which it supports.

Regarding ASEAN's role in regional frameworks with the Southeast Asian region, the fact that an invitation has not been extended to the EU to join the EAS was mentioned by a number of interview respondents. An EU official working in Brussels stated that the reason for this lack of invitation was due to the fact that, 'ASEAN is internally focused' at the moment (I11 EO, 2011). However, others outside of Brussels gave different reasons for the EU's lack of invitation. An EU official in Southeast Asia stated that not receiving an invitation to the EAS from ASEAN is 'a big frustration for colleagues in Brussels', but in fact the 'EU would be useless in the EAS' (I8 EOA, 2011). According to this EU official, a contributing factor to the EU's lack of invitation was the fact that ASEAN asked the EU what their role would be in the EAS and 'the EU could not give a straight answer'. In addition, the message from ASEAN was 'you are never here. You are in the ARF and you never come. Why would you come to the EAS?' (I8 EOA, 2011). According to this official, another concern of ASEAN's is the fact that although changes with the Lisbon Treaty have aimed to provide a more coherent "face" to the EU's external relations, the former Secretary General of ASEAN, Surin Pitsuwan, at the 1st EU–ASEAN Business Summit expressed the sentiment that he would still 'like to see this EU 'face'' (I8 EOA, 2011). Pitsuwan also enquired as to why the EU continuously makes reference to an invitation to the EAS and this official stated that Pitsuwan's message to the EU was 'do your homework first and wait until you are invited' (I8 EOA, 2011).

Another interview respondent also mentioned that a concern within ASEAN was, 'who is going to represent the EU?' This respondent stated that ASEAN's message to the EU was that the EU cannot expect China or the US, for example, to be represented by one leader when the EU cannot decide by whom it will be represented. Whilst the EU's response, according to this official, has been that ASEAN must understand that the structure of the EU does not allow for just one leader to represent the EU, ASEAN has responded by explaining that 'that is for you (the EU) to decide, fight, go and find a solution for yourself and go and come back on our terms' (S3 AA, 2011).

Similar to the EU, ASEAN's motivation to engage with the EU can also be interpreted in terms of enhancing its legitimacy and relevance as a regional organisation. This is not only evidenced by how ASEAN engages with the EU but also by instances where ASEAN asserts its authority and places conditions on, for example, EU membership in regional groupings. This contributes to its legitimacy by demonstrating that interregional dynamics have a significant role in international relations and also that ASEAN has the authority to negotiate the conditions upon which the EU and ASEAN can cooperate.

High expectations

It has been claimed that the more the EU grows in size and economic power, the more is expected of it (Söderbaum and Hettne, 2005). Although its economic viability has been under stress as a result of the current crisis, based on surveys conducted by the European Commission it appears that the EU is considered sufficiently established to be regarded as the main actor which should address the crisis. That the EU is seen as the preferred actor to fight against the financial crisis and also that the EU is considered to have sufficient power and resources to defend its economic interests in the global economy by its citizens demonstrate that certain expectations have been placed on the EU to act in the global arena (European Commission, 2009b). In addition, Eurobarometer 71 found that Europeans want more decision-making at the EU level. The fight against terrorism and the promotion of democracy and peace in the world are the two areas in which it is believed to be beneficial to have greater decision-making at the EU level (European Commission, 2009a). Interestingly, although the results showed that Europeans believed that there should be more EU-level decision-making, it was also apparent that overall, it was thought that the EU was not acting satisfactorily in these areas (European Commission, 2009a). These statistics show that the growth of the EU also involves greater expectations of its citizens.

Increased expectations of the EU as it develops come from both internal and external forces. Internally, the EU has needed to give itself a more visible and effective global identity as a means to justify its existence, expressed in statements such as the following, 'to ensure our security and meet the expectations of our citizens, we must be ready to shape events. That means becoming more strategic in our thinking, and more effective and visible around the world' (European Council, 2008: 2). Transformations to the organisation and the structure of the EU under the Lisbon Treaty attempted to achieve this. The appointment of a High Representative of the Union for Foreign Affairs and External Policy, who also holds the position of Vice-President of the Commission, aims to create a more visible and accessible EU representative. In addition, the EEAS was established as a way to streamline EU external policies and to make them more coherent. As a result of these transformations, there is the expectation that they will contribute to the EU being more effective at the global level. However, as was discussed in this chapter with regard to the EU's invitation to the EAS, the EU continues to be perceived as an incoherent actor with no clear representative with whom its interlocutors can engage.

Externally, the more a regional body such as the EU claims and attempts to create an external image and interact with external actors, the more expectations rise and the more the EU needs to fulfil its promises. Chaban, Elgström and Holland (2006) provide an example of this through their explanation of the link between power and the expectation of leadership. Through a study involving interviews with representatives at three multilateral meetings, they were able to determine some common observations made by external parties.[6] Of note is that respondents from all three negotiations, the United Nations Forum on Forestry (UNFF), the Convention on International Trade in Wild Flora and Fauna (CITES) and the World Trade Organization (WTO), considered the EU to be at least as influential as the US. In addition, because of the recognition of the influence of the EU, the expectation of the EU to be a leader was also present (Chaban, Elgström and Holland, 2006). Nevertheless, it was universally recognised that the EU did not fulfil this expectation for a number of reasons. One reason was that the EU was often ambiguous and unclear in transmitting its messages. Another, possibly linked to the first, was that the EU was often too internally divided or unable to make any firm or concrete decisions (Chaban, Elgström and Holland, 2006). Also, the EU was not perceived to be an effective leader due to its inflexibility. Due to the fact that it took a lot of time and negotiation for the EU to come to a decision as a result of its internal structure, it was viewed as uncompromising. This in turn led to the impression that it is very hard for other actors to influence or change the opinion of any decisions previously made by the EU (Chaban, Elgström and Holland, 2006). In general terms, external actors saw the EU as 'defensive' and 'reactive' mostly due to the fact that its internal decision-making processes were complicated (Chaban, Elgström and Holland, 2006: 253).

In the WTO specifically, the EU did not fulfil expectations of being a coherent actor or a leader. Incoherence related to the fact that although it promoted free trade and the economic development of third countries, it simultaneously pursued what was considered a self-interested and protectionist agricultural policy in the form of the Common Agricultural Policy (CAP) (Chaban, Elgström and Holland, 2006). Similar to the observation made earlier in the chapter relating to the dilemma of the EU simultaneously promoting its values and pursuing its own strategic interests, the same observation has been made by Chaban, Elgström and Holland (2006) with relation to the tension between the EU's support of free trade and its own interests.

Additionally, it is becoming increasingly apparent that EU policy objectives cannot be met without external cooperation. The *Guidelines on the EU's Foreign and Security Policy in East Asia* (Council of the EU, 2012a) present the EU's desire for international cooperation and the need to cooperate with Southeast Asia to address the EU's global objectives. They state that,

> The policies and actions of the major East Asia players are also increasingly important to the EU's wider global agenda. The EU needs, and seeks to promote, multilateral solutions to global challenges and the attitude of the major East Asian players are increasingly important to the EU's wider global agenda. (Council of the EU, 2012a: 6)

The document also states that as the political and economic weight of the Southeast Asian countries increases internationally, they become increasingly influential in the effort to achieve global objectives such as an open and free trading system, the promotion of human rights and good governance, the prevention of the proliferation of weapons of mass destruction, the fight against terrorism and international cooperation on migration, sustainable development and climate change (Council of the EU, 2012a). Therefore, the EU needs to actively seek the cooperation of its Southeast Asian partners to address these issues and be seen as acting in the multilateral manner that it promotes.

To date, the expectations of ASEAN have mainly been expressed with reference to the role of ASEAN. For example, discussions on whether ASEAN is a 'consultation conclave' (Simon, 2008) or a 'talk shop' (Eaton and Stubbs, 2006; Acharya, 2009) reflect an ongoing discourse centred on the expectations of ASEAN's function and responsibilities. Acharya (2009: 497) claims that ASEAN's most important assertion of its relevance has been 'the pacific management of disputes and non-use of force'. Increasingly, however, ASEAN's role has been expanding to include contributions to issues beyond the ASEAN region and most significantly to its ability to be an actor which engages with others such as the EU.

Furthermore, ASEAN has received pressure, at times from the governments of its member states, and increasingly from civil society groups, to address concerns which have not been explicitly on its agenda. For example, the state of human rights and democracy among its members has only recently been incorporated into the ASEAN Charter and the

ASEAN Political-Security Community, and not without contestation. Even before these developments, however, ASEAN had often been judged according to the state of human rights and democracy within its member states and its contribution to improving the state of human rights and democracy (Ciorciari, 2012). The main example of this being ASEAN's inability to engender concrete changes in Myanmar (Davies, 2012; Cook, 2010).

Expectations regarding ASEAN's adherence to its norm of non-interference have also been diverse among ASEAN's members. For example, Indonesia's proposal for an ASEAN peacekeeping force in 2004 was opposed by a number of ASEAN member states, particularly by Singapore (Caballero-Anthony and Haywood, 2011; Acharya, 2009). The concept of a peace-keeping force which could intervene in conflicts within ASEAN member states was contentious and thought to be in potential violation of ASEAN's non-intervention norm. Nevertheless, despite the concern for adherence to the norm of non-intervention, ASEAN received criticism for its inability to prevent the violence which occurred in East Timor in 1999 and for not intervening once the violence had erupted (Caballero-Anthony and Haywood, 2011).

According to Acharya (2009), domestic transitions and democratic change are accountable for member states being 'more receptive to institutional strengthening of ASEAN' and, based on the examples provided for this argument, heightened expectations for ASEAN to move beyond its norm of non-interference. The first example provided by Acharya (2009) is Indonesia's regard for Surin Pitsuwan's proposal of 'flexible engagement'. During the Suharto dictatorship, Indonesia opposed Pitsuwan's suggestion; however, after Suharto, Indonesia became the strongest supporter of the ASEAN Political-Security Community and proposed the aforementioned ASEAN peace-keeping force (Acharya, 2009). The concept of 'flexible engagement' is discussed in further detail in Chapter 6. Another example provided by Acharya is the correlation between democratic development within Indonesia and varied political attitudes towards how to engage Myanmar, which included calls for Indonesia to take more severe and interventionist measures than had been present previously (Acharya, 2009).

Additionally, differing approaches to this norm, and, consequently, the expectations of ASEAN's role as a security actor responsible for peace and stability among and within its member states, is often contingent upon whether intervention occurs at the member state or ASEAN level. On an individual basis, intervention by ASEAN member states in other

ASEAN member states has occurred. A significant example includes Indonesia's consent to the intervention of ASEAN member states on a humanitarian basis to support the Australian-led International Force for East Timor (INTERFET) (Caballero-Anthony and Haywood, 2011).[7] Another example is the participation of Singapore, Malaysia, Thailand, the Philippines and Brunei Darussalam in the EU's Aceh Monitoring Mission (AcMM) to implement the *Memorandum of Understanding* between Indonesia and the Gerakan Aceh Merdeka (GAM, the Free Aceh Movement) (Caballero-Anthony and Haywood, 2011). A final example is the monitoring of a ceasefire between the Filipino government and the Moro Islamic Liberation Front (MILF) in Mindanao during which the monitoring team was predominantly led by Malaysian peacekeepers who had been invited by the government of the Philippines (Helmke, 2009; Caballero-Anthony and Haywood, 2011).

References to a capability–expectation gap in ASEAN, and also the EU, demonstrate an ongoing dynamic, whereby expectations placed on an organisation are constantly beyond their current capacity. This is because the more an organisation becomes established, and the more it projects its aspirations, whether they are idealistic hopes or concrete objectives, the more rapidly the expectations of its citizens and interlocutors rise. Increasing pressure placed on the EU and ASEAN from civil society groups, for example, and results of polls such as the Eurobarometer discussed above attest to this fact. Whilst this increase in expectations results in criticism of an organisation's inability to have a significant role, it is also beneficial in propelling the development of these organisations and preventing them from becoming stagnant or irrelevant.

Issues of coherence and tensions among motivations

The EU has expressed its determination to manage and influence globalisation and the international order more broadly. Conclusions made at the European Council meeting in Laeken 2001 stated a new position and direction for the EU in relation to globalisation and provided evidence of the EU's intent to engage with external actors. The statement asked the following question:

> Does Europe not, now that it is finally unified, have a leading role to play in a new world order, that of a power able both to play a stabilising role worldwide and to point the way ahead for many countries and peoples? (European Council, 2001: 20)

This question expressed the view of the European Council that firstly, the EU has finished the process of unification and secondly that the EU is a global actor with the power to lead and stabilise other parts of the world. What is missing from this question is a recognition of whether the rest of the world indeed view the EU in the same way. In addition, there is no mention here, or elsewhere in the document, as to how the EU would hope to achieve this ambition. It does, however, give an explanation for the EU's attempts to be present and engaged in other parts of the world, including Southeast Asia.

The following section of the Presidency Conclusions of the Laeken meeting expresses a clear message that the European Council considers the EU a power in the world with the ability and responsibility to shape the world order. It is clear in the statement below that the EU is not considered a product of globalisation but an actor that influences, drives and manages globalisation according to its own set of criteria and 'moral framework'.

> Now that the Cold War is over and we are living in a globalised, yet also highly fragmented world, Europe needs to shoulder its responsibilities in the governance of globalisation. The role it has to play is that of a power resolutely doing battle against all violence, all terror and all fanaticism, but which also does not turn a blind eye to the world's heartrending injustices. In short, a power wanting to change the course of world affairs in such a way as to benefit not just the rich countries but also the poorest. A power seeking to set globalisation within a moral framework, in other words to anchor it in solidarity and sustainable development. (European Council, 2001: 20)

One major observation is whether the proposed moral framework is universal or specific to the EU context. Another question that this approach raises is whether other actors within the global order feel that the EU is legitimate in pursuing this objective or is relevant to the management of globalisation.

The sentiments expressed in the Presidency Conclusions of 2001 demonstrate that the European Council believes that the EU is explicit in its ambitions to have a strong presence at the international level. Its relations with Southeast Asia and its advocacy of regional integration, interregionalism and multilateralism demonstrate this. The European Council Conclusions of September 2010 have reaffirmed the Council's position that the EU must have a defining and influential role externally.

> The European Union must be an effective global actor, ready to share in the responsibility for global security and to take the lead in the definition of joint responses to common challenges. A strong economy and internal cohesion will strengthen the Union's ability to project its influence in the world. (European Council, 2010: 1)

The conclusions continue on to state that,

> In accordance with the Lisbon Treaty, and in line with the European Security Strategy, the European Union and its Member States will act more strategically so as to bring Europe's true weight to bear internationally. This requires a clear identification of its strategic interests and objectives at a given moment. And focused reflection on the means to pursue them more assertively. (European Council, 2010: 2)

Similar to the statements presented by the European Council in its 2001 and 2010 conclusions, former Commission President Barroso, in 2007, stated the capacity and responsibility of, and the need for, the EU to provide the world with solutions based on EU values.

> To remain master of our own destiny, we have to shape globalisation in accordance with our values. We in Europe have the capacity to do this, to propose solutions to the rest of the world based on our experiences of working together (e.g. standards, competition). We have to engage with the world and help give real meaning, at a global level, to the rule of law, democracy, human rights and multilateralism. (Barroso, 2007)

Such statements by the European Council and Commission, however, have not always aligned in intensity or policy direction with those of officials working within the EU. Consequently, incoherence and inconsistence are present in the EU's relations with ASEAN. For example, in contrast to the assertive role for the EU advocated by the European Council in the statements at Laeken (European Council, 2001), an interview respondent at the EEAS presented a more benevolent role for the EU. One EEAS official stated that when the EU engages with actors such as ASEAN by promoting regionalism, it does not do this in its own interest and is therefore not perceived as intimidating or overtly forceful. As this official stated, 'we are not seen as ... imposing our own interests. We are probably more of a preacher. Like a missionary, but a missionary is not a threat, normally speaking' (I4 EO, 2011).

Results of the survey conducted have also indicated that there is the perception that the EU's external role may not be as assertive as suggested in Council and Commission statements. To the survey question, 'the EU has said in a number of statements that it has a leading role to play and that it can point the way ahead for other countries. Do you agree or disagree?'; participants which responded with 'agree' only accounted for 33.3%, with 30.3% answering 'disagree' and 27.3% answering 'unsure', demonstrating a significantly mixed response to the EU's external role. The details of the survey question are shown in Figure 3.5 below.

In addition, interview respondents located in Europe and Southeast Asia referred to the differences between EU and member state interests, which at times have the potential to fragment the EU's international role and voice. One official at the EEAS stated that the member states are 'not so much in conflict with each other than with the Union' (16 EO, 2011).

Furthermore, in EU–ASEAN economic relations, one interview respondent referred to the fact that the EU's member states have a 'strange' combination of protectionism and free trade as a result of differing member state interests. This respondent gave the example that the UK and the Scandinavian countries are relatively open to free trade, whereas the Mediterranean countries such as Italy have been more

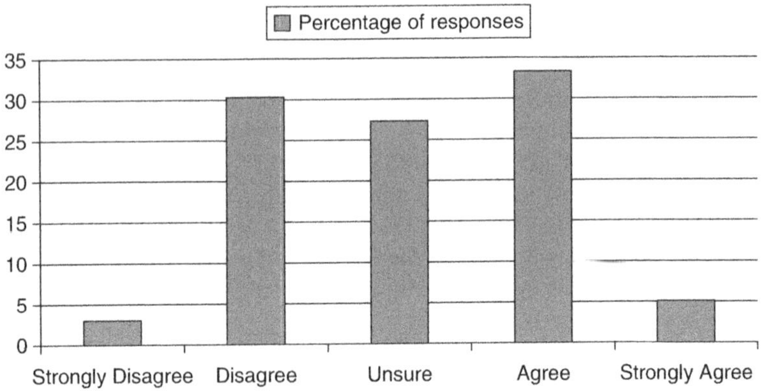

Figure 3.5 The EU has said in a number of statements that it has a leading role to play and that it can point the way ahead for other countries. Do you agree or disagree?

protectionist in their approach (I9 EO, 2011).[8] This respondent stated that the larger EU member states were more interested in, and supportive of, engagement with ASEAN at the EU level. This view was supported by survey respondents, who identified the UK (thirteen survey respondents), Germany (twelve survey respondents) and France (nine survey respondents) as the member states with the most significant impact on the EU's Southeast Asian policy. After these three member states, two respondents mentioned the Netherlands, one respondent mentioned Denmark and one respondent mentioned Sweden as having an impact on the EU's Southeast Asian policy.

Focusing on the two most prominent responses as examples, Germany has often played an 'intermediary role' between the EU and ASEAN (Bersick and Pasch, 2007: 2). Germany's Council of the EU presidencies in particular have driven developments in EU–ASEAN relations and have been significant supporters of interregional dialogue. During its presidency in 1978, Germany proposed to institutionalise the dialogue between the EU and ASEAN at the ministerial level (Bersick and Pasch, 2007). The German presidency of 1994 also supported the development of this dialogue. In the same year as the presidency, the EU released its *Towards a New Asia Strategy* (European Commission, 1994). The *Nuremberg Declaration of an ASEAN–EU Enhanced Partnership* (2007–2012) (ASEAN–EU, 2007a) was also established during a German presidency in 2007. According to Bersick and Pasch (2007: 11), German foreign policy towards Southeast Asia focuses on 'the advancement of democracy, cooperation in security policy including steps for military training, as well as the promotion of German foreign economic interests', and the goals of Germany's foreign policy include 'poverty reduction, the protection of resources and the environment, reusable energy sources, the democratisation of countries and governments, as well as crisis prevention and peaceful conflict resolution'. Germany is also involved in military and civilian training programmes where European or German experiences in realising regional stability are examined and discussed (Bersick and Pasch, 2007).

Germany also has a number of initiatives which derive impetus from the state level as opposed to the interregional. It is especially committed to supporting Cambodia, Lao PDR, Myanmar and Vietnam (CLMV) as a way to reduce the development divide between ASEAN countries (ASEAN, 2013a). In 2013, an appraisal mission was organised in Indonesia to assess how Germany can support this goal. Germany has, in 2013, committed 6 million euro to assist the CLMV countries (ASEAN, 2013a). It has been suggested by ASEAN that this support from Germany is moving from a sectoral approach to a more strategic dimension (ASEAN, 2013a). An interview respondent also referred to Germany's role, stating that it is 'very much involved and that it is politically supportive' and 'has its own ASEAN capacity and political will' to work with ASEAN and its member states. This respondent explained that a driver of this cooperation was the fact that Germany has 'interests there and big investors' in the region (I7 EO, 2011).

The UK, which had the most prominent response to the question, 'which member states have a significant impact on the EU's Southeast Asian policy?', appears to have a more bilateral approach to ASEAN relations, despite declaratory support for the development of EU-ASEAN relations. The year 2012, especially, saw a large number of initiatives by the UK to strengthen its relationship with ASEAN and its member states. In statements made by UK ministers, the UK is progressively putting emphasis on its economic, trade and business relations with the states of ASEAN, and in this regard the UK actively encourages the negotiation of EU free trade agreements (FTAs) with ASEAN and its member states (Hague, 2011; Browne, 2012). However, this ambition of FTAs at the EU level is also accompanied by UK initiatives for trade, investment and business support. Since 2011, the UK–ASEAN Business Council (UKABC) has been operative which complements the ASEAN–UK Business Forum and the 'Headstart' programme which provides support to UK businesses seeking to export to Southeast Asia (Lun and Rogers, 2013).

In a speech UK Foreign Office Minister, Jeremy Browne mentioned that 2012 had the largest number of UK ministerial visits to the ASEAN region, diplomatic staff in the region had increased by over forty and an embassy in Vientiane had been reopened after 27 years (Browne, 2012). The UK now has an embassy in every ASEAN member state.

Alongside the UK's support for cooperation with ASEAN, there is also the aim to pursue bilateral arrangements. For example, Browne reaffirmed the UK's support and continued participation in the Five Power Defence Arrangement.

> With regard to security, the UK is involved in the Five Power Defence Arrangement with Singapore and Malaysia and also aims to promote maritime security and assist counter-terrorism through its defence engagement with Vietnam and Brunei Darussalam. (Browne, 2012)

The UK's determination to maintain its bilateral arrangements has been emphasised by officials in the Southeast Asian region. According to the UK Ambassador to Brunei Darussalam, the UK seeks 'to be seen as the international partner who 'gets' ASEAN better than the rest of the international community' (Fenn, 2012). This, according to Fenn, 'is not because we want to 'tidy up' this part of the world, in the hope that dealing with a group of countries would be easier than dealing with them one by one' (Fenn, 2012). Such a position does not fit particularly well with the EU position of promoting interregional dialogue and regionalism in Southeast Asia.

Nevertheless, Browne stated that the UK does have aspirations to develop the interregional relationship between the EU and ASEAN and stated in his speech of 2012 that

> Britain cannot solve these problems (regulating the world economy, tackling climate change, preventing proliferation of nuclear weapons, preparing for natural disasters) by itself. Neither can Cambodia, or China or even the United States. However, if the UK coordinated action with the rest of the EU, Cambodia coordinated action with the rest of ASEAN, and the EU and ASEAN coordinated action together, we could begin to have a meaningful impact. (Browne, 2012)

Additionally, in UK parliament, Browne stated that the UK's support of the EU's accession to the TAC and the attendance of the UK Secretary of State at the EU–ASEAN Ministerial Meeting in 2012 are testament to the fact that the UK supports engagement with ASEAN at the interregional level (Lun and Rogers, 2013). However, unlike Germany, which has refrained from becoming a signatory of the TAC (Bersick and Pasch, 2007), the UK has sought to complement its support for interregionalism concurrently with its own bilateral arrangements with ASEAN and its member states. With regard to Germany's approach to the TAC, analysts have stated that, 'such a development (Germany signing the TAC) can set in motion or encourage the re-nationalisation of the EU's interregional Southeast Asian policy. Germany should not become part of this process, but rather should continue to push ahead and strengthen the Europeanising of its Southeast Asian policy' (Bersick and Pasch, 2007: 19).[9]

In an interview with a former Secretary General of ASEAN, the interplay between the bilateral relations between EU and ASEAN member states and the interregional EU–ASEAN relationship was explained. This interview respondent stated:

> They will continue to try to preserve whatever they have with all the countries here. And to do so, they will probably do more bilaterally,

> that means, the British and Malaysia, Singapore and Britain, France and Vietnam or the Netherlands and Indonesia. Because the EU collective is so troubled by so many troubles that they have, I see the individual countries such as the UK, France, Germany, (and the) Netherlands becoming more and more prominent. (I1 AO, 2011)

However, this respondent expressed the desire for ASEAN to continue engaging with the EU at the regional level, stating that these bilateral relations cannot replace what has already been established between the EU and ASEAN.

> So these other individual countries in Europe will have to find a way to bring the rest of the European countries, as (the) EU, to engage ASEAN. So it will be an interesting situation where at the bilateral level you will see a lot of activities between say, France and Vietnam, or France and Laos, but the French will also be lobbied by the Vietnamese and the Laotians to do more for ASEAN, because otherwise, the Vietnamese and Laotians will say that the ASEAN agenda will be weakened. It would be in the interest of everybody to continue to have a European presence. (I1 AO, 2011)

In the context of ASEAN, incoherence and inconsistency are not of the same nature as the EU's due to ASEAN's intergovernmental governance structure and decision-making style based on consultation and consensus. However, the diversity among ASEAN's member states is often referred to as a factor affecting the development of ASEAN and the nature of its relations with external actors. For example, Chia (2011) attributes the slow pace of economic integration to the differing levels of economic development, competitiveness and liberalisation among the ASEAN member states. In contrast, Severino (2007b) argues that the recent members of ASEAN, which have smaller and less developed economies, namely the CLMV countries, do not impede economic integration. Rather, economic integration has been hampered by the 'foot-dragging' of the strong economies to implement initiatives designed to further economic integration, such as the delay in the inclusion of Malaysia's motor vehicles into the ASEAN FTA (Severino, 2007b: 38). However, Severino (2007b) does argue that the development divide among ASEAN's member states has implications. For example, the Initiative for ASEAN Integration's (IAI)[10] success and effectiveness was hampered by 'inadequate coordination' of initiatives, 'insufficient participation' of the CLMV countries and a lack of ownership or a sense of ownership of these programmes by the CLMV countries and no 'follow-through for implementation, for the effective dissemination of knowledge or skills gained' or the project's assessment (Severino, 2007b: 40–41).

One of the most notable areas where ASEAN's diversity has negatively affected its interaction with the EU has been the range of human rights standards and democracy levels within ASEAN. Most significantly, Myanmar's past human rights abuses and lack of democracy have created instances where meetings between the EU and ASEAN have been stalled based on Myanmar's membership in ASEAN. This issue is analysed and discussed in greater detail in Chapter 6; however, it is worth noting here that the diversity of human rights standards and democracy, and ASEAN's norm of non-interference have, at times, affected ASEAN's ability to interact with the EU in certain contexts and also to further regionalise.

The differences in approaches of the EU member states, as evidenced by the UK's and Germany's different views on signing the TAC, divergent member state opinions on free trade and also the deviating opinions on the EU's role among its institutions and officials reveal a fragmented actor striving for interregional relations. Similarly, ASEAN's internal diversity, if not in practice at least in perception, strongly influences its interregional dynamics. These are inescapable fragmentations which require the best possible management by the EU and ASEAN in order for the two organisations to have a workable relationship.

Conclusion

Increasingly, the EU is recognising that ASEAN 'is too big to ignore' and whilst the relationship has formally existed for over 30 years there are still strong motivations for these organisations to accord each other greater priority (I8 EOA, 2011). For this to occur, however, both parties must consciously take pro-active steps to overcome the obstacles impeding a greater intensity of interaction between the two. Even beyond a donor–recipient dynamic, and a 'partnership' with Southeast Asia (European Commission, 2003), the EU must prove that it has the capacity and willingness to engage ASEAN despite its internal crises and also that its contribution is valuable to ASEAN. Meanwhile, ASEAN, although it is increasingly asserting its position as an established actor with the capacity to engage the EU on its own terms, must still ensure that it gives adequate priority to the EU and retains its attractiveness as a destination for investment, trade and development aid.

Through an analysis of the multifaceted motivations for EU–ASEAN engagement, an overarching theme of self-interest emerges as a basis for engagement for both actors. Admittedly, this is a potentially delicate observation, as to a certain extent it challenges the values of multilateral cooperation and interregional dialogue. Although these values are not completely lost, a tension often arises between promoting these ideals and pursuing strategic interests, which include trade maximisation and the consolidation of their legitimate position and role in global affairs. Whether stated explicitly or not, EU–ASEAN involvement is predominated by considerations of what will benefit the EU and ASEAN.

The focus on EU self-interest affects the coherence of the EU's Southeast Asian policy and its external relations more generally. Rosamond (2005) refers to the EU's lack of predictability and consistency in external affairs. He also mentions the difficulty for third parties to try to determine EU interests (Rosamond, 2005). This is likely due to the fact that the EU does not interact in a consistent way with external actors such as ASEAN.

In relation to the motivations of the EU to engage ASEAN, the lack of coherence in its behaviour potentially sabotages any other motivations the EU has. Incoherence and inconsistency are inherent, and arguably inescapable, aspects of the EU. This is mainly due to the EU's multi-level and multi-faceted design as a supranational entity and the complexity and range of interests and processes which this creates. In the context of EU–ASEAN relations, the EU's policy inconsistencies and incoherence are not managed sufficiently and therefore affect their relationship. One example is the EU's lack of receipt of an invitation to the EAS based on arguments by ASEAN that it is not clear who would represent the EU. Another is the varied positions of the EU's member states on levels of open and protectionist trade policies. Based on the arguments by Farrell (2009) and Söderbaum, Stålgren and Van Langenhove (2005) that the promotion of regionalism is one way in which the EU can validate and legitimise its own existence and structure, its confusing and, at times, hypocritical actions reduce the value of its attempts at promoting regionalism. This applies not only to the promotion of regionalism but also to the efforts of the EU to transfer its norms more generally. Farrell states that, 'the success of the strategy of promoting norms internationally depends in large measure upon the willingness of the rest of the world to endorse these norms, and this is also linked to the EU's credibility with other international and regional actors' (Farrell, 2009: 1180).[11] Chaban, Elgström and Holland echo this sentiment.

> Were the EU able to demonstrate a positive international role, and one that is widely recognised and appreciated by third countries

> and international organisations, then the prospects for increased popular legitimation for the European project might ensue, and thereby further bolster the EU's international actor capacity. The case for a more coherent EU approach to public diplomacy seems undeniable. (Chaban, Elgström and Holland, 2006: 262)

In the case of ASEAN, its diversity has also affected its ability to be viewed as a unitary, coherent actor. However, expectations of a regional actor have a significant impact on its relations with external partners, and due to the fact that the ASEAN does not demand that it be unified in the same sense as the EU, the expectations of ASEAN to have similar levels of coherence and consistency are not present. Nevertheless, expectations of ASEAN to address major issues within its member states are rising and affect its external relations, as the state of the EU–ASEAN relationship demonstrated during critical moments in Myanmar when human rights abuses and a lack of democracy were prevalent.

The mutual self-interested motivation to consolidate their relevant and influential positions will continue to drive the interregional relationship between the EU and ASEAN. Officials in the EU and in ASEAN have expressed the need to afford each other high priority, and the EU especially is currently in a precarious position to lose attention from ASEAN as it moves to other partnerships with actors such as the US, China, Australia and New Zealand. As one interview respondent stated,

> So one very interesting line of thinking is that, as we grow economically, can ASEAN, and Australia and New Zealand become more integrated economically? If we can do that, we are in a better position to compete with China. ASEAN, Australia, New Zealand, competing with China, or servicing the Chinese market. Similarly, servicing the Indian market. Because, if you look at the economy of ASEAN, and Australia and New Zealand, we are actually quite complementary ... So if we can map this out and crystallise some of the inherent potential and strength, we might see a little bit less of the Europeans. (I1 AO, 2011)

For both actors, a more committed investment in the relationship appears to be at the forefront of those in the two organisations. Addressing their incoherent and inconsistent images is one way in which to do this; another is to increase their presence in their partner's region. The ASEM process is one such way in which this is being attempted; another is the EU's promotion of regionalism to ASEAN.

4
The EU, ASEAN and Economic Integration

> The EU is the most integrated market, so it has a role to play for those who want to pursue economic integration, but the EU is not a 'model' across the board.
>
> Survey Respondent 31, Academic within the EU, 2012.

> ... we believe that a united and self-confident ASEAN, proceeding with its own integration and able to transcend binary strategic choices, is good for regional stability, security and prosperity – and hence good for us.
>
> David O'Sullivan, Chief Operating Officer of the EEAS, speech at the GRIPS Forum, Tokyo, 12 February, 2013.

Neofunctional interpretations of economic integration in the EU and ASEAN

The EU's endeavours to create a single market have resulted in the creation of a distinct economic entity. The level of economic integration of the EU has not been matched elsewhere and continues to require and provide innovative approaches to economic governance. This distinctiveness, however, has both advantages and disadvantages for the EU when it attempts to export or promote its experience beyond its borders. The EU's relevance to the development of ASEAN's economic community and its ability to be viewed as an international actor are heavily influenced by this distinctiveness. To be considered an actor with valuable lessons of economic integration for the Southeast Asian region, the EU requires its distinctiveness to be perceived as worthy of inspiration or replication. The EU's unique path to economic integration has advantages for promoting its experience to ASEAN as although the EU single market is most definitely an unfinished project, it has demonstrated that creative alternatives to economic structures and agreements are possible. The disadvantages lie in the fact that as a consequence of its uniqueness, the EU cannot be viewed as entirely relevant to ASEAN due to the differences in their contexts. In addition to this, the current economic crisis in Europe has illustrated the complexities and implications of an economic entity such as the EU and aspects of the EU's single market which are problematic and still require further development. Moravcsick (2012) has pointed out that although EU members decided back in 1992 with the Maastricht Treaty on monetary union, the current crisis demonstrates that this has not occurred sufficiently. The challenge, he states, is to make

> European economies converge, that is, assuring that their domestic macroeconomic behaviours are sufficiently similar to one another to permit a single monetary policy at a reasonable cost. For this to happen, both creditor countries, such as Germany, and the deficit countries in southern Europe must align their trends in public spending, competitiveness, inflation, and other areas. (Moravcsik, 2012: 1)

The main problem, according to Moravcsik (2012), is the fact that there are imbalances between the economies of the member states despite the fact that a single monetary policy and single exchange rate are applied. Others, such as Grant (2010: 1) and Youngs (2010), have discussed the fact that the crisis has the potential to tarnish the international reputation of the EU and to diminish its 'ability to act effectively'. These observations place ASEAN in a position to assess where the EU can and cannot play a role in assisting ASEAN in its development of economic integration.

I argue in this chapter that the EU's attempt to promote its economic integration experience is the most successful of the three areas of regionalism promotion analysed in this book.[1] This position has been reached through an examination of the primary projects in which the EU has been involved that focus on economic integration assistance in ASEAN. In addition, perception analysis based on the data gathered from interviews and surveys has also contributed to the determination that the EU's promotion of economic integration, although not without its criticisms, has experienced the greatest success when compared to the promotion of institutional or political aspects of regionalism support by the EU. The economic integration projects in which the EU is involved and perception analysis of qualitative data are discussed in detail in sections three and four of this chapter.

Another tool with which to assess the EU's ability to be an international actor with regard to its promotion of economic integration to ASEAN is the examination of neofunctionalism with regard to the EU and ASEAN. Neofunctionalism has not been without its critics and its popularity has fluctuated over time. Nevertheless, it has continued importance and relevance to a discussion on economic integration. However, there is a limit to the determinism that a neofunctional logic often suggests, especially in the case of ASEAN. This argument is discussed in full detail in section three of this chapter. In the context of ASEAN, this 'neofunctional determinism' is potentially an inaccurate description of what actually takes place during the development of economic integration and also a detrimental prescription of the paths that economic integration should take.

Nevertheless, when analysing the development of economic integration in the EU and ASEAN, certain principles of neofunctionalism are useful explanatory tools. As a starting point, a key question of neofunctionalism as presented by Cini and Borrogán (2010: 74) asks 'whether and how economic integration leads to political integration and if so, what kind of political unity will result'. Although neofunctionalism is a theory within a set of integration theories which emerged in the context of the EU, this question is more far-reaching than the EU and has applicability to an examination of ASEAN's economic integration. It is not so much the concepts of neofunctionalism which are specific to the EU, but rather the findings and the outcomes of the application of these theoretical concepts. Therefore, as I will explain in this chapter, neofunctional assumptions can also be useful to ASEAN's economic integration path and considerably beneficial in this respect as much of the literature to date on ASEAN has focused more on description rather than discussions based on theoretical frameworks (Acharya and Buzan, 2007; Acharya, 2011b). Through examining this question and the central principles of neofunctionalism, there is provision for a more thorough understanding of how the EU exports its economic integration experience and the implications this has on its actorness.

By analysing the question above posed by Cini and Borrogán (2010), the central components of neofunctionalism become significant considerations. Firstly, as a point of departure from functionalism, neofunctionalism moved to incorporate political interests, objectives and integration impetus into developments of economic integration (Wunderlich, 2007).

Secondly, a central principle of neofunctionalism, spillover,[2] is also notable within economic integration developments in the EU and ASEAN. I argue in this chapter that ASEAN has pro-actively encouraged the spillover effects which have occurred during its integration processes in contrast to those of the EU which have often had a more deterministic momentum of their own. Moreover, even the EU's approach to supporting ASEAN economic integration often takes a spillover logic, and considering the fact that ASEAN's approach to spillover is different from the EU's, I argue that this may not always be the appropriate method.

A third main observation within neofunctionalism is the process of elite socialisation, which involves the process of elites, and especially those working in regional organisations such as the EU and ASEAN, progressively working in the interest of the organisation as opposed to any other level of governance, for example, the level of the member states (Haas, 1968). Interview and survey responses conducted for this study suggested that this concept is apparent in the EU and ASEAN yet has produced different results. As manifest in the EU's structure and presence of supranational institutions such as the European Commission, elite socialisation has, to a certain degree, resulted in a transfer of interests and loyalties to the EU level. In the ASEAN case, elite socialisation processes occur, yet they do not result in supranational interests to the same extent as the EU as a result of ASEAN's core norms, which include protection of sovereignty, non-interference and intergovernmentalism.

Finally, another concept within the neofunctional framework is a focus on regional integration as a process and means to an end rather than an end goal in itself (Haas, 1968). This, in fact, is a pertinent and accurate observation for the EU and ASEAN. It can be argued that both the EU and ASEAN were initially established in order to foster and protect peace and stability in their respective regions. This, in time, became coupled with the objective of promoting economic stability and growth and increasingly better living standards for their citizens.

Whilst the EU and ASEAN embarked on regional integration projects in different manners,[3] the consideration of regionalism as a means to an end is common to the two organisations. As Article 2 of the Treaty Establishing the European Community (TEEC) states,

> The Community shall have as its task, by establishing a common market and progressively approximating the economic policies of

> Member States, to promote throughout the Community a harmonious development of economic activities, a continuous and balanced expansion, an increase in stability, an accelerated raising of the standard of living and closer relations between the States belonging to it. (European Economic Community (EEC), 1957)

ASEAN's Bangkok Declaration of 1967 similarly makes the statement that ASEAN aspires to

> Establish a firm foundation for common action to promote regional cooperation in South-East Asia in the spirit of equality and partnership and thereby contribute towards peace, progress and prosperity in the region. (ASEAN, 1967)

In this regard, despite the different contexts in which economic integration has taken place in the EU and ASEAN, one similarity which they share is the neofunctional view that integration is a process rather than an end goal.

However, as mentioned above, neofunctional frameworks can be imprecise or even detrimental when it comes to explaining or proposing steps towards economic integration. Critiques of neofunctionalism, which have been voiced even by Ernst Haas (2001), its initial and main proponent, have included a recognition that the theory focused too heavily on supranational structures and interests and that spillover effects are not necessarily automatic and are, as Wiener and Diez (2009: 52) suggest, 'fair-weather' processes. Beyond a descriptive purpose, if neofunctionalism is taken as an approach to integration, its potentially short-sighted, incremental path dependency steps do not give significant or adequate space for long-term projections or comprehensive and systematic planning.

Despite these shortcomings, neofunctionalism in this chapter is beneficial as a preliminary framework from which to begin the discussion. It places the following analysis within a theoretical context which can be used to improve the effectiveness of analysing the EU and ASEAN in relation to each other. The following section of the chapter moves on to present the major developments of EU and ASEAN economic integration.

The EU and economic integration

The *Spaak Report* of 1956 is one of the first key documents which sets out the aspirations of a single market for Europe. This report was the basis for a convention held in Brussels in 1956 to draft what became in 1957 the Treaty of Rome, or the TEEC (Spaak, 1956). Many of the proposals made in the *Spaak Report*, which included guidelines on the establishment of a customs union, harmonisation of national legislations, rules on competition, proposals on transport services and transport rates, as well as the development of a European investment fund, served as basic principles underpinning the creation of a single market within the EU (Spaak, 1956). With the adoption of the Treaty of Rome, the basis of a customs union was established, with the objective of creating a zone that would allow for the free movement of labour, services, capital and goods in a single market, largely achieved in 1993,[4] as well as endorsing that a number of policies, such as those relating to transport and agriculture, be regulated at the EU level (EEC, 1957).

Although the Treaty of Rome contributed to developments within the context of economic integration, barriers and obstacles to a single market persisted. Many of these obstacles related to the emergence of new technologies and products in the 1960s and 1970s which resulted in new standards and the protection of these standards, especially at the national level. In addition, preferences continued to be given to local and domestic markets, and differences in national policies, industrial cultures and operating rules which protected and supported local producers and suppliers remained (Wallace and Young, 1996).

However, prior to the crisis which affected Europe in the 1980s, during which a number of EU member states entered into recession, two major contributors to creating a single market were the policy of harmonisation and the role of the ECJ.[5] Whilst being a major key in organising the structure and functioning of the economic community, harmonisation, as chiefly set out in Article 100 of the TEEC (EEC, 1957), also revealed the complexity and challenges of the creation of a single market. Article 100 states that:

> The Council shall, acting unanimously on a proposal from the Commission, issue directives for the approximation of such provisions laid down by law, regulation or administrative action in Member States as directly affect the establishment or functioning of the common market. The Assembly (European Parliament) and the Economic and Social Committee shall be consulted in the case of directives whose implementation would, in one or more Member States, involve the amendment of legislation. (EEC, 1957)

However, the Commission, in its role to propose directives in the area of policy harmonisation, soon realised the enormity of the task, and rather than uniformly and comprehensively applying the principle of harmonisation, began to insist on directives that supported harmonisation only 'where it could be specifically justified' (Wallace and Young, 1996: 129). At this stage, moves towards creating a regulatory system faced two obstacles. The first was that the Commission, when drafting its directives, often consulted working groups, European-level pressure groups and private standard-making bodies such as the European Committee for Standards (CEN) and the European Committee for Electrical Standards (CENELEC). However, the technical assistance which was provided by these private bodies was often insufficient and inappropriate (Wallace and Young, 1996). The second difficulty was the use of unanimity decision-making by the Council on the directives proposed by the Commission as specified in Article 100 of the TEEC. As a consequence of national interests, approaches and objectives, results and decisions were often delayed and unambitious (Wallace and Young, 1996).

Rulings by the ECJ in the 1970s contributed to the future direction of the creation of the EU single market. The most oft-cited cases are the *Dassonville* ruling of 1974 and the *Cassis de Dijon* case of 1979. The *Dassonville* case refers to a case where the Belgian government was found to be in breach of European law by restricting trade on whisky purchased by a Belgian trader in France based on the fact that Belgium required such whiskey to have a certificate of authenticity. The ECJ ruled that this restriction by Belgium had the equivalent effect of quantitative restrictions on trade and was therefore hindering intra-regional trade and competition (ECJ, Case 8/74, 1974). The *Cassis de Dijon* case ruled that a liqueur, *Cassis de Dijon*, should not be restricted from being sold in Germany as liqueur even though its alcohol percentage rate did not classify it as a liqueur under German law (ECJ, Case 120/78, 1979). A major contributor to the single market as a result of this ECJ ruling was the principle of mutual recognition which allowed member state regulations to be viewed as equal and comparable where appropriate, avoiding the need to impose an EU standard in such cases and also to remove restrictions on intra-regional trade.

The late 1970s and early 1980s saw the increase in trade imbalances and deficits in the EU (Senior Nello, 2005). As previously mentioned, many of the member states entered into recession and inflation and unemployment increased. This was compounded by a rise in oil prices after the Iranian Revolution (Senior Nello, 2005). European firms lost competitiveness relative to firms in the US and Japan, and American direct investment into the EU began to decrease (Wallace and Young,

1996). In response, many member states maintained or increased national regulations to protect national industries which either stagnated or negated previous harmonisation developments (Cini and Borrogán, 2010). A number of initiatives took place in the early 1980s in order to address the concerns of member states and EU institutions regarding the state of the single market. For example, in 1982 the Council created an Internal Market Council to discuss issues related to creating the single market, and in 1983 the European Roundtable of Industrialists (ERT) was established.[6]

In the following year the EP adopted a draft treaty on the EU, based on the *Spinelli Report* by Altiero Spinelli. This report, a draft treaty establishing the EU, was, however, rejected at subsequent European Council meetings and not endorsed by all of the national parliaments of the EU's member states. The federalist approach which Spinelli proposed called for greater policy harmonisation among the members and suggested that neither functional integration on economic matters nor an intergovernmental approach was sufficient. Whilst his report was not accepted by the European Council, it has been attributed to providing the impetus and inspiration for developments agreed upon at the 1984 European Council meeting in Fontainebleau, and the report presented by the Dooge Committee (Murray and Rich, 1996; Europa, 2013b).

The Conclusions at the European Council at Fontainebleau called for a renewed commitment to the single market project. The Conclusions covered a number of 'guidelines for the reactivation of European cooperation' (European Council, 1984). These included implementing processes that addressed any budgetary burdens carried by member states and the arrangement to balance out the budgetary contribution paid by the UK to the EU. It also covered guidelines for the accession of Spain and Portugal, called for a single document for the movement of goods, the abolition of police and customs formalities for people moving within the EU and a system to allow for the recognition of diplomas and qualifications in certain cases (European Council, 1984). It also set up an *ad hoc* Committee on Institutional Affairs, the Dooge Committee, which presented a report in 1985 that proposed to 'set out the objectives, policies and institutional reforms which are necessary to restore to Europe the vigour and ambition of its inception' (Dooge, 1985). Regarding economic integration, the report stated that a primary objective was to create a homogenous internal economic area through the creation of an internal market, a competitive European economy, economic convergence of member states, the creation of a technological community, the strengthening of the European Monetary System and the mobilisation of resources through budgetary control (Dooge, 1985).

In addition, a White Paper, *Completing the Internal Market,* written by Lord Cockfield, then Commissioner for the Single Market, outlined the steps which needed to be taken in order to achieve a single market by 1992. A single market had been called for by Jacques Delors in his inaugural speech as head of the European Commission (European Commission, 1985). In its conclusion, the White Paper made a statement for a Europe that went beyond a free trade area.

> Europe stands at the crossroads. We either go ahead – with resolution and determination – or we drop back into mediocrity. We can now either resolve to complete the integration of the economies of Europe; or, through a lack of political will to face the immense problems involved, we can simply allow Europe to develop into no more than a free trade area. (European Commission, 1985: 55)

The White Paper presented the measures necessary to address physical, technical and fiscal barriers to trade and emphasised that the objectives of the internal market were three-fold and included merging the markets of the member states, ensuring that the single market was growing and not static and ensuring that the market was flexible so that capital and investment flowed into the areas of economic advantage (European Commission, 1985).

The following year, at the Council meeting in Milan, an Intergovernmental Conference was proposed which aimed to examine how the European single market could be achieved. This conference supported the White Paper, *Completing the Internal Market*. The result of the intergovernmental conference was the agreement of treaty reforms to enact the Single European Act (SEA). The SEA restated previous objectives that had lost momentum, stating that a single market should be 'an area without internal frontiers in which the free movement of goods, persons, services and capital is ensured' (European Community, 1986: Article 8a). Significant developments within the SEA that impacted the creation of a single market included the adoption of qualified majority voting (QMV) as opposed to unanimity on decisions relating to the single market and increased powers given to the EP to reject and amend proposals on single market issues (European Community, 1986).

Shortly after the SEA in 1986, the *Cecchini Report* of 1988 outlined the 'costs of non-Europe', or, in other words, the cost of not establishing and developing a single market. A summary of the report concluded that:

> The completion of the internal market will, if appropriately reinforced by the competition policies of both the Community and Member States, have a significant and positive impact on economic performance and employment. The size of this impact, in terms of the potential for increased non-inflationary growth – an economic bonus of ECU 200 billion at 1988 prices and the creation of millions of new jobs – should be sufficient to transform the Community's economic performance from a less than brilliant one to an outstanding one. (European Commission, 1988)

However, despite the proposals made in Lord Cockfield's White Paper and the persuasive, yet potentially overly ambitious arguments within the *Cecchini Report*, obstacles towards the completion of the single market remained. Tax and fiscal harmonisation were met with resistance by member states, and the White Paper did not address social or politically sensitive issues. However, it soon became apparent that economic integration within the EU had social, welfare and political consequences and that national governments could no longer address social and welfare concerns independent of the EU.

In response to this recognition, the Treaty on European Union (TEU), or the Maastricht Treaty of 1993, broadened the scope and structure of the EU by introducing a pillar structure which covered economic, social, political and security sectors.[7] This was also the year when the single market was formally introduced. The TEU also laid out a number of initiatives which aimed to make economic and monetary union (EMU) and the use of the Euro possible. The central element was the creation of the Maastricht Criteria,[8] which outlined the criteria which needed to be met in order for member states to adopt the Euro.[9]

Even after the TEU, challenges remained to further developments in economic integration. For example, national governments and the business sector were ill-prepared and in some cases lacked commitment to implement EU regulations and rules, which were often complicated and difficult to interpret. Initiatives in the mid to late 1990s aimed to rectify this situation. In 1996, the European Commission launched a programme entitled the Simpler Legislation for the Internal Market (SLIM). SLIM was a programme in five stages which recognised the complexity of EU legislation and therefore worked to streamline internal market legislation between 1996 and 2002 (European Commission, 2012a).

The *Action Plan for a Single Market* (European Commission, 1997a) also addressed issues necessary for the improved functioning of the single market by 1999. Its four objectives were: make 'the rules of the single market more effective (proper enforcement and simplification of rules at Community and national levels)'; deal 'with key market distortions (tax and anti-competitive behaviour)'; remove 'sectoral obstacles to market integration (new legislative measures and changing national administrations' attitudes)'; and deliver 'a single market for the benefit of all citizens (the social dimension of the single market)' (European Commission, 1997a: 1).

A third initiative in the late 1990s was the introduction of a single market scoreboard, a six-monthly report which has the purpose of presenting the current state of the single market and assessing the degree to which member states and EU institutions are meeting targets and complying with regulations (European Commission, 1997b). At the European Council meeting in Amsterdam in 1997, the Treaty of Amsterdam was approved which consisted of amendments to the TEU (European Council, 1997). The Council meeting also resulted in the resolution on the Stability and Growth Pact, which was based on a proposal by the German Finance Minister of the mid 1990s, Theo Waigel. The pact was essentially a follow-up of the Maastricht Criteria as it ensured that once a member state had adopted the Euro they continued to meet the requirements set out in the Maastricht Criteria and the pact (European Commission, 2012b).

The subsequent treaties, the Treaty of Nice (2003) and the Lisbon Treaty (2009), largely built upon the major developments that had previously occurred regarding the single market. The Treaty of Nice was chiefly designed to accommodate EU enlargement to the East,[10] and institutional reforms and decision-making processes aimed to enhance the functioning and efficacy of the single market in an enlarged EU. Of note within the Lisbon Treaty (2009), also known as the Treaty on the Functioning of the European Union (TFEU), was the emphasis on the social implications of a single market. The European Economic and Social Committee (EESC) released an opinion in 2011 which stated that, 'the Lisbon Treaty seems to give to the internal market more social aims' by working towards 'a social market economy, aiming at full employment and social progress' (EESC, 2011: 1).

Decision-making powers and processes under the Lisbon Treaty are revised, and 'ordinary legislative procedure' becomes the new term for the co-decision process which involves both the Council and the EP.[11] National parliaments have also been given a strengthened role in decisions pertaining to the internal market. Although they have no voting powers, by virtue of the fact that they are sent proposals, there is increased opportunity for them to inform their national representative at the Council of the EU and to some extent their counterparts at the EP on their opinions.

> All proposals from the Commission, initiatives from a group of Member States, initiatives from the European Parliament, requests from the Court of Justice, recommendations from the European Central Bank and requests from the European Investment Bank for adoption of a legislative act are to be sent to the national Parliaments at the same time as they are sent to the co-legislator (Council and Parliament). (European Commission, 2012c)

However, it is widely recognised that the single market is by no means accomplished nor is absent of difficulties, the least of which being the economic and financial crisis of recent years. Mario Monti's report, *A New Strategy for the Single Market* (2010), outlined the challenges facing the single market and how it can be reinforced and consolidated. The three main challenges, according to Monti, are 'the erosion of political and social support for market integration in Europe' which are exacerbated by 'integration fatigue' and 'market fatigue', 'uneven policy attention given to the development of the various components of an effective and sustainable single market' and 'a sense of complacency' in the sense that the single market is considered completed and therefore not a political priority (Monti, 2010: 6).

Recommendations to address these concerns include 'strengthened delivery, enforcement and governance' of the single market (Monti, 2010: 8). Moreover, drawing on the Lisbon Treaty's emphasis on the social implications of economic integration, Monti (2010) suggests reconciling the relationship between economic freedoms and workers' rights, effective use of social services, a developed public procurement policy, a conciliation of tax coordination and national tax sovereignty, a balance of competitiveness and cohesion in regional development policies, a functioning industrial policy and initiatives which ensure that the EU single market remains 'open, but not disarmed *vis-à-vis* competitors at a global level' (Monti, 2010: 6).

Partially in response to Monti's report, and along with the report by Louis Grech from the EP, *Delivering a Single Market to Consumers and Citizens* (Grech, 2010), which echoed many of the claims made by Monti, the Single Market Act (European Commission, 2011a) put forward twelve actions for growth and development of the single market. The twelve areas are access to finance for small business, citizen mobility, intellectual property rights, consumer empowerment, services, networks, the digital single market, social entrepreneurship, taxation, social cohesion, the regulatory environment for businesses and public procurement.

In 2012, the Commission issued a working document entitled, *Delivering the Single Market Act: State of Play* (European Commission, 2012d). This document elucidates the areas of the EU's single market which are still in need of further attention and development. The *Delivering the Single Market Act: State of Play* document covers such issues as introducing legislation on venture capital funds, revising the system for the recognition of professional qualifications, adopting legislation on pensions, adopting legislation on unitary patent protection, adopting legislation to combat piracy and counterfeiting, amending customs regulations, modernising trademark systems, adopting legislation on alternative dispute resolution, ensuring transparency of bank fees, revising legislation on the European standardisation system, adopting energy infrastructure legislation and transport infrastructure legislation, resolving cross-border taxation problems, introducing legislation clarifying exercise of freedom of establishment/services alongside fundamental social rights and revising procurement directives (European Commission, 2012d).

The EU's development of its single market has, since the *Spaak Report* of 1956, been primarily driven by functional developments to enable intra-regional trade and economic cooperation and development. What is apparent, however, is that despite the aim to achieve economic integration through an overtly functional design of initiatives and goals, such as the harmonisation of national legislations, revising transportation infrastructure to complement and facilitate intra-regional trade and developing standards for products, national member state interests and priorities and economic and financial crises have significantly affected the realisation of the single market. Furthermore, the solidarity implied by economic integration has come under pressure in recent years, suggesting that processes of elite socialisation become compromised in times of crisis (Jenkins, 2012). Certain initiatives, such as the Treaty on Stability, Coordination and Governance signed at a European Council meeting in 2012, have aimed to reinvigorate and consolidate this solidarity. However, the ability of these initiatives to transform rhetoric into concerted action and mutual responsibility is still affected by the pressure of economic turmoil. The ongoing debate and disjuncture of opinions regarding the usefulness and limits of austerity measures within the EU's member states demonstrate the current strains on EU solidarity.

In the EU context, the ECJ has had a substantial role in overcoming national differences in order to allow for the single market to be realised. Rulings on product harmonisation and mutual recognition attest to this fact. Largely due to the fact that the EU has been pioneering in its endeavours to create a single market, such issues raised by the *Dassonville* and the *Cassis de Dijon* cases were novel and unique to the creation of a single market and were therefore difficult to be anticipated with any preventative measures. These cases demonstrate the ECJ's role in resolving issues raised during the processes of developing a single market. An interview respondent stated that the EU is persistent in delivering and reviewing issues and referred to the EU's tendency towards continual implementation and subsequent reassessment until they are resolved and approved, often with the assistance of the ECJ (I11 EO, 2011). According to this official, ASEAN, in contrast, devises initiatives but when they are found to be too difficult they develop completely new proposals. This official stated, 'they (ASEAN) keep changing their plan when things get too difficult' (I11 EO, 2011). Whilst these responses illustrate the differences in approach by the EU and ASEAN, an incremental developmental process is common to the two organisations.

Despite their shared incrementalism, the neofunctional processes of spillover have been left to acquire their own momentum in the EU whilst ASEAN has taken a more pro-active approach. Haas (2001) himself came to acknowledge that the concept of spillover could not be an assumed dynamic of regional integration. Nevertheless, many EU developments in economic integration have tended to rely on an assumed impetus for spillover, as the discussions on the ECJ rulings have shown. The EU's continual review of developments regarding the single market, such as the decisions made on mutual recognition of products after problems arose with sales of products in other member states and the creation and subsequent abolition of the pillar system, illustrates the uneven path that functional spillover processes have experienced in the EU context. In addition, I contend that the necessity of the ECJ in ensuring the correct implementation of single market policies is also a result of this approach.

ASEAN, conversely, has taken the approach of trialling certain proposals and then subsequently deciding on whether to formalise or reject these initiatives. As one interview respondent remarked,

> Here in ASEAN, we are still just coping with informal arrangements and we hope that if the benefits are recognised and quite

> substantial all the countries will say, 'yes, it is time to establish the ASEAN Institute for Standards for Cosmetics or the ASEAN Centre for Biodiversity or the ASEAN Centre for Mitigating Climate Change and so on and so forth'. (I1 AO, 2011)

In this sense, as will be argued further below, ASEAN acknowledges that spillover does not run on its own momentum and therefore regards functional spillover as a concept which must be actively initiated and guided by preparing for subsequent spillover effects rather than allowing them to occur on their own. This is the case for two main reasons. The first is that ASEAN has the advantage of not being the first economic integration project and can therefore use the EU experience to understand how to best develop regional economic integration. The second is that ASEAN norms of interaction, based on consultation, informality and consensus, allow for the informal adoption of initiatives which can then be reviewed, adapted, rejected or eventually institutionalised.

With regard to crises, two reactions are evident within the context of the EU. Firstly, an initial response has been to call for more federalism within the EU. In response to the economic turmoil of the 1980s, the *Spinelli Report* brought Spinelli's preference for increased federalism within the EU once again to the fore. Similarly, José Manuel Barroso's State of the Union speech of 2012 referred to a more federal EU in response to the economic and financial crises of recent years.

> Let's not be afraid of the words: we will need to move towards a federation of nation states. This is what we need. This is our political horizon. This is what must guide our work in the years to come. Today, I call for a federation of nation states. Not a superstate. A democratic federation of nation states that can tackle our common problems, through the sharing of sovereignty in a way that each country and each citizen are better equipped to control their own destiny. (Barroso, 2012b: 11)

The second response to crises which has been evident in the EU is the reassertion of national priorities. In the current crisis, the UK Prime Minister David Cameron's call for a national referendum to decide if the UK should remain a member of the EU is one such example. Yet another example was the preliminary result of Italy's 2013 elections, whereby the centrist coalition party, led by Mario Monti, only received 10% of votes. The coalition was clearly rejected by the Italian public which instead voted for parties with a eurosceptic stance such as Silvio

Berlusconi's centre-right allegiance of the *Il Popolo Della Liberta* and the *Lega Nord*, the populist protest party, *Cinque Stelle*, initiated by comedian Beppe Grillo, who called for a referendum on Italy's exit from the Eurozone and the centre-left coalition led by Pier Luigi Bersani (British Broadcasting Cooperation, 2013; Deutsche Welle, 2013).

ASEAN's responses to crises have resulted in a reinvigoration of economic integration but not in the form of increased supranationalism or federalist developments. Indeed, as discussed in greater detail in the subsequent section, ASEAN's reaction to the financial crisis in Asia in the late 1990s was to enhance its mechanisms for future crisis aversion and independent, self-help processes. Moves towards more supranational structures were not evident, and ASEAN revived its processes of economic integration whilst still maintaining its core norms of cooperation.

The differing processes of elite socialisation within the EU and ASEAN, as discussed in the introduction of this chapter, are evidenced in their distinct reactions to crisis. The elite socialisation processes are present in both ASEAN and EU leaders calling for renewed energy in developing regional integration. The differences lie, however, in the socialisation of preferences for specific norms of integration, which result in distinct suggestions for further development of their respective organisations.

ASEAN and economic integration

Another feature of ASEAN's economic integration, in addition to the aspects discussed in the previous section, is the flexible approach which has been provided to its members largely because of the differing political economies and levels of development among the ASEAN member states. This flexibility is evident in the range of deadlines to meet agreed-upon targets such as tariff rates and product harmonisation for member states with different levels of economic development. In the ASEAN experience, various deadlines have been reduced, extended or eliminated, a current example being the deadline for the ASEAN Economic Community (AEC) in 2020, which has since been brought forward to 2015, with some member states having until 2018 to fulfil implementation requirements.

Whilst this flexibility has allowed ASEAN states with a variety of economic situations and approaches to interact and cooperate, it has also been a contributor to a common criticism of ASEAN's economic integration development – slow implementation and low utilisation of initiatives. Not only have the developing economies of Cambodia, Lao PDR, Myanmar and Vietnam been given more time to implement measures such as tariff reductions, the more developed economies have also, at times, been selective in their compliance with initiatives at the ASEAN level (Severino, 2007b).

An additional significant factor in the development of ASEAN's economic integration has been the fact that external events and pressure have been major driving forces for increased economic integration. As an interview respondent stated,

> ... we also have internal tensions, we still have border issues, we still have maritime sovereignty issues ... so we did not have a strong internal push to establish a community like the European Union in the initial years. It is only now, I would say, since the Charter, (that) ASEAN has started to take integration very, very seriously because if we want to be relevant in the region we really need to integrate because we have an external push. I would say normally ASEAN reacts to external pressure ... (This is) because we are competing for investment, we are competing for trade. ASEAN realised that it cannot function anymore as 10 different countries, we need to come together as one single entity. So that is the reason why our integration process, I would say, is very much driven by external pressure. (I2 AO, 2011)

Until 1977, ten years after ASEAN's inception, despite the fact that economic development and prosperity had been stated in the founding ASEAN documents, geopolitical and security issues had been the priority for the organisation (Chia, 2011). Frost (2008) rightly points out that whilst ASEAN recognised the need for economic cooperation, at its inception and during its early years it did not want to engage in policies which would produce tension and unnecessary competition among its members, especially since a number of them were at the stage where they were developing their fragile and emerging national economies.

In 1977, the first major recognition of ASEAN's determination to embark upon economic integration became manifest in the ASEAN Preferential Trading Arrangement (APTA) (DeRosa, 1995). The APTA, which aimed to reduce tariffs and non-tariff barriers (NTBs) to intra-regional trade through a system of tariff negotiations and preferences, only resulted in minor increases in intra-regional trade. During this period ASEAN also established the ASEAN Industrial Projects scheme in 1976, the ASEAN Industrial Complementation Programmes in 1981 and the ASEAN Industrial Joint Ventures in 1983 (Chia, 2011). These programmes, similar to the APTA, yielded only negligible results. The lack of economic integration and increased intra-regional trade at this time have been attributed to the protection of national economic interests of ASEAN member states that were in a stage of economic stabilisation and development (DeRosa, 1995). There was also potentially insufficient external pressure for ASEAN at this stage to elicit a committed response by those within the region to economic integration. The 1990s, however, provided such impetus.

Exogenous events and pressure in the 1990s included the uncertainty as to the results to be reached at the GATT Uruguay round (DeRosa, 1995) and the competition facing ASEAN by the North American Free Trade Agreement (NAFTA) and the development of the single market in Europe. As a result, ASEAN decided to initiate an ASEAN Free Trade Agreement (AFTA) in 1992 for trade in goods (Chia, 2011). The AFTA aimed to liberalise and eliminate intra-ASEAN tariffs through the Common Effective Preferential Tariff (CEPT) programme. The CEPT, however, was not used extensively by the ASEAN member states (Chia, 2011). Reasons given for its low utilisation include the presence of NTBs and either no or negligible difference between most favoured nation (MFN) tariff rates and CEPT tariff rates (Chia, 2011).

Similar to the APTA, however, the AFTA has also had limited effects and implementation and progress has been slow (Beeson, 2009). Beeson (2009: 339) accredits the 'modest impact' of the AFTA to the divergent capacities and political systems of the member states and the differing levels of economic development which contribute to the difficulty of reaching consensus on economic integration issues and also the adoption of lowest common denominator decisions and initiatives. Moreover, the economies of the ASEAN member states have often been described as competitive as opposed to complementary (Beeson, 2009; Chia, 2011). This was especially significant in the years following ASEAN's inception during which ASEAN economies had competing natural resources and were heavily reliant upon competing labour-intensive manufacturing (Chia, 2011).

The AFTA and CEPT were followed in 1995 by the ASEAN Framework Agreement on Services (AFAS) and the ASEAN Investment Area (AIA) in 1998. The AFAS has not experienced the same amount of development as the AFTA. Chia (2011) asserts that a considerable number of barriers continue to exist and that negotiations have proceeded slowly. ASEAN initially prioritised financial services, maritime transport, air transport, telecommunications, tourism, business services and construction. Negotiations and initiatives have since expanded, and to date commitments under the AFAS include packages for business services, professional services, construction, distribution, education, environmental services, health care, maritime transport, telecommunication and tourism (Chia, 2011: 53). Demonstrating the flexible approach pursued by ASEAN mentioned previously, within the AFAS, ASEAN has adopted an 'ASEAN minus X' approach, whereby two or more countries can start to negotiate trade liberalisation for services with other members joining at a later stage (Chia, 2011). This approach has continued to be an element of ASEAN policy initiation and implementation, and whilst it can be interpreted as a mechanism to overcome the need for consensus, the integral decision-making process within ASEAN, it is also an instance of the accommodating nature of ASEAN economic integration, especially towards the weaker economies within the region.

The purpose of the AIA is to ensure that ASEAN remains an attractive destination for FDI, which has been essential to the development of the economies of ASEAN. One of its primary methods of facilitating investment in the ASEAN region is the plan to ensure that national treatment is granted to ASEAN and non-ASEAN investors by 2020. Whilst the AIA has been criticised for its long time frame and list of exclusions, it has progressively been expanding its coverage and has also initiated investment promotion programmes (Chia, 2011).

As well as the efforts made to reduce and eventually eliminate tariffs among the ASEAN member states, the reduction of NTBs also became a priority for ASEAN. Chia (2011) explains that it took a substantial amount of time for ASEAN to compile its list of NTBs which mainly included barriers related to different product standards and regulations and differing customs regulations and procedures. Such barriers proved difficult to overcome due to the development gap among member states and the more developed economies imposing more stringent standards than the developing member states. With regard to customs harmonisation, the ASEAN Agreement on Customs was established in 1997, but again the progress was slow for the agreement to be implemented, and it took until 2003 for the ASEAN Harmonised Trade Nomenclature (AHTN) Protocol, which assisted customs procedures, to be signed (Chia, 2011). Other agreements and arrangements aimed at reducing and eliminating NTBs were the ASEAN Industrial Cooperation (AICO) scheme which replaced the industrial schemes initiated in the 1970s and early 1980s, initiated in 1996, the ASEAN Framework Agreement on Mutual Recognition Arrangements, signed in 1998 and the e-ASEAN Framework Agreement of 2000 (ASEAN, 2009b).

ASEAN was criticised for its inability to predict and manage the Asian Financial Crisis (AFC) of 1997. Developments related to economic integration, however, did occur, and Tay (2001) does attribute increased economic cooperation among the ASEAN member states to a reaction to the AFC. Economic cooperation was largely a reaction to the perceived inability of external actors, including the International Monetary Fund (IMF), to adequately remedy the effects of the crisis and support the states within ASEAN. Greater commitment was declared to accelerate the achievement of free trade throughout ASEAN and to increase investments across borders (Tay, 2001). In an interview with the author a Deputy Secretary General of ASEAN remarked that, 'the financial crisis is the first time I think, in 97, 98, when ASEAN really started looking at some of these integration issues' (I2 AO, 2011).

Partly in response to the crisis, in 1997 ASEAN adopted the *ASEAN Vision 2020*, which set out the direction of the Association up to 2020 and stated that it aims for

> A concert of Southeast Asian nations, outward looking, living in peace, stability and prosperity, bonded together in partnership in dynamic development and in a community of caring societies. (ASEAN, 1997)

In the following year, at the ASEAN Finance Ministers Meeting in February, the establishment of an ASEAN Surveillance Process (ASP) was agreed upon, with the Terms of Understanding for establishing the ASP signed in October 1998. The objectives of the ASP included information exchange, the provision of an early warning system and 'a peer review process to enhance macroeconomic stability and the financial system in the region', the encouragement of unilateral or collective actions to prevent crisis and the monitoring of 'global economic and financial developments which could have implications on the region' and proposals of regional and national actions in response to such developments (ASEAN Finance Ministers, 1998).

Also in 1998, the *Ha Noi Plan of Action* set out the priority areas and key measures which should be implemented in order to fulfil the *ASEAN Vision 2020* and included the importance of establishing and supporting the ASP. With reference to economic integration more generally, the *Ha Noi Plan of Action* specified measures for strengthening macroeconomic and financial cooperation and enhancing greater economic integration (ASEAN, 1998).

However, also evident during this time was a range of national responses which did not always necessarily align with the aspirations of ASEAN. In reaction to the AFC, Tay (2001) explains that some ASEAN member states moved towards more protectionist policies whilst others opened up their markets further as a way to revitalise their economies. Malaysia, for example, moved from being a relatively open market to experimenting with implementing controls over capital and currency rates during this period (Tay, 2001). Vietnam, Lao PDR and Cambodia also did not make significant efforts to open their markets at this time. Thailand and Singapore, in contrast, reacted differently from these aforementioned states and moved to open up their markets in the face of the crisis (Tay, 2001). Such diverse approaches and opinions on how best to rectify the conditions that contributed to the AFC proved difficult for consensus to be achieved at the ASEAN level, despite proclamations of renewed impetus for regional economic integration.

Strengthening the APT process was viewed as another way to reinforce a regional commitment towards combating financial crises.[12] Starting with its initial meeting in 1997, the APT, which included ASEAN, China, Japan and South Korea, began to meet regularly and in 2000 agreed to establish the Chiang Mai Initiative (CMI), a process that allows for currency-swap agreements which allow governments to pool their hard-currency reserves if another regional economic crisis were to occur (ASEAN, 2010a; Webber, 2001). A statement released at the APT Finance Ministers Meeting in 2000 stated that:

> In order to strengthen our self-help and support mechanisms in East Asia through the APT framework, we recognised a need to establish a regional financing arrangement to supplement the existing international facilities. As a start, we agreed to strengthen the existing cooperative frameworks among our monetary authorities through the 'Chiang Mai Initiative'. The Initiative involves an expanded ASEAN Swap Arrangement that would include all ASEAN countries, and a network of bilateral swap and repurchase agreement facilities among ASEAN countries, China, Japan and the Republic of Korea. (APT, 2000)

This statement also set out additional proposals by the APT, which included establishing a regional surveillance system in East Asia, monitoring mechanisms for capital flows and establishing a network of research and training institutions (APT, 2000). In 2003, the APT also set up the ASEAN Bond Market Initiative (ABMI), largely in reaction to the AFC and as a way to foster increased domestic savings and initiatives for investments within the ASEAN region.

Another exogenous factor, the economic development of China and India, has provided sufficient impetus for ASEAN to continue to drive economic integration despite the slow progress which it had been experiencing. In 2003, the decision to embark upon the creation of the AEC was made to spur further economic integration (Severino, 2007b; Chia, 2011). ASEAN's *Bali Concord II* declaration stated that:

> ASEAN is committed to deepening and broadening its internal economic integration and linkages with the world economy to realise an ASEAN Economic Community through a bold, pragmatic and unified strategy. (ASEAN, 2003)

Additionally, the *Bali Concord II,* in reference to the AEC states that:

> The ASEAN Economic Community shall establish ASEAN as a single market and production base, turning the diversity that characterises the region into opportunities for business complementation making the ASEAN a more dynamic and stronger segment of the global supply chain. (ASEAN, 2003)

In the same year as the *Bali Concord II,* to address persistent NTBs, ASEAN also initiated a 'green lane system' for CEPT products, adopted the WTO agreement on customs valuation and committed themselves to establishing a 'single window' for trade document processing, with the Agreement to Establish and Implement the ASEAN Single Window signed in 2005 (Chia, 2011). Additional developments included the Protocol Governing the Implementation of the ASEAN Harmonised Tariff signed in 2003 and the ASEAN Framework Agreement for the Integration of Priority Sectors of 2004 (ASEAN 2013b, 2013c).

In 2007, ASEAN released an AEC blueprint which set out the necessary steps for realising the AEC by the proposed date, 2015, and when and how these measures should be implemented. The AEC blueprint states that ASEAN is 'determined to achieve higher levels of economic dynamism, sustained prosperity, inclusive growth and integrated development of ASEAN' (ASEAN, 2007a: 2). According to the blueprint, the underlying principles of the AEC are an 'open, outward-looking, inclusive, and market driven economy consistent with multilateral rules as well as adherence to rules-based systems for effective compliance and implementation of economic commitments' (ASEAN, 2007a: 4).

The ASEAN Charter reiterated ASEAN's commitment to economic integration and stated that a central aim of ASEAN is

> To create a single market and production base which is stable, prosperous, highly competitive and economically integrated with effective facilitation for trade and investment in which there is a free flow

> of goods, services and investment; facilitated movement of business persons, professionals, talents and labour; and freer flow of capital. (ASEAN, 2008)

The Eminent Persons Group (EPG) which was formed to draft a report on the ASEAN Charter made recommendations as to the economic integration development of ASEAN. However, a number of its suggestions were either changed and diluted or did not become part of the Charter. For example, the EPG report emphasised the importance of reducing and eliminating the development gap among ASEAN's member states to facilitate the AEC. The report suggested the creation of a special fund which could be created through member state contributions, from a portion of sales or excise taxes or airport or visa fees. However, this fund was not implemented as part of the ASEAN Charter (ASEAN Eminent Persons Group (EPG), 2006).

Furthermore, with respect to decision-making, the EPG report suggested allowing for voting on non-sensitive issues if consensus was not achieved. It stated that consensus 'should not be allowed to hold up decisions or create an *impasse* in ASEAN cooperation' (ASEAN EPG, 2006: 18). The report also endorsed the 'ASEAN minus X' and '2 plus x' systems, whereby member states could proceed on initiatives at different rates. Whilst these systems continue to be utilised by ASEAN, voting as suggested by the EPG was not adopted.

Finally, the EPG was explicit on the need for ASEAN to address compliance and implementation. The report suggested dispute settlement mechanisms for all policy areas which should have monitoring, advisory and consultative functions in addition to being enforcement mechanisms (ASEAN EPG, 2006). Whilst ASEAN has a dispute settlement mechanism for economic matters,[13] it has not been utilised to date, is not an obligatory mechanism for the settlement of disputes and the ASEAN Charter did not provide a significantly enhanced system when compared to the protocol signed in 2004.

In the same year as the ASEAN Charter, the ASEAN Trade in Goods Agreement (ATIGA) was launched. It is built upon the existing agreements on trade in goods and aims to provide a more cohesive and comprehensive agreement in trade in goods. In this sense, it is more of an agreement reorganising current provisions rather than providing for an agreement with innovative inclusions.

The ASEAN Comprehensive Investment Agreement (ACIA) came into force in 2012 and replaced the ASEAN Agreement for the Promotion and Protection of Investment of 1987 and the Framework Agreement on the

ASEAN Investment Area of 1998 (ASEAN, 2012a). The ASEAN Annual Report 2011–2012 describes the ACIA as 'a single investment document covering the liberalisation, promotion, and protection of investments by both ASEAN investors and ASEAN-based foreign investors (ASEAN, 2012a: 48). Its principal aim is to improve ASEAN's competitiveness as a destination for investment.

According to the ASEAN Annual Report 2011–2012, the realisation of the AEC by 2015 was on track. The report, however, also mentions that there are challenges to the implementation of certain aspects of the AEC and that of significant importance is the need to 'engage the private sector, strengthen connectivity, address the development divide, and build stronger institutional support and better macroeconomic and policy coordination' (ASEAN, 2012a: 37). With regard to services, the report acknowledges the need for a more strategic perspective on ASEAN's approach to trade in services and refers to the fact that the AFAS is currently being reviewed (ASEAN, 2012a). Concerning trade in goods, the report refers to the fact that import duties have been eliminated, with the exception of goods under certain lists such as the General Exception List, the Sensitive List and the Highly Sensitive List, since 2010. For the CLMV countries, tariffs are currently at 0–5%, with the majority being eliminated by 2015, with the concession that 7% of tariffs can be eliminated by 2018 (ASEAN, 2012a).

The ASEAN Economic Community Scorecard of 2012 has set out the extent to which the necessary measures for the AEC have been implemented. The AEC is structured into distinct pillars which cover establishing ASEAN as a single market and production base, creating a competitive and economic region, achieving equitable economic development and integrating ASEAN into the global economy (ASEAN, 2012b). The ASEAN Economic Community Scorecard of 2012 has surmised that there have been delays in the implementation of a number of measures and that this is largely due to 'the ratification of signed ASEAN-wide agreements and their alignment into national domestic laws as well as delays in implementation of specific initiatives' (ASEAN, 2012b: 21). The scorecard argues that ASEAN member states need to increase their commitment, implying that a lack of political will is hindering the realisation of the AEC. In some cases, the lack of implementation at the member state level was delaying the realisation of regional level initiatives (ASEAN, 2012b). Suggestions made by the scorecard included greater private sector engagement and a review of legislative and regulatory limitations which are impeding intra- and extra-ASEAN commitments (ASEAN, 2012b).

The scorecard states that 67.5% of targets have been achieved. 65.9% of measures related to creating a single market and production base have been achieved; 67.9% of measures concerning the establishment of ASEAN as a competitive economic region have been achieved; 66.7% of measures related to equitable economic development have been implemented and 85.7% of measures for ASEAN's integration into the global economy have been achieved (ASEAN, 2012b).

According to the scorecard, fundamental to the AEC is 'political will, coordination and resource mobilisation, implementation and arrangements, capacity building and institutional strengthening and public and private sector consultations' (ASEAN, 2012b).

An interview respondent stated that they believed the AEC to be realisable by 2015, but, similar to the 2012 scorecard, was concerned about the depth and extent of implementation of necessary measures.

> Yes, it is achievable. But you see, it can be achieved; the design and the broad strokes will be there. My concern is how deep will the integration be? You can meet all those requirements but the depth of integration is something that ASEAN will have to look at ... I think that by 2015 we will have the community but if we want to be substantive then we really have to look at the nuts and bolts inside of that framework. (I2 AO, 2011)

Chia (2011) is less optimistic and believes that it would be difficult for the AEC to be realised by 2015. A major factor contributing to meeting the 2015 deadline is, according to Chia (2011), lack of political will as a result of the difficulties faced when attempting to convince various parties, including legislators, the private sector and the public, of the benefits of trade liberalisation.

In response to the GFC, ASEAN again made proclamations of reinvigorating economic integration (Pitsuwan, 2009; Rillo, 2009). Since the AFC, ASEAN states had implemented national measures to prepare for a future crisis such as the GFC and most had account surpluses, foreign currency reserves and had implemented stimulus packages to combat the effects of the crisis (Nair, 2011). Nevertheless, intra-regional trade did decline and export dependent states such as Singapore, Malaysia and Thailand had falls in growth as a consequence of the GFC (Nair, 2011). In addition to the national responses to the GFC, ASEAN also took measures to brace the region against the impact of the crisis. Building upon what had been implemented during and after the AFC, in 2010 ASEAN expanded the CMI from $24 billion

US dollars to $120 billion US dollars under the Chiang Mai Initiative Multilateralisation (CMIM), which aims to 'address balance of payment and short-term liquidity difficulties in the region, and supplement the existing international financial arrangements' (ASEAN +3 Macroeconomic Research Office (AMRO), 2013). Also, in 2012, the ASEAN +3 Macroeconomic Research Office (AMRO) was opened with the objective of creating an 'independent regional surveillance unit to monitor and analyse regional economies and support CMIM decision-making' (AMRO, 2013).

However, similar to the response by ASEAN member states to the AFC, national policies and practices did not always align with the position of ASEAN, which once again supported further economic integration cooperation and a strengthening of the mechanisms already in place such as the ABMI and surveillance and monitoring systems (Rillo, 2009). Nair (2011) presents an example of this misalignment of regional and national priorities by explaining that Indonesia, when seeking financial support in 2009 for its budget gap, sought assistance from the World Bank, Australia, Japan and the Asian Development Bank rather than asking Singapore or Malaysia, who would have been in a position to assist. Furthermore, Nair (2011) and Rillo (2009) have asserted that some member states such as Indonesia and Malaysia have resorted to more protectionist policies in the wake of the GFC despite ASEAN's support for increased free trade and economic integration. For ASEAN to counteract these protectionist approaches, Rillo (2009) suggests that ASEAN must continue to develop domestic demand and investment.

Throughout ASEAN's economic integration experience, slow implementation, flexible participation and commitments and avoidance of formal and legal dispute settlement mechanisms have been evident. I argue that the slow progress of ASEAN's economic integration can be explained by ASEAN's version of a neofunctional approach to economic integration as discussed in the previous sections. With regard to spillover, ASEAN's approach of trialling and then later formalising its initiatives has been present, which is evident in the flexible commitments available to its members. The elite socialisation processes, which have been influenced by ASEAN's norms of interaction, have also had a significant impact. As an association which has emphasised consolidating modes of interaction, rhetorical norms and principles and peaceful and consensual participation in its policies, it is to be expected that firm obligations, bold policy developments and swift implementation of economic measures have not been especially evident. The disparity between the recommendations of the EPG report on the ASEAN Charter and the final contents of the Charter with regard to economic integration measures is one example where the elite socialisation of ASEAN norms has influenced developments within the Association.

Additionally, NTBs have been particularly problematic and persistent. The different speeds of economic development and differing opinions on the value of integration have resulted in a diversity of approaches among the member states, none the least being the recent agreement between Singapore and Thailand, the Singapore–Thailand Enhanced Economic Relationship (STEER). Singapore, Thailand and Malaysia have been the main drivers of economic integration (Severino, 2006), but they have also had moments, especially during post-crisis periods, when they have reverted to more protectionist and nationalist policies. Especially since the AFC, ASEAN has attempted to strike a balance between, on the one hand, remaining an outward-looking economic region, with a number of export-driven economies and ensuring that it is an attractive destination for FDI and, on the other, implementing measures to ensure the economic independence and self-help capabilities of the region through initiatives such as the ABMI and the CMIM.

Predominant throughout ASEAN's approach however has been its determination to respond to external events and pressure by continuing along the path of economic integration. The observations and arguments made thus far demonstrate that whilst the endeavour to integrate their respective regions is true for the EU and ASEAN, differences exist. Understanding these differences aids in comprehending the impact the EU has had on ASEAN economic integration which will be discussed in the following sections.

As discussed below, a major concern regarding the EU's efforts to promote and support regional integration to ASEAN has been the dissatisfaction of EU officials with the implementation of initiatives. Through an examination of ASEAN's path towards economic integration, it becomes apparent that concerns over implementation have been a recurring theme. Whilst some of these concerns are valid, I suggest that this concern is often a result of a misunderstanding of the role of ASEAN and the organisational norms underpinning the Association. The root cause of dissatisfaction has often been the existence of expectations of ASEAN unfitting for its purpose and function. If there is a desire on the part of the EU for greater efficacy and efficiency of implementation of initiatives in ASEAN, a thorough assessment of ASEAN's norms of interaction is required rather than the imposition of inappropriate expectations.

The EU's promotion of economic integration to ASEAN

The 19th ASEAN–EU Ministerial Meeting held in April 2012 launched two cooperation programmes to support ASEAN integration. These two programmes are the ARISE programme and the Regional EU–ASEAN Dialogue Instrument (READI) (Council of the EU, 2012b). READI, in fact, is not a new programme, and the statement at the 2012 meeting is a reconfirmation of its continuation.[14] The ARISE programme focuses on EU–ASEAN cooperation on economic integration and support for the development of the AEC.

> The overall objective of the ASEAN regional integration support by the EU (ARISE) is to support the ASEAN economic integration process through contributing to the implementation of the ASEAN Economic Community (AEC) blueprint for the realisation of the AEC. The purpose is to enhance the capacities of the ASEAN Member States in harmonising and implementing policies and regulations in the economic and trade sectors and implement them effectively drawing on EU experience, so as to contribute to the realisation of the AEC. (Devex, 2012)

The ARISE programme aims to strengthen the overall ASEAN economic integration process, assist in the achievement of free flow of goods within ASEAN and strengthen the capacity of the ASEAN Secretariat (Devex, 2012).

Prior to these initiatives, the most significant project to date through which the EU has supported the economic integration of ASEAN was the APRIS programme. The APRIS programme expanded on, and gave practical application to, the decisions laid out in the *Plan of Action to Implement the Nuremberg Declaration on an EU–ASEAN Enhanced Partnership* (ASEAN–EU, 2007b) and the *Phnom Penh Agenda for the Implementation of the ASEAN–EU Plan of Action* (2009–2010) (ASEAN–EU, 2009). APRIS was managed in two phases, APRIS I and APRIS II, and was run in conjunction with the Trans-Regional EU–ASEAN Trade Initiative (TREATI) and READI. David Martin, the head of the APRIS programmes, stated that, 'APRIS is aimed at supporting regional needs in relation to the agreement and delivery of current and future trade agreements, in the deepening of integration and in the improvement of regulatory frameworks that are "pro-trade"' (Martin, 2009: 89).

APRIS I commenced in September 2003 and finished in September 2006. Its budget consisted of a 4 million euro contribution from the

EU and 0.5 million euro contribution from the ASEAN Secretariat. Following on from APRIS I was APRIS II, which ran from 2006 until November 2009. The funding for APRIS II in relation to APRIS I was increased, with 7.3 million euro being provided by the EU and 1.1 million euro being provided by ASEAN (Martin, 2009). APRIS I's primary focus was the creation of policy papers and analysis and training for economic cooperation. The structure of APRIS I bore strong hallmarks of EU economic integration design and processes. The stages of APRIS I followed the EU logic of first establishing a single window for customs throughout the region, followed by plans to abolish NTBs and align the external tariffs for all ASEAN members. Developments on NTBs and the establishment of common external tariffs were followed by moves to establish processes that aimed to harmonise production and product standards, common production statistics and classifications, and systems to study intra-regional trade and production patterns.

APRIS I also assisted in the creation of a consultation process, which gave the private sector the possibility to refer to a consultation body, the ASEAN Consultation to Solve Trade and Investment Issues (ACT) for businesses 'encountering operational problems on cross-border issues related to the implementation of ASEAN agreements in trade and investment' (ASEAN, 2007b: 1). The third component of APRIS I created a framework to increase the organisation, functioning and capacity of ASEAN to work towards economic integration. This included training ASEAN Secretariat staff, developing management systems and performance indicators and auditing procedures.

APRIS II encompassed more specific initiatives and included programmes which covered technical regulations and standards, customs and trade facilitation, investment and capacity building. In contrast to APRIS I, which placed primary emphasis on policy formulation and cooperation, APRIS II moved towards an increased emphasis on implementation and integration (Martin, 2009). Within APRIS II, one example of action under the technical regulations and standards component was the support for the implementation of the ASEAN Cosmetics Directive (ACD) (APRIS II, 2012a).[15] Within the cosmetics industry, ASEAN regulators were trained by APRIS officials who participated in workshops and visited Europe in order to see how EU directives work in practice. APRIS II also promoted the development of an ASEAN Cosmetic Testing Laboratory Network (ACTLN), trained those within the industry on Good Manufacturing Practice (GMP) and helped businesses within the industry to understand the ACD (APRIS II, 2012a).

Regarding customs and trade facilitation, APRIS II supported the increase of intra-regional trade in ASEAN by assisting ASEAN member state officials in creating a system through which exporters can 'self-certify' the origin of their goods as a way to save costs and move goods more efficiently and quickly.[16] Prior to this development, exporters had to prove the origin of their goods before they were shipped and obtain a certificate of origin from the local ministry for trade. As this is often expensive, time-consuming and complicated, the 'self-certification' system aims to save time and also money on unnecessary tariffs paid as a consequence of the complexity of the original system (APRIS II, 2012b).

APRIS II also helped ASEAN develop an ASEAN Customs Declaration Document (ACDD) which aims to reduce clearance times for goods across borders (APRIS II, 2012c). APRIS II officials developed a *Guide to Use of the ASEAN Customs Declaration Document* and also helped ASEAN member states, through workshops and seminars, harmonise their data to comply with the ASEAN Customs Data Model (APRIS II, 2012c).

A third area in which APRIS II assisted in trade facilitation and customs throughout ASEAN was with the development of a report on the advantages of a regional transit transport regime and the design of a computerised ASEAN Customs Transit System (ACTS). These initiatives were designed to reduce the costs and time of intra-regional movement of goods.[17]

ASEAN has recognised the role EU law has played in creating a competitive market within Europe. Although it does not have an institution such as the ECJ, ASEAN has committed itself to a 'rules-based' integration process and to this end has been developing the Enhanced ASEAN Dispute Settlement Mechanism (EDSM) since 2003.[18] As mentioned earlier in the chapter, this mechanism has not been used to date and is not a compulsory mechanism for dispute settlement. ASEAN has called on the EU to improve the effectiveness of this mechanism, and APRIS II's support to the EDSM included training and networking, process development and the establishment of operational guidelines. Legal experts from APRIS also worked with officials from the ASEAN Secretariat and trade ministries from the member states to explain the EDSM. Study tours were organised to the WTO Secretariat and to the European Commission's legal services. APRIS officials also produced the *Guidelines Aimed at Supporting the ASEAN Secretariat in the Management of the EDSM System*, and they also reviewed notification arrangements and provided legal advice (APRIS II, 2012e).

TREATI, part of the fifth component of APRIS II, aimed to develop closer cooperation in trade between the EU and ASEAN and create a framework for future trade relations between the two (European Commission, 2003). It focused on developing trade regulatory convergence between the two regions and also furthering the economic integration of ASEAN (European Commission, 2003). The initial focus of TREATI in 2003 included programmes and workshops covering trade facilitation, investment facilitation and promotion, sanitary and phytosanitary standards, industrial product standards and technical barriers to trade, Intellectual Property Rights, trade and the environment and tourism and forestry products (European Commission Directorate General for Trade, 2007). In 2004, these focus areas were redefined to also cover sanitary and phytosanitary standards in agricultural and seafood products, technical standards for electronics and wood-based industries, cross-sectoral cooperation on trade facilitation and investment (European Commission Directorate General for Trade, 2007). During APRIS II, some of the key projects within TREATI were a workshop on automotive product standards which involved officials from the EU and ASEAN, representatives from the private sector and from ASEAN member state ministries of transport (APRIS II, 2012f).[19]

Responses to the EU's promotion of economic integration

Overall, the programmes discussed in the previous section have been seen to have had a positive impact on ASEAN's economic integration development (Martin, 2009), and interview participants working in the EEAS and the ASEAN Secretariat were positive about the results of the EU's programmes to support economic integration. An official from the EEAS said that the programmes were 'much appreciated by the ASEAN Secretariat and the ASEAN member states' (I7 EO, 2011). In addition, an ASEAN official stated that:

> It was a successful programme (APRIS), focusing on some of the key trade facilitation areas, like customs standards and so on. That helped us introduce some of those key concepts in terms of trade facilitation and transport facilitation. It was helpful in the sense that we modernised the way that we look at some of the trade facilitation measures. (I2 AO, 2011)

Additionally, in response to the question, 'how successful do you think APRIS has been?' 60% of the respondents answered 'moderately successful' from the following options: 'not successful', 'solid but minimal', 'moderately successful' and 'very successful'. The response to this question is illustrated in Figure 4.1 below.

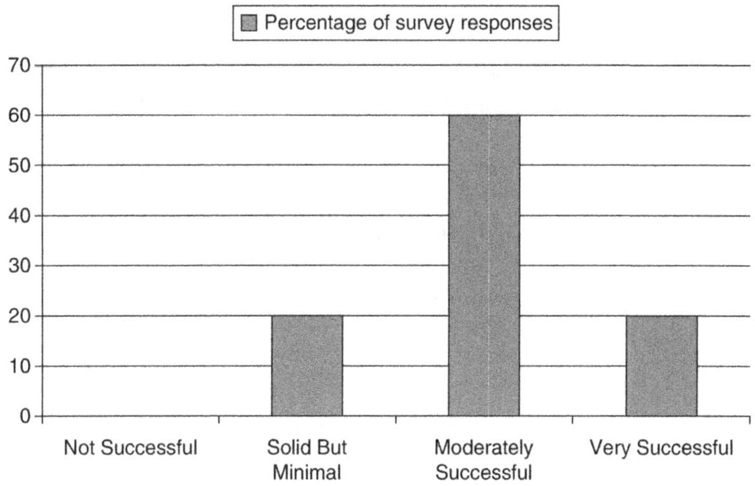

Figure 4.1 How successful do you think the APRIS programme has been?

In response to the question, 'could other components have been included in APRIS II?' four respondents answered this question and two were generally satisfied with the contents of the programme based on the resources available. For example, one respondent stated that, 'it was good that the programme focused on a limited number of areas' (S16 EOA, 2012). This respondent expressed the opinion that other components should not have been included due to limited resources (S16 EOA, 2012). Similarly, another respondent stated that 'there is a limit to resources', and therefore other components were not feasible (S5 EOA, 2012). As to the other two respondents, one suggested 'cultural dialogue for better understanding' as a possible inclusion (S20 EAA, 2012), and the other respondent mentioned energy and environment as possible inclusions into APRIS II (S13 EOA, 2012).

However, it was also pointed out that there were limits to the EU's support of economic integration to ASEAN, and there were some criticisms of the programmes that had been initiated. Two main areas of concern became apparent through an analysis of the interviews. The first is that there is a divergence of perceptions between officials and academics related to the EU and those connected to ASEAN of the EU as an actor that supports the economic integration of ASEAN. The second is that although there is common concern for implementation and impact assessment of the initiatives under APRIS I and II, respondents working with and in the EU, and those connected to ASEAN, have differing views on the reasons for this.

As to the first observation, perception divergence of the EU's role was discussed in relation to its regulatory power. A respondent from the EEAS was explicit in stating that the EU 'is not seen as imposing its interests' (I4 EO, 2011). Although it may be true that the EU is not considered a threat by those in ASEAN, ASEAN officials and scholars working in Southeast Asia did not necessarily perceive the EU as a benevolent actor. An ASEAN official stated that 'we urge the Europeans to go beyond their rigidity, you don't have to look for institutions to partner to develop some of these programmes. It could be done in an informal way, as ASEAN works in a very informal way.' (I1 AO, 2011)

Although it was not the intended outcome of programmes such as APRIS, the EU is often perceived as an actor that is rigid and inflexible in its approach to economic integration support. A scholar based in Southeast Asia noted that although the EU is often proud to be a regulatory power, there is the perception in Southeast Asia that 'it tends to regulate itself to death' (I3 AA, 2011). This academic also stated that the EU functions with 'a degree of inflexibility that is not very healthy' and that in this respect it is often perceived as a 'nuisance' to its interlocutors in ASEAN (I3 AA, 2011).

With regard to implementation, EU officials expressed frustration concerning the fact that developments under the APRIS programme had not happened as quickly as the EU would have liked. An EEAS official stated that ASEAN 'takes what they like, but in an inefficient way' and that 'up until recently, ASEAN has not been serious about APRIS' (I7 EO, 2011). It was also said that, 'the ASEAN Secretariat are trained to death, and training is ineffective if not used immediately and if there is no implementation' (I7 EO, 2011). According to this EEAS official, delays in the implementation of APRIS initiatives have been attributed to the capacity of the ASEAN Secretariat: 'There is a lack of personnel and resources, the mandate is weak, it doesn't have executive powers and members are travelling all the time' (I7 EO, 2011). Another EU official said of the ASEAN Secretariat, 'the member states don't put a lot of resources in; it's too small, it's not very well-managed, it's stumbling by' (I8 EOA, 2011). One official at the EEAS had concerns for the current programme, ARISE, as although the budget has increased, because there have not been any significant changes to the capacity and mandate of the ASEAN Secretariat, it is unsure as to whether these funds will be utilised to their full capacity (I7 EO, 2011).

ASEAN officials also referred to concerns regarding the implementation of programmes under APRIS. Although ASEAN officials admitted that there was a need for increased connectivity between ASEAN member states in terms of transport and transit infrastructure and customs harmonisation, it was reiterated that some of the initiatives supported by the EU were unworkable in the ASEAN context. In addition to this, one official at the ASEAN Secretariat emphasised that:

> EU officials need to work closely with those in ASEAN as I don't think that many EU experts understand ASEAN. So they will have to work closely with ASEAN experts, actually, when implementing some of these key projects. I think the EU will have to work closely with us, understand our needs, and implement accordingly. (I2 AO, 2011)

According to this ASEAN official, another reason why there had been concerns with implementation was that fact that national and regional initiatives were not coordinated to their full effect. An ASEAN official stated that:

> What I think is important is if you want to set up a regional platform for cooperation, you must also ensure that at the national (level) they (the member states) can implement. I think the EU should also put emphasis on that. Otherwise, if you create a regional platform ... if you don't set up the necessary mechanisms, then, you can't have the system. (I2 AO, 2011)

This official emphasised the need for greater synergy between regional initiatives and implementation at the ASEAN member state level in order for programmes such as APRIS to be realised to their full potential.

A final issue regarding implementation which was raised by ASEAN officials was the fact that there was not enough emphasis by the EU on impact assessment for programmes such as APRIS. One ASEAN official stated that in order to know if a programme or initiative had been implemented effectively, or if there was room for improvement, it was necessary to 'give some time and then really look at the impact of the programme on ASEAN integration' and that this is something in which the EU should be involved (I2 AO, 2011).

By analysing the results achieved through the EU's support for ASEAN economic integration, and the responses by officials and academics, it is apparent that the technical and economic integration steps taken by the EU as reflected in the APRIS and ARISE programmes are seen to be of merit by ASEAN. Nevertheless, problems exist in the approaches taken and also, at times, in the results that are expected.

A neofunctional spillover logic is evident in the EU and ASEAN through the approach to develop economic integration in the two regions. However, as argued earlier in this chapter, this spillover process in ASEAN differs from the EU in two main ways. Firstly, as a result of looking towards the EU experience for inspiration, ASEAN is actively pushing this spillover rather than allowing it to have a deterministic momentum of its own, which has been the case in certain areas of EU economic integration. One example of the EU approach is the changes in decision-making processes throughout the EU economic integration process, which moves from unanimity to qualified majority voting, and now, under the Lisbon Treaty, co-decision processes which have allowed for new divisions of power within the EU institutions. The SLIM initiative discussed earlier in the chapter is also an example of a project attempting to rectify negative consequences of EU economic integration, in this case overly-complex legislation, in order to ensure that processes within the single market function correctly. Another example of this is the fact that the EU itself consists of two types of member states, those within the Eurozone and those outside, potentially creating a barrier to intra-regional trade.

Additionally, although ASEAN has experienced similar developments to the EU in eliminating tariffs, customs facilitation, harmonising external tariffs, abolishing NTBs and enhancing trade facilitation, ASEAN is neither a customs union nor a single market in the same sense as the EU as it does not have the same level of capital and labour mobility, nor the same amount of policy harmonisation (Chia, 2011). Therefore, the way in which the EU promotes economic integration to ASEAN based on its own style of functional development and interpretation of spillover processes has not always suited ASEAN's approach to economic integration. This has resulted in the frustrations and concerns expressed by interview and survey respondents.

Economic integration and the EU as an international actor

The EU is an international actor with regard to the promotion of its economic integration norms, and its norm entrepreneurship role is recognised by elites in Europe and Southeast Asia. According to the EU's official statements and documents, and also responses in surveys and interviews, the EU does consider itself to have the capacity and responsibility to promote its economic integration experience despite the recent turmoil it has been experiencing as a consequence of the economic and financial crisis. When survey participants were asked how important aspects of regional integration were for the EU to promote, on a scale which included 'minor', 'important', 'very important' and 'vital', 'economic integration and cooperation' was considered 'very important' by the majority of respondents. Furthermore, in comparison with the other aspects of regional integration the respondents were asked to evaluate, 'economic integration' received the highest number of responses for 'very important'. For this question there was a response rate of 91%. The results of this survey question are detailed in Figure 4.2 below.

As discussed and analysed in this chapter, the EU has offered material and financial resources in the form of programmes such as APRIS. Similar support is ongoing in the form of ARISE, and the monetary contribution by the EU has increased. In addition to this, the number of visits by high-level officials increased dramatically in 2012. In this sense, the EU has utilised its resources to a considerable extent regarding economic integration support for ASEAN. However, as mentioned earlier in the chapter, there are concerns as to whether these resources have been used sufficiently due to issues with implementation.

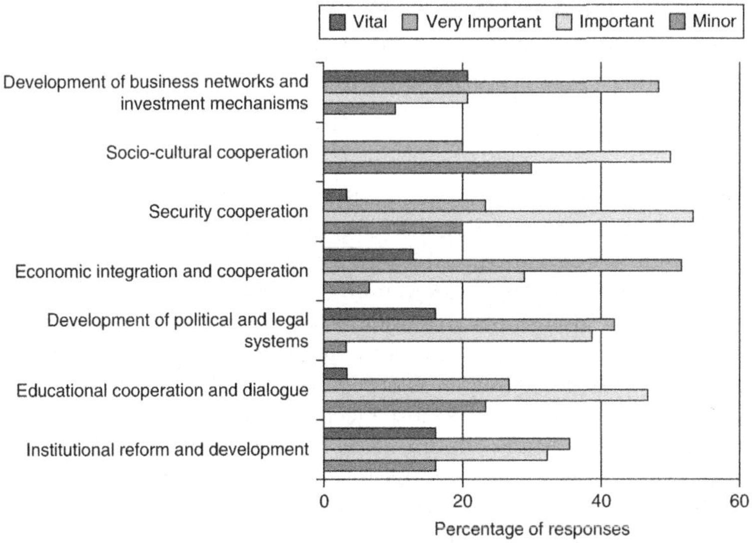

Figure 4.2 How important is it for the EU to promote the following aspects of regional integration to Southeast Asia?

Whether the EU has been able to transform the 'target' environment, a large number of ASEAN developments in economic integration correlate with components of the APRIS programmes. Therefore, it can be surmised that the EU has been able to transform the target environment with regard to ASEAN's economic integration developments. The most recent evaluation of the EU's cooperation with ASEAN, commissioned by the EuropeAid Co-operation Office, the Directorate-General for Development and the Directorate-General for External Relations found that support from the EU had 'significantly contributed to regional economic integration' and that the APRIS programme had assisted in increasing the capacity and ability of the ASEAN Secretariat 'to promote policy dialogue and deal with routine matters' (Particip GmbH, 2009: 9). However, it also found that 'APRIS was not in a position to bring about far-reaching dramatic changes in the course of regional integration'. The report attributed this to the presence of 'major bottlenecks to break-through ASEAN reforms' which were present in 'numerous country level political stumbling blocks' (Particip GmbH, 2009: 9). Areas in which the EU made a significant contribution to ASEAN economic integration, according to the evaluation report, included sanitary and phytosanitary harmonisation, simplification of customs procedures, intellectual property rights and strengthened dialogue on trade and integration (Particip GmbH, 2009: 9).

Finally, whether approaches and results have been deemed successful, internally and externally, according to the responses gathered in the interviews and surveys, the programmes initiated to support and promote economic integration in ASEAN have been regarded as successful, despite a number of reservations mainly related to implementation. As has been mentioned earlier in the chapter, 60% of survey respondents believed the APRIS programme to have been moderately successful. Aspects of the APRIS programme which were considered to be the most effective were training in standards and conformance and training in customs and trade facilitation. This is demonstrated in Table 4.1 below, which shows the results of the question, 'APRIS II focused on the following areas of regional integration. Which aspects do you think have been the most effective?' Respondents were asked to number their choices, with one being the most effective and six being the least effective. However, the low response rate to this question, with only 32% of participants answering this question, possibly indicates a low awareness of the details of the APRIS programme among survey respondents.

Table 4.1 APRIS II focused on the following areas of regional integration. Which aspects do you think have been the most effective?

APRIS II instruments by order of preference	Percentage of responses within each rank (number of responses in brackets)							Mean	Adjusted mean*
	1	2	3	4	5	6	Not ranked		
Training and standards conformance	27(3)	27(3)	9(1)	27(3)	9(1)	0(0)	0(0)	**2.6**	
Training in customs and trade	27(3)	27(3)	18(2)	0(0)	9(1)	9(1)	0(0)	**3.3**	
TREATI	9(1)	27(3)	18(2)	27(3)	9(1)	0(0)	9(1)	2.72	**3.4**
READI	9(1)	18(2)	18(2)	9(1)	18(2)	0(0)	18(2)	2.3	**3.5**
Capacity building and strengthening	9(1)	0(0)	18(2)	27(3)	27(3)	18(2)	0(0)	**4.3**	
Training in investment	0(0)	9(1)	9(1)	36(4)	18(2)	18(2)	9(1)	3.9	**4.5**

*The adjusted mean has been chosen as the more accurate result for this question due to the fact that a rank of 7 was given to a participant who chose not to rank an instrument (as opposed to a rank of 0 used to calculate the mean) for this calculation. It was assumed that not ranking an instrument indicated that it was considered less effective than instruments which were ranked. This was determined by the following factors: participants had been previously asked if they were aware of APRIS, and therefore lack of knowledge could not be a reason for a non-response; also, the opportunity to rank effective APRIS instruments was given, which ensured that a non-response would not be given to effective instruments.

The evaluation on EU–ASEAN cooperation from 2009 also reflects the findings of the data analysis conducted for this research project as it states that there has been 'tangible progress' towards economic integration which would not have been as substantial in the absence of a programme such as APRIS (Particip Gmbh, 2009: 9). Also, the evaluation stated that there was a positive reaction to the appropriateness of the EU's engagement when analysed against the priorities of the EU as set out in documents such as *A New Partnership with South-East Asia* (Particip Gmbh, 2009: 9).

According to the criteria established in Chapter 2 to assess actorness in this study, the EU does have the potential to be perceived as an actor with regard to its economic norms of regional integration and the promotion of its norms to ASEAN. A policy of promoting economic integration norms to ASEAN does enable the EU to be an international actor. As a norm entrepreneur, therefore, the EU's role is effective in diffusing norms to ASEAN, despite the fact that there are a number of issues and concerns such as a lack of understanding of the ASEAN context and the need to ensure that implementation and impact assessments are conducted.

Economic integration and the EU as a norm entrepreneur

The EU's norm entrepreneurship role in the promotion of economic integration to ASEAN has involved a number of norm diffusion processes. The main diffusion processes which have been present with regard to the EU's promotion of economic integration are transference and overt diffusion. The technical assistance provided through the APRIS and ARISE programmes demonstrated a high level of transference. As has been detailed in this chapter, these programmes have had an impact on ASEAN's economic integration, with ASEAN and EU officials positively responding to an approach which involves an exchange of technical assistance and knowledge transfer. A number of technical developments, such as customs declaration procedures and ASEAN directives on certain products, demonstrate a high level of transference. Overt diffusion is also a characteristic of the EU's approach of promoting economic integration through the presence of EU officials in Southeast Asia conducting workshops and seminars to train ASEAN officials. Additionally, the TREATI programme, with its emphasis on facilitating trade between the EU and ASEAN, has also involved transference and overt diffusion processes through workshops and training programmes.

Procedural diffusion in the case of economic integration support and economic cooperation is also evidenced in the presence of institutionalised meetings such as the ASEAN Economic Ministers and EU

Trade Commissioner Meetings (AEM–EU) and the ASEAN–EU Senior Economic Officials Consultation Meeting (SEOM–EU). The latest SEOM–EU was held in March 2013 in preparation for the AEM–EU, and discussed economic and trade relations between ASEAN and the EU as well as items which were to be included on the agenda of the AEM–EU. At the most recent AEM–EU meeting in March 2013, statements were made regarding the EU's support for ASEAN's economic integration and economic cooperation between the two organisations.

> The Ministers and the EU Trade Commissioner were pleased to note the status of the implementation of the various ASEAN–EU economic cooperation programmes in support of ASEAN's economic integration, institutional capacity-building, statistics, ASEAN's FTA negotiating capacity, intellectual property rights and air transport. The Ministers and the EU Trade Commissioner welcomed the ASEAN Regional Integration Support by the EU (ARISE) project which is aimed at supporting the realisation of the ASEAN Economic Community (AEC) by enhancing the capacities of ASEAN Member States and the ASEAN Secretariat. The Ministers and the EU Trade Commissioner agreed that the experience drawn from the EU's economic integration would substantially benefit ASEAN. (ASEAN, 2013d)

Prior to 2012, criticism had been voiced by EU officials based in Southeast Asia (I8 EOA, 2011) and analysts (Islam, 2011) that the level of significance given to ASEAN by EU officials was inadequate. Whilst EU official documents stated the importance of economic integration support for ASEAN and economic cooperation with ASEAN, the EU's priorities and informational diffusion processes were often perceived as insufficient. The year 2012, which experienced an unprecedented number of official visits from the EU, an increase in statements claiming the EU's recognition of the importance of ASEAN's economic integration and the EU's relations with Southeast Asia have resulted in an increase in informational diffusion processes in the form of strategic communications between the two organisations.

The cultural filter has also had an impact, especially on the level and rate of implementation of EU initiatives. Regarding technical and functional aspects of economic integration policy, norm learning is evident, with a number of developments reflecting those within the EU. However, with regard to implementation, results and ASEAN's overall approach to economic integration, norm diffusion processes have been significantly influenced by ASEAN's pre-existing norms and principles. This chapter has analysed the differences between the EU and ASEAN concerning neofunctional aspects of integration and also reactions to crises, with ASEAN displaying contrasting effects of elite socialisation and spillover. There is also within ASEAN the propensity to implement preventative and self-help mechanisms such as the CMIM and the ABMI. These aspects of ASEAN's economic integration have resulted in the direction of ASEAN economic integration differing from the EU's despite normative diffusion occurring with regard to a significant number of technical developments.

Due to the fact that the EU's approach to promoting its economic integration experience has been explicit and concrete, there is limited evidence of unintentional diffusion of the EU's economic integration norms. Normative contagion has also been limited because of ASEAN's recognition of the relevance of the EU's support and its willingness to draw upon aspects of the EU's economic integration experience.

Whilst the role of the EU as a norm entrepreneur with regard to economic integration has been reasonably robust, ASEAN as the norm recipient has not been passive. This is especially noticeable in ASEAN's interest in obtaining support from the EU for its dispute mechanism system even though ASEAN is determined not to create a legal body comparable to the ECJ.

The EU's norms of economic integration resonate with the existing norms of ASEAN to the extent that ASEAN has declared economic integration a key principle. As presented in this chapter, whilst economic integration and development were stated in the Bangkok Declaration of 1967, the early years of ASEAN's existence were primarily focused on political and security issues. Once security concerns had largely abated, and especially after the AFC, economic integration norms were of increased importance for ASEAN and consequently resonated with the EU's position regarding the benefits of economic integration. Especially with regard to the technical aspects of economic integration, ASEAN's aims and norms have resonated with the EU's. How ASEAN has incorporated members with different levels of economic development and also the flexibility with which it has pursued initiatives, however, have differed from the EU.

The current Secretary General of ASEAN, in his inaugural speech, stated the benefits of economic integration. 'The more open flow of investments, capital, labor, goods and services will pose different challenges and opportunities for our Member States, indicating that local actors do see the benefit in norms of economic integration. But it will also have a tremendous multiplier effect on the region' (ASEAN, 2013e). Additionally, former Secretary General, Surin Pitsuwan, in a speech at a Workshop on Benchmarking and Monitoring Progress of the ASEAN Economic Community in 2011, stated the goals and benefits of economic integration. 'Since regional economic integration is not an end by itself, but a policy instrument designed to achieve development goals, greater macroeconomic and policy coordination is needed' (ASEAN, 2013f). At the ASEAN level, indeed, there is the consideration that economic integration is of benefit and, similar to the EU, ASEAN maintains that not only the lowering of tariffs but also the need to reduce NTBs is of critical importance. Nevertheless, at the member state level, there is still the need to address the differing levels of political will among the ASEAN members. In the same speech by Surin Pitsuwan as quoted above, he stated that:

> To ensure that the AEC is achieved by 2015, ASEAN will need to strengthen the implementation of programs at both regional and national levels. In this regard, commitments to integration matter most. ASEAN Member States are being urged to ensure that regional commitments are transposed into national commitments through appropriate domestic processes ... the real test of how far integration should go depends on individual countries' commitment. (ASEAN, 2013f)

However, despite the commitment to economic integration, certain aspects of the existing economic structure of the ASEAN region are considered inadequate and in need of new norms and mechanisms of economic integration. One example of this is the level of connectivity among ASEAN member states with regard to creating an integrated region. An interviewee referred to this fact by stating:

> To me, what is more important for ASEAN now is making sure there is enough connectivity. That means we are building a single market production base, so we need to be connected physically. By land, sea and air and then we need to be connected ... in terms of trade facilitation, transport facilitation and things like that and people to people (connections), including tourism. So that is one way that's important to build an ASEAN community. (I2 AO, 2011)

After the AFC, the legitimacy and authority of ASEAN with regard to the economic stability and prosperity of the Southeast Asian region was questioned. Not only did this event raise expectations of ASEAN to play a role in the economic stability of the region, it also made those within the region realise the need for regional mechanisms which ensured independent management of any future crises. However, this had to be done whilst still maintaining the openness and accessibility to external markets and especially the continuation of growth for those ASEAN markets which were export driven. Norms of economic integration, therefore, were considered by ASEAN, as evident in the commitments within the *Ha Noi Plan of Action* and the *Bali Concord II*, as crucial and advantageous to ASEAN's economic objectives and able to make a contribution to ASEAN's legitimacy and authority. This, to a certain extent, included economic norms of integration inspired by the EU.

With trade with external partners and FDI flows into ASEAN from outside the region as ASEAN priorities,[20] a functioning, stable and integrated market for ASEAN has the ability to enhance ASEAN's profile, especially in the sense that it creates an attractive destination for investment and trade. Furthermore, ASEAN's commitment to increasing the economic well-being of its citizens and reducing the development gap among its members are also objectives which are hoped to be achieved through increased economic and financial integration. Therefore, it can be surmised that economic integration norms have the potential to contribute to ASEAN's aims as stated in its policy and legal documents such as the ASEAN Charter.

Whilst this is the case, rather than replacing pre-existing norms, ASEAN's flexible approach to economic integration aims to take into account the norms which are already entrenched within the Association. This is one of the reasons why whilst ASEAN is aiming to create an economic community, it does not aim to create a customs union with a common external tariff (Balassa, 1967), at least at this stage, and ambitions for a full common market with a high level of policy harmonisation and free flows of capital and labour, or even a monetary union, are only for a possible, distant future (Chia, 2011). For example, as one interview respondent stated regarding a common external tariff, 'there's a question mark there because Singapore has (a) zero tariff for most things ... so how do you bridge the gap?' (I2 AO, 2011). Another interviewee referred to Singapore's policy of having no external tariff in comparison with other ASEAN member states such as the Philippines.

> In some countries like the Philippines, the constitution says foreign goods are subjected to (a certain) amount of tariff. Now, if you say,

> the ASEAN single market is free (of tariffs), immediately they will (need to) do a constitutional amendment in congress, which is almost impossible. Things like that, we have to take into account. (I1 AO, 2011)

Only in the sense that member states have had different reactions to protectionist policies and opening up their markets do norms of economic integration have the potential to threaten ASEAN's identity and norms. From concerns regarding national implementation of regional initiatives and the institutional capacity of ASEAN, instances emerge where ASEAN's existing norms, and also the normative structures of its member states, do not align with agreed upon norms of economic integration, and those promoted by the EU. I contend, however, that ASEAN's style of economic integration development, with the inclusion of members with different political economies and levels of economic development, and the flexible adoption and time frames given to these member states to implement initiatives enable the incremental adoption of economic norms. This reduces the threat to ASEAN's identity and pre-existing normative framework. This is not to say that criticisms of national implementation and alignment with ASEAN priorities are absent, but ASEAN's overall approach has accommodated ASEAN's member states where necessary.

Considering the EU's norms of economic integration, there is little chance that these norms would increase instability in ASEAN for two main reasons. Firstly, ASEAN is only progressing at a pace and in a style which it believes to be appropriate. Certain economic integration norms found within the EU, none the least being the adoption of a common currency, are not considered by ASEAN. The FTA negotiations between the EU and ASEAN also support this argument. As one interviewee stated:

> They (the EU) have put in certain things for which ASEAN is not really ready. Government procurement for example, we are not ready to put in anything on government procurement in the FTA. And other issues, like competition, consumer protection. Yes, we are interested, but we don't have the capacity as of now to implement some of those things. (I2 AO, 2011)

Secondly, the adoption of economic integration mechanisms which resonate with those promoted by the EU and also those initiated by ASEAN are complemented by a number of precautionary mechanisms if instability were to occur. The CMIM and the ABMI are two such examples of these preventative measures which have been established by ASEAN that do not necessarily resonate with the EU's approach.

Finally, regarding functional and technical instruments related to economic integration, supporting and strengthening behaviours, as part of Acharya's (2011a) subsidiarity framework, have been evident within ASEAN. In terms of customs and product harmonisation, increased transport infrastructure and efficient systems for determining the origin of goods, norms emanating from the EU's experience have been adopted and strengthened by ASEAN.

Nevertheless, some challenging/resisting behaviours are also evident. The previously mentioned ASEAN initiatives which refer to preventative measures, such as the CMIM, have been established in response to EU and global economic and financial norms to ensure ASEAN's independence in the face of a crisis. Such a mechanism was mentioned by an interviewee as an instrument which ASEAN could potentially export to other regions such as the EU. As an interviewee stated:

> One good example would be the multilateral swap agreement that we have. You see, because, we had it first, and only when the crisis struck in Greece, (did) leaders come together and start pooling their resources into a fund. But we already have something like that in the region. An early-warning system. (I2 AO, 2011)

Whilst not directly a matter of EU–ASEAN relations, the recent release of the text for the EU–Singapore FTA on 20 September 2013 also displays a combination of supporting/strengthening behaviours and is closely linked to the EU's aspirations for future FTAs in the region with individual states and ASEAN. The final text for the EU–Singapore FTA also bolsters the argument for the EU as a norm entrepreneur regarding economic norms, especially due to the fact that much trade is facilitated by the mutual recognition of EU product standards for traded goods. Within the agreement the alignment and greater recognition of EU standards on industrial and agricultural products such as cars have been negotiated, ensuring that EU standards are accepted and likewise facilitate the sale of Singaporean products which also meet EU standards and regulations.

Other aspects of the deal which have contributed to fulfilling EU interests are the fact that this FTA, together with the EU's FTA with South Korea, strengthens the EU trade agenda in Asia and that the agreement helps to protect EU exporters against a loss of competitiveness *vis-à-vis* other FTAs, including the Trans-Pacific Partnership and the Regional Comprehensive Economic Partnership (European Commission, 2013). Also, the FTA with Singapore focuses on green growth, thereby meeting aims of the EU's *2020 Strategy* for a competitive economy by boosting trade and investment in 'environmental technologies and promoting green public tendering' (De Gucht, 2012b: 1).

For the Europeans it has been clearly stated that the agreement with Singapore is a step towards further trade agreements in Southeast Asia. A memo released by the European Commission stated that, 'an ambitious FTA with Singapore has the potential to open the door to other FTA partners in Southeast Asia, and ultimately an agreement in the regional framework with the ASEAN group' (European Commission, 2013: 2). EU Trade Commissioner, Karel De Gucht stated that:

> Singapore is a dynamic market for EU companies and is a vital hub for doing business across Southeast Asia. This agreement is a gateway to the region and can be a catalyst for growth for EU exporters. After our agreement with South Korea, sealing this deal with Singapore clearly puts the EU on the map in Asia. But we do not intend to stop here – I hope it will open the doors for FTAs with other countries in the ASEAN region. (De Gucht, 2012b: 1)

Supporting and strengthening EU economic norms by accepting EU product standards as conditions for trade has likely occurred due to the benefits which Singaporean exporters will receive as a result of the agreement. While tariffs on Singaporean goods and services entering the EU are to be eliminated within five years, Singapore will only need to eliminate a few remaining duties on goods entering Singapore from the EU, such as beer. With Singapore now having access to a market containing 28 states, the Singaporean Trade Ministry anticipates benefits for local exporters of electronics, pharmaceuticals, chemicals and processed food products (Bloomberg, 2013). Largely due to the differences in market size, the increase of GDP over the next 10 years is considerably larger for Singapore than for the EU, with Singaporean GDP expected to rise by 2.7 billion euro and EU GDP to rise by 550 million euro. It is envisaged that the FTA will increase EU exports to Singapore by 1.4 billion euro and Singaporean exports to the EU by 3.5 billion euro (European Commission, 2013).

Whilst the agreement is expected to be mutually beneficial, the strategic impact of the agreement for the EU in terms of facilitating future agreements appears to allow for expected concessions, none the least in the petroleum sector. There are concerns on the European side that the removal of tariffs on petroleum products will increase petroleum shipments from Singapore to the EU as Singapore has one of the largest oil refining centres in the world (Reuters, 2013). Whilst the oil refiners must meet certain EU conditions in order to ship the oil tax-free to Europe, a managing director at a Swiss-based petrol company stated to the Bloomberg press that 'this could be disastrous for European refiners, the FTA with Korea is already taking crude out of Europe and increasing the cost for it for Europeans, now you have another challenge for them with competition for distillate flows from Singapore. It is already bad for them and it is getting worse' (Bloomberg, 2013: 1).

ASEAN's norm recipient role has involved the localisation of a number of EU economic integration norms. This is due to the fact that these norms are not seen to threaten the existing normative framework of ASEAN. Existing norms have not been replaced by the introduced norms of the EU because they were not challenged and only considered inadequate in most cases, as the example of ASEAN's need for greater connectivity demonstrates. Especially regarding the technical aspects of economic integration, acceptance of norms which resonate with EU norms have occurred. Yet ASEAN has also created its own economic norms of cooperation in order to ensure its independence where this has been deemed necessary. ASEAN has also expressed where aspects of the EU's economic integration experience are either inappropriate or unsuitable for the current state of the ASEAN economies, such as in the case of a common external tariff, demonstrating its proactive role as a norm recipient.

Conclusion

The EU's distinctiveness regarding its economic integration experience has provided ASEAN with a unique point of reference as it develops its own economic community. The analysis of the EU's support to ASEAN's economic integration efforts has demonstrated that the EU has been considered a source of inspiration, and the EU's efforts to promote economic integration to ASEAN have been welcomed by those within ASEAN.

The EU has had a considerable amount of success with supporting and promoting economic integration to ASEAN, which has in turn contributed to its international actorness. Interview and survey responses have indicated that the contribution made to ASEAN integration as a result of the APRIS and ARISE programmes has been of benefit and that ASEAN continues to refer to the EU for support in this area, albeit under its own conditions. This has allowed the EU to be a recognised and consequential actor in the realm of economic integration within Southeast Asia. However, this strength of the EU's actorness has been more significant with regard to ASEAN's consideration of the EU as a reference (Wong, 2012) and its willingness to accept the EU's support for its economic integration process than with regard to the actual impact and implementation of efforts to promote economic integration in ASEAN. Interview and survey responses have shown that there have been concerns on the EU side regarding the pace of implementation and development. Frustrations on the ASEAN side were related to some contents of the EU's support programmes which were not applicable to the ASEAN context. This is explained by the dichotomy between the EU's focus on outcomes and ASEAN's emphasis on processes. It is also explained by the differences between the EU and ASEAN which have been made apparent through the utilisation of a neofunctional framework of analysis in this chapter. Of particular significance is the finding that whilst the EU and ASEAN have progressed incrementally with regard to economic integration, spillover has been considered differently by the two organisations. ASEAN has trialled economic integration developments before formalising them. The EU's formalisation of developments and an assumed spillover momentum, has, at times, required subsequent revision and modification of EU economic integration initiatives. For this reason, some EU initiatives have been received as too ambitious for ASEAN at its current stage of economic integration. As a Deputy Secretary General of ASEAN stated in an interview for this study, 'ASEAN really is looking at incremental development, we are not going into a big bang in terms of community building' (I2 AO, 2011).

Additionally, differences exist between the EU and ASEAN with regard to the results of elite socialisation based on two differing normative contexts. It therefore follows that EU and ASEAN elites have had different priorities concerning economic integration and also different responses to crises. Due to the frustrations and misunderstandings that are persistent within the EU's policy of promoting economic integration to ASEAN, a balance must be struck between support to the process and expectations of the outcomes.

5
The EU, ASEAN and Institutionalisation

> Another important difference between ASEAN and the European Union is in the Western way. The typical approach is to institutionalise certain important processes, whereas in Southeast Asia, the general way is, well, if you think this is good, let's work together first, and if we like it, then we find some formal way to root it into the system and have an institutional process.
>
> Interview Respondent 1, Former Secretary General of ASEAN, 2011.

> ... in Europe we are so obsessed with institutions. Agencies creating and informing institutions ... this creates something that is stable and you can actually work within these structures. Now the downside of course in Europe is that it's considered to be too bureaucratic these days, which is probably true.
>
> Interview Respondent 4, Official at the EEAS in Brussels, 2011.

Paths to institutionalisation and historical institutional analysis

Attempts by the EU to promote institutionalisation, which include governance structures, decision-making processes and legal frameworks, to ASEAN have had a moderate and fragmentary impact. There is evidence that certain institutional developments within ASEAN appear to have been a result of the EU's promotion efforts. However, the outcomes have not been as significant as in the area of economic integration promotion discussed in Chapter 4. As with the EU's promotion of economic integration, the distinctiveness of the EU is a factor determining the receptiveness level of ASEAN and the degree to which ASEAN finds the EU's institutionalisation relevant to ASEAN.

ASEAN has actively referred to the EU for inspiration regarding its institutional development, which has resulted in the creation of institutions and processes which can be seemingly attributed to the EU experience yet are distinctive to ASEAN. With regard to institutionalisation, ASEAN's active role in evaluating what is relevant to its institutional path of development is more evident and tangible than the EU's efforts to promote institutionalisation. The EU is willing to provide ASEAN with support and information on its institutional structure, yet interview and survey responses have indicated that there are limitations with regard to the EU's promotion of institutionalisation. As one EEAS official stated,

> We can explain to you what we are doing here, but of course, you (ASEAN) do it in your own way. We can just give you an example of how we have been working ourselves for 50, 60 years now. But we do this also because we don't want to be seen as though we are imposing our standard of regional integration or how the EU functions is the model for the world ... I would say that it's sometimes very difficult, from an EU perspective, not to speak about a model that can be exported to the world. (I4 EO, 2011)

Institutional structures, political organisation, decision-making processes and fundamental norms and practices of the EU and ASEAN are distinct from one another in many ways (Stubbs, 2008). Drawing on the discussion on bureaucracies developed by Barnett and Finnemore (2004), the EU and ASEAN in this chapter are both classified as bureaucracies, deviating slightly from the common conclusion that the EU is bureaucratised to a larger extent than ASEAN. This is due to the fact that Barnett and Finnemore (2004: 3) define a bureaucracy as 'a distinct social form of authority with its own internal logic and behavioural proclivities'. It therefore follows that both the EU and ASEAN are bureaucracies with their own internal logics and behaviours. Barnett and Finnemore (2004) explain that the rules which a bureaucracy follows and creates are the constitutive substance of that bureaucracy, even to the extent that their rules may have the potential to be detrimental if an organisation follows its predetermined rules. This is regardless of whether these rules prove to be the most efficient means of addressing an issue or problem.

As regional organisations in constant flux and development, ASEAN and the EU have emerged with their own organisational rules and institutional structures. In order to explain how ASEAN has actively implemented the knowledge it has gained from examining the EU's regionalism experience, an analysis of the EU's and ASEAN's paths towards regionalism is crucial. When such an analysis is viewed through the lens of historical institutionalism, their paths can be largely understood by their historical contexts, the issues which they have had, and have to address, the internal nature of their member states and the institutional choices which have been made which have subsequently influenced further developments.

This chapter utilises the definition of institutionalisation and institutions which is widely accepted among scholars who have developed and applied historical institutional analysis. March and Olsen (1998: 948) define an institution as 'a relatively stable collection of practices and rules defining appropriate behaviour for specific groups of actors in specific situations'. Similarly, Hall (1986:19) states that an institution comprises 'the formal rules, compliance procedures, and standard operating practices that structure the relationship between individuals in various units of the polity and economy'. This has been expanded by some scholars (Pollack, 2004) to also include informal norms and practices as part of an institution. Institutionalisation is, therefore, the 'emergence of institutions and individual behaviour within them' (March and Olsen, 1998: 948).

The historical institutional approach is embedded within the 'new institutionalism' scholarship which emerged in the 1980s and 1990s which also included rationalist choice and sociological institutional traditions. It has been recognised by scholars such as Fioretos (2011) that the field of international relations has not paid significant attention to historical institutionalism. I maintain in this chapter that it is of considerable benefit to the study of the institutional development of the EU and ASEAN, as well as the examination of the EU's efforts to promote institutionalisation to ASEAN.

This is due to historical institutionalism's claim that institutions have the ability to influence and determine political strategies and political outcomes (Steinmo, Thelen and Longstreth, 1992). This theoretical approach contends that institutions matter due to their ability to shape the strategies and goals of actors, mediate cooperation and conflict and structure political situations (Steinmo, Thelen and Longstreth, 1992). In other words, not only are institutions the context in which actors can exert their influence and power, they also determine the nature of the context in which these actors can perform. Fioretos (2011: 369) summarises the function of historical institutionalism as stressing

> The type of processes that often characterise international relations, including the legacies of founding moments in shaping long-term power relations and whether new ideas become consequential, the ubiquity of unintended consequences, and especially the prevalence of incremental reform over stasis and fundamental transformations.

In contrast to rational choice theory, where actors are considered utility maximisers with their preferences assumed and given to be based on the pursuit of self-interest, historical institutionalism claims that actors are not solely motivated by self-interest but are also influenced by the rules, habits, values and processes by which they are surrounded (Pollack, 2004). Sociological institutionalists also claim that actors are influenced by their environment yet differ from historical institutionalism in its emphasis on time and how once processes are established within an institution, how this then constrains and affects actors (Pollack, 2004).

Therefore, in order to adequately understand the behaviour of actors, and institutional change and development, it is necessary to examine the context in which these actions occur. Pollack (2004) has argued that historical institutionalism rejects purely functionalist explanations of the emergence and development of institutions. Although there are elements of functionalist reasoning that can explain certain aspects of regional organisations, attention must also be paid to the historical context in order to understand the current and future policy processes and outcomes of regional organisations. This is important to understand the reasons not only why a regional organisation such as the EU or ASEAN came into existence but also how a regional organisation has developed and possesses certain structures and norms.

Historical institutionalism has been criticised for considering institutions as overly static (Steinmo, Thelen and Longstreth, 1992). However, its inclusion of historical analysis has, in fact, allowed scholars to develop theories which avoid 'institutional determinism' and explain institutional change and development. Theories on institutional dynamism and change are pertinent to an analysis of the EU's promotion of institutionalisation to ASEAN. In this regard, Krasner's (Krasner, 1983) 'punctuated equilibrium' framework is of significance yet requires further elaboration. An argument by March and Olsen (1998) reflects

Krasner's framework as they observe that institutional change often occurs when an institution is seen to fail. Explaining that institutions experience periods of stability 'punctuated' by sudden and substantial change in times of crisis is acknowledged yet is not the only dynamic which can be attributed to institutional change. It also does not explain slower, incremental change or unexpected change. Steinmo, Thelen and Longstreth (1992) present four ways in which institutions can change. The first is through contextual change, in which a previously latent institution may become more active or important. Secondly, an old institution, through an internal change or pressure from within the institution, may be given a new purpose. The third process is similar to the second, yet the impetus for change is exogenous rather than endogenous. The fourth change refers to a change in strategy of political actors within an institution as a result of institutional change.

From a historical institutional perspective, institutional change can be seen to include certain phenomena. Of note are sequencing, path dependence and unintended consequences. Sequencing refers to the process by which previous events often hold more importance or legitimacy than later ones, often because they are more familiar to actors and are therefore considered efficient based on their being embedded (Fioretos, 2011). Path dependence explains that previous decisions will determine the nature of later decisions and developments, and potentially preserve the previous institutional structure and processes, even if newly presented alternatives could be more efficient, appropriate or beneficial (Pollack, 2004). Furthermore, unintended consequences are acknowledged within the framework of historical institutionalism, and this often occurs when practices which were efficient at their time of implementation become inefficient or irrelevant due to a change in circumstances.

However, although institutions evolve and change, there is also the recognition that there is a certain level of robustness attributed to their constitution and processes. In addition, incremental change is also viewed as an addition to Krasner's 'punctuated equilibrium' supposition. Fioretos (2011: 377) states four factors which contribute to this robustness and incremental change. Firstly, practices can be 'locked-in' and therefore habitualness and familiarity make it difficult for the institution to change. Secondly, positive feedback in the form of positive externalities makes it difficult to foster a willingness for change, as does the third factor, increasing returns, in which institutions experience increasing benefits from their pre-existing structure, identity and processes. Finally, self-reinforcing qualities based on 'complementary relationships with other institutions' which enhance an institution's value also contribute to the continuity of an institution, less fundamental change and more gradual transformations.

In the context of EU and ASEAN regionalism development, an institutional approach which encompasses elements of rational choice, sociological institutionalism and historical institutionalism has an important role to play in explaining the policies these two organisations have towards developing their institutional design and structure. This approach also assists in explaining how the EU has been able to promote institutionalisation to ASEAN to some degree. March and Olsen's (1998) discussion on the motivations of actor behaviour is especially relevant to the discussions in this chapter. March and Olsen (1998) split action into two main groups – the logic of consequences and the logic of appropriateness. The logic of consequences, aligning with the rational choice tradition, emphasises that actors are motivated by a calculation of perceived consequences and preferences and the degree to which chosen actions will fulfil the interests of actors. This approach does not take into account factors beyond the interests of actors and it also assumes a certain level of interest coherence among actors, which is often not accurate in reality.

The logic of appropriateness, in contrast, places the importance of identities over interests and rules over rational, utility-maximising preferences (March and Olsen, 1998). An actor is influenced by how it perceives and interprets the rules, norms, processes and values of which it is constituted. March and Olsen (1998: 953) state that:

> Actors enter into new relationships for instrumental reasons but develop identities and rules as a result of their experience, thus shifting increasingly towards rule-based action, which they then pass on to subsequent actors. By this mechanism, instrumental modes of action can be seen as self-limiting, whereas rule-based modes can be seen to be self-reinforcing.

The dynamics through which the EU and ASEAN have developed into distinct regional organisations reflect the interplay between the instrumental motivations for progression and the rule-based behaviour which has emerged. In turn, the self-limiting and self-reinforcing actions of these two organisations strongly determine their institutional structures and how they will evolve in the future. March and Olsen (1998: 952) also state that:

> When preferences and consequences are precise and identities or their rules are ambiguous, a logic of consequences tends to be more

> important. When identities and their implications are clear but the implications of preferences, or expected consequences are not, a logic of appropriateness tends to be more important.

This framework of differing logics makes it possible to understand to a greater degree the motivations behind the policy choices of the EU and ASEAN, and also their institutional developments. In this chapter I examine the EU and ASEAN using this framework which allows for a comprehensive explanation of why the two regions differ in terms of their institutional structures.

The EU's support for further institutionalisation of ASEAN is a constitutive element of its policy with the region. A part of the EU's policy towards ASEAN, the promotion of institutionalisation and support for ASEAN's institutional development have been detailed in official documents. The European Commission's 2003 *A New Partnership with South-East Asia* states,

> The EU must stand ready to fully support ASEAN's integration efforts with an open mind and in the fields where assistance is requested. In particular the EU can share its half-century's worth of experience in regional integration and provide technical assistance that is needed to reinforce ASEAN institutions. (European Commission, 2003: 15)

In addition, the most recent guidelines released in 2012 from the Council of the EU state that the EU should strengthen its relationship with ASEAN and mentions 'peer support for ASEAN institutions (where requested)' (Council of the EU, 2012a: 9). It also states, with regard to regional security architecture, that:

> The EU's long-term aim should be to support the development of increasing regional integration and the emergence of strong regional institutions based on clear recognition of shared interests. These should embody closer cooperation on foreign and security policy objectives across East Asia in line with international norms. (Council of the EU, 2012a: 15)

The *EU–ASEAN Nuremberg Declaration on EU–ASEAN Enhanced Partnership* (2007) also makes reference to the fact that the EU and ASEAN will

> Cooperate to strengthen ASEAN capacity and institution building processes that will contribute to achieving the goal of the ASEAN

> Community consisting of ASEAN Security Community (ASC), ASEAN Economic Community (AEC), ASEAN Socio-Cultural Community (ASCC) through, among other steps, exchange of information and experience between the EU and ASEAN on community building. (ASEAN–EU 2007a: 2)

Similar to the arguments presented in Chapter 3, the EU promotes regionalism and the development of institutionalisation in ASEAN because supporting other regions of the world to follow a similar path to the EU bolsters its legitimacy and value and also facilitates political dialogue and trade relations. One interview respondent stated that the EU is a 'club' and a 'force for good', and it therefore tries to find as many 'emulators' as it can worldwide (I9 EO, 2011). This respondent stated that the reason why the EU aims to support further integration of ASEAN and therefore engage the states of Southeast Asia at the regional level is because 'we (the EU) are a club and we want to relate to other clubs. The difficulty at the moment is that ASEAN is not integrated enough to be able to deal with properly' (I9 EO, 2011). With reference to economic relations, this respondent stated that 'economically speaking, the more ASEAN countries break down their national barriers the easier it is for European businesses to conquer the region' (I9 EO, 2011).

Institutionalisation in the EU

The EU has been noted for its high level of institutionalisation, its rule-based community stemming from its *aquis communautaire*[1] and its extensive administration. Olsen (2007: 9) has explained that the EU more than any other regional organisation is a rule-based polity and that it 'bears the imprint of the legalistic tradition of continental Europe and its belief in the importance of rule-driven Weberian bureaucracies'. In comparison with ASEAN, the EU is an organisation which is centred around formal and legally defined decision-making processes. It has even come under criticism for being an elite-driven process and overly technocratic and bureaucratised (I4 EO, 2011).

This formalised and legalistic approach is often attributed to the bureaucratised nature of its founding member states, reflecting the path-dependent, historical institutional frameworks presented earlier in the chapter. The EU's tendency towards pooling sovereignty and creating supranational institutions has been attributed to the legacy of the liberal democratic traditions of which the EU member states were associated. The answer to the need to address the post-war circumstances in which Europe found itself, as well as the negative sentiments towards overtly nationalistic political systems, was to create supranational bodies which allowed for responsibilities and decision-making to be mandated to specialists whose interests were not solely for the state to which they belonged.

Olsen (2007) and Jetschke and Murray (2012) have explained that the EU is a political community which has partly emerged and developed based on a functionalist logic of addressing issues and concerns and the maximisation of peace, stability and welfare within its region. The process of institutionalisation within the EU has often been to formulate policies and then create, alter or mandate institutions to fulfil these policies (Olsen, 2007). This progressive, open-ended approach to institutional development has been largely influenced by a logic of consequences, and actions have been reactive in nature in that institutional developments have occurred as a result of past events, and as means to address past or current problems rather than as pre-emptive measures.

Yet the functional development of EU institutions has occurred simultaneously with a more constructivist logic of appropriateness. The concurrent attention given to established norms, processes and institutional structures has also influenced the way in which the EU's institutional structure has emerged and developed. Schuman's proposal for a Coal and Steel Community in 1950 is an example of the interplay between consequences and appropriateness which has influenced all subsequent policies and institutional structures. The European Coal and Steel Community (ECSC) Treaty (1951) expressed the principles of economic integration in order to rebuild Europe. It stated that the signatories recognised

> That Europe can be built only through practical achievements which will first of all create real solidarity, and through the establishment of common bases for economic development. (ECSC, 1951: 3)

It also stated that the signatories were

> Resolved to substitute age-old rivalries with the merging of their essential interests; to create, by establishing an economic community, the basis for a broader and deeper community among peoples long divided by bloody conflicts; and to lay the foundations for institutions which will give direction to a destiny henceforward shared. (ECSC, 1951: 3)

The initial desire to achieve the normative ideals of peace and stability after World War II by creating a supranational economic community created a legacy which has arguably permeated the majority of subsequent EU institutional developments, policy-making and policy implementation.

Consistent criticisms of the EU, including policy incoherence, governance gaps, limited international actorness, and democratic deficits are, at least in part, attributed to the tension between appropriateness and consequences and the approach of the EU to address the two simultaneously. Moreover, often the logic of consequences, and especially the pursuit of economic interests in the EU, have been subsumed or concealed within a rhetoric of normative posturing. This has inevitably led to policy incoherence and limited capacity to pursue either economic or normative policies.

Another contextual factor which has been attributed to the EU's initial approach to regionalism, the dual pursuit of economic and normative ideals and the obstacles which affected the full realisation of both, was the involvement of the US. Historians and scholars on European integration have explained the position of the US as being one of support for the creation of supranational structures of governance and an economic single market in Europe after World War II (Carolan, 2008). Unlike Britain, which favoured a more intergovernmental approach, the US framed its willingness to provide aid for the restructuring of Europe within the conditions of integrated plans proposed by the Europeans for how they were to utilise the aid offered under the European Recovery Plan (ERP), also known as the Marshall Plan.

Reasons given for the US's desire to support a supranational proposal for reconciliation and economic development included the belief that economic prosperity was a deterrent against communism, the desire to contain Soviet power in Western Europe and the belief that integration was the best way to ensure that Western German relations with its neighbours were peaceful and economically beneficial (Carolan, 2008; Acheson, 1949).

The then US Secretary of State Dean Acheson's letter to US Ambassadors in Europe in 1949 said that, 'the key to progress towards integration is in French hands ...' and that 'France and France alone can take the decisive leadership in integrating Western Germany into Western Europe' (Acheson, 1949: 2). In Acheson's final paragraph, he sums up the position of the US with regard to European integration.

> I have in mind the earliest possible decision by the Europeans as to objectives and commitments among them on a timetable for the

> creation of supra-national institutions, operating on less than a unanimity basis, for dealing with specific economic, social, and perhaps other problems. We do not intend to propose the precise character and scope of these institutions. The nature of the problem and the means for dealing with it are obviously more clearly understood in Western Europe than here. Institutions, if they are to last, must be created by the countries who are to participate in them. But I do wish to emphasise that, in my opinion, they would fall short of the needs of time if they did not involve some merger of sovereignty. (Acheson, 1949: 3)

The US eventually gave Schuman a deadline of May 1950 to present a proposal, which eventuated in the *Schuman Plan* and the subsequent creation of the ECSC (Carolan, 2008). Reflecting Acheson's letter, US reactions to Schuman's proposal and the creation of the ECSC were viewed positively by US officials.

Ensuing developments of the EU have built upon the initial structure of the ECSC. A pooling of sovereignty, the creation of supranational mechanisms and the interplay between interests at different levels of governance have been the hallmarks of the European integration experience. Distinctive to the EU is its development of compliance dispute settlement mechanisms to ensure that EU laws are implemented among its members. EU principles in this regard have differed greatly from any in ASEAN. The EU has a system of dispute resolution which has a legal basis and is manifest in the supranational institution, the ECJ (Henry, 2007). According to Henry (2007), the role of the ECJ has contributed greatly to the creation and unification of Community law, the creation of the single market and the protection of individual rights under EU law. As one interview respondent stated, 'the single market in Europe would not have been possible without the ECJ' (I7 EO, 2011). Another respondent commented,

> Without the Court of Justice the EU would be basically nowhere. It's quite interesting that one of the first court cases ... was brought by member states which basically claimed the EU Treaty or, the EC Treaty, was never meant to be what was written in there. And the Court of Justice said ... you have to subscribe to this and I'll give you the interpretations. And they abided by that and that was basically the kick off for the whole integration (process). (I4 EO, 2011)

As opposed to dispute resolution referring to compliance and rights protection under EU Community law, dispute resolution in ASEAN has largely referred to the establishment and maintenance of peaceful interaction and cooperation (Henry, 2007). A judicial process whereby winners and losers are created, as explained by one interview respondent, 'are values that you would see in Europe' and are present because 'European predictability, accountability and transparency come from a sense of security and a sense of self-confidence about each of the countries in Europe' (I1 AO, 2011). According to this ASEAN official, within ASEAN

> They are afraid to bring (cases) to court because if you go to court, there is always a winner or loser. The winner, of course, would be happy. For the loser, the government may be whacked by the citizen ... no win, no lose, it's ok. But if you go to court there is always a winner and loser and this is not acceptable. (I1 AO, 2011)

Rather than a judicial body such as the ECJ, ASEAN has taken the approach of initiating agreements and treaties, such as the TAC, discussed earlier in this book, to manage relations and cooperation among its members and to ensure regional peace and stability. If a state is at risk of failing to comply with the terms of the TAC, it can be submitted to the High Council, which consists of a representative of ministerial rank from each member state (Henry, 2007). However, this process of dispute resolution has never been used and the International Court of Justice has been the preferred mechanism, especially since non-ASEAN members are now signatories of the TAC (Henry, 2007). Although ASEAN does not have a comparable enforcement mechanism to the ECJ, in economic matters concerning the AFTA, if disputes are not resolved via consultation and mediation, they may be referred to a panel of experts nominated by the Senior Economic Officers Meeting and the ASEAN Secretariat (Henry, 2007). This mechanism is not mandatory, but once it has been utilised its decision is binding (Henry, 2007). Such options for ASEAN demonstrate that it does not give a central role to a jurisdictional body such as the ECJ, but, especially in the instance of intra-regional trade, it has initiated rule-based frameworks which suit ASEAN's norms of interaction.

The most recent institutional changes and developments within the EU are evident in the Lisbon Treaty (EU, 2009). Scholars and EU officials have noted that a significant development of EU institutionalisation as a consequence of the Lisbon Treaty has been the change in mandate of the European and national member state parliaments in decision-making processes of the EU (Dinan, 2010; Dinan, 2011; Buzek, 2011).[2]

The Lisbon Treaty has attempted to reconcile ongoing concerns regarding the EU's governance structure. For example, it has aimed to improve the EU's democratic legitimacy by making changes to the balance of responsibility and the mandates of the EU institutions and the EU member states (Borrás, 2009; Borrás and Radaelli, 2011), and in particular providing the EP with more mandate (Sjursen, 2011; Tonra, 2011). This has also had an effect on the functioning of multi-level governance structures, especially with the national parliaments being given new roles in decision-making processes, and Borrás and Peters (2011) have found that the Lisbon Treaty has triggered institutional changes at the national government level.

According to a former President of the EP, the EP has 'gained enormously' from the Lisbon Treaty (Buzek, 2011: 12). This is especially attributed to the development of the EP having co-legislative authority with the Council on the majority of policy areas (Buzek, 2011). Buzek (2011) also refers to the *Framework Agreement for 2009–2014* between the EP and the European Commission as a positive development towards greater accountability of the Commission. This agreement includes the Commission's recognition of equal treatment of the EP and the Council on budgetary and legislative matters, which reflects the principle of co-legislation introduced by the Lisbon Treaty (Buzek, 2011). For the former President of the EP, European democracy has been improved as a result of the institutional developments within the Lisbon Treaty. The inclusion of national parliaments in the legislative processes, whereby they must be consulted, is intended to facilitate the effective realisation of the principle of subsidiarity. The national parliaments are in the best position to decide if a policy or legislation should be actioned at the EU or national level which in turn gives them a greater sense of ownership and involvement in the EU legislative process. The advantage of the inclusion of national parliaments in the process is the positive effect this would have on the implementation of policy and legislation at the national level, as according to Buzek (2011), the fact that the national parliaments had been actively involved would increase their willingness and efficiency to implement EU directives. A final institutional development regarding increased democratic and inclusive decision-making is the creation of the European Citizens' Initiative, whereby one million signatures from residents in a quarter of member states, under certain conditions, would prompt the Commission to take action (Miller, 2011).

Nevertheless, in the face of the economic and financial crisis, Buzek's (2011) calls for greater political deepening to complement institutional deepening and a stronger political party system at the EU level have not come to fruition, and instead, the central role of the European Council, especially during tumultuous periods, is apparent. Whilst debates centred on EU intergovernmental and supranational governance structures are often considered to be analyses of the past, within the institutional structure of the EU, a battle for power and authority among the institutions continues to be negotiated. The Lisbon Treaty has attempted to reconcile institutional imbalances, yet there remains opportunity to develop the EU's democratic accountability mechanisms. For example, the European Citizens' Initiative, mentioned above, only allows EU citizens to 'invite the Commission to act' and does not change the sole authority of the Commission to initiate legislation even though it would be unlikely that the Commission would not agree to propose draft legislation in these circumstances (Miller, 2011: 326). Furthermore, the mandate afforded to the national parliaments to decide on the principle of subsidiarity has also not changed the fact that existing laws cannot be changed as it applies to legislation and not to laws associated with implementation (Miller, 2011). According to Miller (2011), the Lisbon Treaty has made progress in ensuring the democratic legitimacy of forthcoming EU legislation, but the fact that it is difficult to change or overrule existing laws implies that the Lisbon Treaty has been unable to fully realise the democratic legitimacy of the EU.

Moreover, whilst institutional developments with the Lisbon Treaty are treated favourably by Buzek (2011), Dinan (2011: 105) asserts that the Framework Agreement 'exceeds the terms of the Lisbon Treaty and upsets the EU's institutional balance'. Buzek (2011: 11) states that the EP puts the Commission at the 'centre of the institutional architecture of the EU' and that while 'the European Council might provide for important political impetus', it is the Commission which is 'at the centre of the Union system by leading the day-to-day process of converting priorities into action'. In contrast, Dinan (2010, 2011) argues that the crisis in Europe has demonstrated the centrality of the European Council and that the Lisbon Treaty has readjusted the balance among the institutions with the European Council increasing its authority. Additionally, the example of selective summits held by a few EU member state leaders to work out common positions before European Council summits demonstrates an inequality among the member states. They also demonstrate that there are challenges to a proper functioning of a European Council comprising 28 member states. As Dinan stated, 'in theory all countries are equal in the EU; in practice, when it comes to economics and finance, not to mention security and defence, the big countries remain more equal than the others' (Dinan, 2010: 114).

Furthermore, whilst the Lisbon Treaty has been considered by some to be the final major treaty development within the EU (Buzek, 2011; Dinan, 2011), the Commission President has opined that the current economic crisis has revealed the need for further treaty revisions and amendments (Barroso, 2012b). Former President Barroso has called for the development of a federation of member states, stating that a federation would also require a new treaty in the future (Barroso, 2012b: 11). The Commission President also explained his position on the current institutional structure of the EU which involves retaining the core decision-making and legislative processes which place the Commission at the centre of legislative proposals, defending his role as Commission President.

> ... our proposals will be based on the existing Union and its institutions, on the Community method. Let's be clear – there is only one European Union. One Commission. One European Parliament. More democracy, more transparency, more accountability, is not created by a proliferation of institutions that would render the EU more complicated, more difficult to read, less coherent and less capable to act. (Barroso, 2012b)

The latest institutional developments with the Lisbon Treaty have coincided with a time of crisis and pressure for the EU. Such a combination of events has emphasised not only the interplay of powers and interests among the EU's institutions but also the remaining gaps in its democratic legitimacy. By no means is the EU's institutional journey complete and the current issues which are prominent as a result of the Lisbon Treaty and the crisis in Europe demonstrate that the EU's actions of appropriateness and consequence – its fundamental normative ideals and economic and political interests – remain intertwined, providing for institutional development but also perplexing and complicated approaches to accountability, democracy and transparency.

Institutionalisation in ASEAN

Despite arguments of ASEAN's irrelevance and incapacity to be an international actor which have arisen throughout its existence, especially after the AFC of 1997–98, it has also been referred to as a model of regionalism rather than a reflection of another, external exemplar (Jetschke and Murray, 2012; Stubbs, 2008). ASEAN has experienced its own distinct path of institutionalisation and community building and is often seen by scholars as an alternative, non-western prototype for regional integration (Stubbs, 2008).

An observation of note that has had a strong impact on Southeast Asian regionalism is the fact that when new modes of political organisation have been established through processes such as colonisation, decolonisation and regionalism, elements of historical institutionalism's path dependence have been present in the sense that pre-existing structures have been built upon in order to allow a new system to emerge. For example, during periods of colonisation, Tarling (2001) argues that the Western powers not only challenged the kingdoms they were replacing in Southeast Asia, they also utilised the structures that were in place. Rather than starting afresh, Western powers sought to build on the arrangements that were already present in Southeast Asia. Similarly, processes of decolonisation used the borders which were put in place during the colonial period as a basis for national independence. Similar to the path dependent processes existent during times of colonisation and decolonisation, ASEAN regionalism is a result of, and closely related to, the context from which it has emerged.

Prior to processes of colonisation and decolonisation, concepts of the state, sovereignty, political order and even geographical demarcation of territories were either non-existent or dramatically different. Every member of ASEAN, excluding Thailand, had experienced periods of colonisation and decolonisation which have subsequently determined the political landscape of the region. From the 16th century onwards, European states started to enter Southeast Asia. Tarling (2001) explains that the European states went in search of increased wealth as a result of heightened rivalry between states within Europe. This rivalry was due to the organisation of the European region into defined, dependent states. This was the earliest motivation for colonial expansion into Southeast Asia which was further fuelled by the Industrial Revolution and positive views on trade liberalisation, product specialisation and the benefits of focusing on products with which a state has a comparative advantage (Beeson, 2004). By the early 20th century the majority of Southeast Asia was either a colony or protectorate of a Western power. With the colonial powers came a reorganisation of Southeast Asia; by 1920 the many kingdoms and peoples of Southeast Asia had been reduced to six states: British Burma, French Indo-China, the Spanish Philippines, British Malaya, the Netherlands East Indies and Siam, which was the only state to not have been colonised by a European state (Beeson, 2004). Not only had the number of states decreased, but the principles of political organisation that these states were based upon were now modelled on European modes of governance. Beeson (2004: 20) provides a succinct description of the colonial construction of Southeast Asian states.

> The state was now in constant contact with Southeast Asians – codifying their traditional law systems, counting and classifying them, surveying their lands, overseeing their customary movements, spying on their political activists, dressing up their officials in colonial uniform, creating new conceptions of laws regarding their land, developing plural legal systems and administrative agencies to enforce ethnic divisions and identities, analysing their cropping techniques and building dams and irrigation systems – and even making sporadic efforts to protect their environment from the demands of the rapidly increasing population – to enhance their prosperity, imposing administrative languages upon them, and generally trying, in various guises and under various paternalistic labels, to 'civilise' them.

One of the most significant results was the establishment of borders that previously had not existed, and which were created in order to avoid conflict between the Western powers in the region (Kingsbury, 2005). Paradoxically, this move to create clearly demarcated territories is seen in sharp contrast to approaches used by the European powers in the post-World War II period, which saw the pooling of sovereignty and regional integration of states as an alternative way to avoid conflict. A consequence of these colonial borders was the elimination of any sense of regional identity or sense of commonality among Southeast Asian states (Beeson, 2004).

However, a strong sense of clearly defined states, and the increasing capacity of states to act autonomously, gave those living within each state more ability to assert their nationalist aspirations. The paradox was that the more colonial states were consolidated through such means as arms, persuasion, railways, the telegraph, the presence of administrative representatives and the creation of national economies, the more they were provided with the grounds for the mobilisation of anti-colonial movements (Beeson, 2004). This was partly due to the fact that the gap between colonial authority and the general populace had become more evident and pronounced. The main issue was that the concept of the state was strengthening, yet there was no national loyalty or identity to reflect and support the governance and governors of the state. Nevertheless, nationalist movements within these Southeast Asian states based their claims for independence on the territorial and political structures that had been put into place by the colonial powers (Kingsbury, 2005). Beeson (2004: 25) makes this point by stating that:

> Indigenous political imaginings relied heavily upon the infusion of Western ideas of political organisation ... Much of the ideological groundwork for these new ways of thinking came from a fertile yet often personally and intellectually confusing conjunction of young indigenous minds and modern Western political tradition and practice.

Therefore, what resulted were nationalist movements which were a combination of oppositional sentiments towards the Western colonial powers due to demands and expectations which could not be met by the colonial rulers and an acceptance of certain aspects of Western ideology and political structures which could be used to their benefit.

Between the 1940s and 1970s the period of decolonisation saw the gradual transfer of state power from colonial rulers to national leaders and movements (Tarling, 2001). The Japanese invasion of the majority of the Southeast Asian region during the 1940s has been described as a major factor in accelerating the retreat of the colonial powers and the creation of independent states in Southeast Asia. Japan's occupation of many Southeast Asian states demonstrated both the weakness of the colonial powers to maintain their authority and the growing strength of the nationalist movements within these states. However, before Japanese authority could be consolidated, the attacks on Hiroshima and Nagasaki brought on Japan's surrender and consequently their eventual retreat from the region (Tarling, 2001).

During the post-World War II period, the concept of a Southeast Asian region was gradually established. The Cold War established commonalities between the communist states and the American allies, respectively. In addition, the Southeast Asian states themselves were progressively coming to consider a regional approach as beneficial. Tarling (2001) attributes this to governments needing to assert forms of allegiance between their governments and citizenry and to limit the differences among themselves as a way in which to consolidate and establish their newly independent nation states, limit intervention from other powers and also adhere to and survive in the global order which had been established primarily by the Europeans and the Americans and was increasingly placing emphasis on regional cooperation and alliances. These new nation states had to prove that they were capable of interaction at the international level as a way to establish their efficiency, legitimacy and power as independent states; regional cooperation was seen as one such way in which they could concretely exert their recently achieved nation-state status.

Of note here is the changing attitude towards the demarcation of territorial borders within Southeast Asia. During the colonial period, borders were established by the colonial powers as a way in which to avoid tension among the colonial powers; in other words, clearly defined borders had a pacifying function. After World War II this attitude changed dramatically. Regionalism, especially in Europe, replaced this view, and consequently became the appropriate method for eradicating inter-state violence and preserving peace. This marked change has had a significant impact on regional dynamics in Southeast Asia. Consequently, accepting regionalism as a way in which to establish peaceful relations between states and also as a way to enhance the legitimacy of Southeast Asian states on the one hand, and the need for Southeast Asian states to consolidate their state autonomy internally on the other, was difficult to reconcile. This challenge has contributed significantly to the normative framework which came to define ASEAN and its institutional structure.

Its establishment in 1967 saw ASEAN's founding members, Indonesia, Malaysia, the Philippines, Singapore and Thailand, look to regionalism as a way to address common concerns among these five states. A major concern was the threat of communist subversion and the need to prevent the region from becoming deeply involved in the Cold War; this was especially felt in Thailand with neighbouring Indochina being under communist rule (Severino, 2007a). Morada (2008) makes the claim that the formation of ASEAN assisted in resolving territorial disputes between the five original members. Examples of sensitive territorial disputes that had an impact in 1967 were the separation of Malaysia and Singapore and the Philippines' continued claim over the state of Sabah, which had come under eastern Malaysian authority (Severino, 2007a). ASEAN's inception is also attributed to the changing political circumstances within Indonesia which saw the cessation of antagonism towards Malaysia and Singapore through the end of its *Konfrontasi* policy (Webber, 2001; Severino, 2007a).[3] In addition, the Vietnam War was of particular concern, given its close proximity to these founding member states, as was Cambodia's and Lao PDR's transitions to communism.

Similar to the creation of the ECSC, it is also possible to attribute the emergent structure and composition of ASEAN to US influence. However, in contrast to the US's support for a supranational approach to reconciliation and development in Europe, the US did not explicitly support a cohesive integration plan in Southeast Asia. This was because US security interests in Asia were largely underpinned by bilateral alliances, unlike in Europe where the North Atlantic Treaty Organisation

(NATO) provided a mechanism for collective security. Acharya and Tan (2006: 9) state that:

> In contrast to the systematic and strategic way in which the United States constructed the liberal international order in post-war Europe, the US approach to post-war Asia and Southeast Asia has been decidedly more ambivalent.

According to Acharya and Tan (2006) the US's ambivalence allowed ASEAN to develop its own distinct form of institutionalisation and role within the region. In addition, once the US withdrew from Vietnam in 1975, even more space was created for ASEAN to pursue and develop its regional role. Although there has been a dominant narrative which has stated that the US balance-of-power approach has contributed to security and stability in Southeast Asia, in comparison with US interests in Northeast Asia, South Asia, the Middle East and Europe, Southeast Asia has not been a major area of interest for the US (Acharya and Tan, 2006). The US's bilateral approach to Southeast Asia has not hindered the emergence of a regional organisation, but the ambivalence which Acharya and Tan (2006) refer to has allowed ASEAN to construct its own regional designs and architectures without the need to create supranational institutions as a result of external pressure and expectations.

Scholars such as He and Feng (2012) and Hemmer and Katzenstein (2002) have presented arguments for why the US supported multilateralism in post-war Europe and preferred to engage Southeast Asia bilaterally during the same period. He and Feng (2012) present an explanation for the divergent approaches of the US based on the perception of the level of threat a situation posed. As the US did not perceive the same threat from the Soviet Union in Southeast Asia as in Europe, the US was willing to take greater risks in pursuing multilateralism in Europe and was more risk-averse in Southeast Asia where they pursued a bilateral approach. In addition, a major contextual difference lay in the fact that the US occupied a divided Germany in which part was occupied by the Soviet Union as opposed to its occupation of Japan in its entirety post World War II. According to He and Feng (2012) multilateralism had the potential to constrain US power and hegemony more than bilateralism and was therefore considered to be the riskier approach; nevertheless, as the risk was evaluated as being higher in Europe, the US was more willing to pursue this approach than it was in Southeast Asia.

Hemmer and Katzenstein (2002) attribute the difference in approaches to the sense of collective identity the US felt with Europe as opposed to

Southeast Asia. They note that a sense of identification was responsible for the US's support for multilateralism in the form of the creation of NATO and the ECSC, which also connects with Acharya's (2005) constructivist arguments that norms prevalent in Asia did not align with ideas of collective defence. Attempts by the US to form multilateral security alliances were viewed as attempts of power dominance and intervention which were unfavourable considering the number of states in the region that had recently experienced decolonisation.

It has been widely recognised that the US pursued a strategy of multilateralism in Europe and a strategy of bilateralism in Asia after World War II. An extensive set of reasons, beyond those discussed in this chapter, has been given to explain these differences. Although the US influence is not the only factor influencing the institutional nature of the EU and ASEAN, the strategies that the US employed post-World War II have affected the subsequent institutional decisions made by ASEAN and the EU, especially in the pursuit of peace and stability through economic integration, as was the case for the EU, or through norms of interaction and cooperation, which occurred in the ASEAN context.

The reasons given for the initial impetus behind the creation of ASEAN fundamentally had a security and political focus. This was reflected in the aims and agenda laid out in its founding document, the Bangkok Declaration of 1967. The declaration made it clear that the founding members were 'mindful of the existence of mutual interests and common problems among countries of South-East Asia and convinced of the need to strengthen further the existing bonds of regional solidarity and cooperation' (ASEAN, 1967).

The importance of regional cooperation was advocated in the following section of the Declaration where the signatories expressed the opinion that they were

> Conscious that in an increasingly interdependent world, the cherished ideals of peace, freedom, social justice and economic well-being are best attained by fostering good understanding, good neighbourliness and meaningful cooperation among the countries of the region already bound together by ties of history and culture. (ASEAN, 1967)

Although the Bangkok Declaration mentioned economic growth and collaboration on trade issues, it is dissimilar to the European approach in which peace and stability was largely framed within the merging of companies and the creation of supranational bodies in order to establish cooperation. In other words, the creation of a peaceful, stable and prosperous region for ASEAN was the means and the ends, as opposed to the European approach which utilised economic means in order to achieve a peaceful and prosperous region. Such a distinction has been a continuous feature throughout the histories of the EU and ASEAN.

The first ASEAN summit meeting did not occur until 1976. Prior to this the ASEAN members had signed the Kuala Lumpur Declaration in 1971, which aimed to create a zone of peace, freedom and neutrality (ZOPFAN) in Southeast Asia by stating

> That Indonesia, Malaysia, the Philippines, Singapore and Thailand are determined to exert initially necessary efforts to secure the recognition of, and respect for, South East Asia as a Zone of Peace, Freedom and Neutrality, free from any form or manner of interference by outside Powers; and that South East Asian Countries should make concerted efforts to broaden the areas of cooperation which would contribute to their strength, solidarity and closer relationship. (ASEAN, 1971)

The Kuala Lumpur Declaration, similar to the Bangkok Declaration, emphasised the importance ASEAN placed on creating rules and norms of interaction and cooperation among its members. These declarations demonstrated ASEAN's process of establishing a logic of appropriateness and norms of interaction, which were to be agreed upon by all member states.

Four years after the Kuala Lumpur Declaration, at the ASEAN summit meeting in Bali, the Declaration of the ASEAN Concord was signed, as was the TAC. As discussed in Chapter 3, the TAC stipulated the norms underpinning ASEAN which are, namely, the

> Respect for independence, sovereignty, equality, territorial integrity and national identity; the right for every state to lead its national existence free from external interference, subversion or coercion; non-interference in the internal affairs of one another; settlement of differences or disputes by peaceful manner; renunciation of the threat or use of force; and, effective cooperation among themselves. (ASEAN, 1976)

From a historical institutional perspective, a number of explanations have been given as to why the norms stated in the TAC became the foundation rules for what was to become known as the 'ASEAN Way'. A major challenge for ASEAN arose when Vietnam invaded Cambodia late in 1978. The challenge was two-fold. Not only did Vietnam's actions challenge ASEAN's newly defined norms of non-interference and rejection of the use of violence and force, it also brought the communist threat up to the borders of an ASEAN member, Thailand, and consequently ASEAN, due to Thailand being a neighbour of Cambodia (Beeson, 2004). ASEAN's handling of the Vietnamese invasion, however, succeeded in reinforcing ASEAN's diplomatic credentials. ASEAN supported Thailand at the UN by pushing for resolutions which condemned the actions of Vietnam and ensured that the Vietnamese government installed in Cambodia was unable to have a seat at the General Assembly. ASEAN also provided military support to the non-communist factions within Cambodia (Beeson, 2004). ASEAN put pressure on the Vietnamese government by making it impossible for it to receive aid from Western powers or international agencies, and it also conducted informal talks in Jakarta with key figures from Cambodia which allowed local regional actors to be actively involved in the peaceful resolution of the crisis (Morada, 2008). Granted, ASEAN was not the only, and perhaps not the most significant, actor in resolving the conflict; however, its role was not completely inconsequential.[4]

The literature on ASEAN frequently mentions that Vietnam's withdrawal from Cambodia and the end of the Cold War prompted a reconsideration of the relevance and purpose of ASEAN. As former foreign minister of Singapore, Kan Seng Wong stated,

> With the end of the Cold War, we cannot assume that the Western powers will continue to woo ASEAN. ASEAN must reassess itself. If ASEAN is inward looking, then our strategic importance to our traditional dialogue partners, including the United States, Japan and the European Community, may very well diminish. We need to transform the substance of both ASEAN and our relations with the major economic and political powers. (Wong, 1991: 3)

Although it is not contested that ASEAN realised that it required a reassessment of its purpose and relevance during this period, another reading of its institutional development is possible. ASEAN from its onset did not look to achieve peace and stability through economic integration. It was primarily a political organisation which, largely as a consequence of the recent histories of its member states and the concurrent political and security issues, prioritised the establishment of collaboration and non-violent and non-intrusive methods of interaction.

As the external security threat had now abated, ASEAN was then able to look towards economic objectives as a way in which to assert its utility and provide for its members. Economic cooperation was now seen as a substantial objective for ASEAN (Freistein, 2005). The 1980s especially had seen substantial growth in the economies of ASEAN member states, due in major part to high amounts of FDI from Japan (Beeson, 2004). As a consequence, ASEAN became an increasingly attractive trading partner for external actors which in turn helped to increase the status and strength of ASEAN (Beeson, 2004).

Nevertheless, a major event which prompted ASEAN to consider its economic role was the AFC of 1997–98. It increased ASEAN's desire to implement the AFTA and spurred the creation of the APT, both discussed in Chapter 4. ASEAN was ineffective in either preventing or managing the AFC (Freistein, 2005; Eaton and Stubbs, 2006). Furthermore, it was felt by those within Southeast Asia that the IMF and the US only compounded the problems caused by the crisis by providing inappropriate solutions. In response to these factors, as argued in the previous chapter, ASEAN realised the importance of an independent regional approach to protecting and developing the economies of Southeast Asia in order to prevent further crises.

The next stage of ASEAN's institutional development is closely related to the steps that were taken in order for the ASEAN Charter to be ratified. The *Bali Concord II* introduced the idea of an ASEAN community and paved the way for further ASEAN initiatives concerning regional cooperation. This was a necessary move to mitigate the blows to ASEAN's utility and credibility which were a consequence of ASEAN's inability to manage the recent crises in the region (Freistein, 2005). The concept of an ASEAN community has also been attributed to strategic responses to the rise of China and the challenges posed by globalisation (Morada, 2008). The structure of an ASEAN community is based on enhancing regional cooperation in three areas – economic cooperation, political and security cooperation and socio-cultural cooperation (Simon, 2008). In 2004, the *Vientiane Action Plan* (VAP) expanded on the concept introduced in the *Bali Concord II* by providing concrete norms, principles and projects that would contribute to the realisation of this three-pillar structure (ASEAN, 2004). The VAP states that ASEAN agrees to

> Pursue the comprehensive integration of ASEAN towards the realisation of an open, dynamic and resilient ASEAN Community by 2020 as envisioned in the Declaration of ASEAN Concord II and

> its annexes in the form of the action plans of the ASEAN Security Community (ASC), the ASEAN Socio-Cultural Community (ASCC) and the Recommendations of the High-Level Task Force on ASEAN Economic Integration. (ASEAN, 2004)

A significant result of the Charter is the recognition of ASEAN as a legal entity (Wah, 2007). In addition, the ASEAN Charter makes specific reference to a commitment by the ASEAN members to democracy, human rights and good governance and also sets up a human rights body, the AICHR (McCarthy, 2009). It also gives the ASEAN Secretariat the authority to suspend certain rights of member states if they do not comply with these principles (Simon, 2008). Nevertheless, an enforcement mechanism such as the ECJ is still not evident within ASEAN, as analysed earlier in the chapter. The Charter also set up three ministerial councils which cover political-security, economic and social concerns. Further developments laid out in the Charter include the continued commitment to setting up an economic community by 2015 and the creation of a CPR (Simon, 2008).

The tension created by following a logic of consequences and a logic appropriateness has influenced the functioning of the EU and is the central element which differentiates the EU's institutional development from ASEAN's. In the context of ASEAN's institutionalisation, there is a clearer distinction between areas in which the logics of consequences and appropriateness have impacted on ASEAN's institutionalisation. ASEAN's establishment, with its primary function of establishing political cooperation among its members in order to mitigate security concerns, was greatly driven by the need to establish a logic of appropriateness for interaction throughout the region, as the aims of the TAC have shown. ASEAN's inactivity in the years following its establishment demonstrate that ASEAN has separated logics of consequences and appropriateness by applying political and security means for political and security ends.

This fact, coupled with the recent histories of states within Southeast Asia experiencing processes of decolonisation and new statehood, has led to the creation of ASEAN's norms of institutionalisation and interaction. Only when ASEAN's logic of appropriateness had been established and security threats had ceased after the Cold War did ASEAN then reassess its utility and embark upon such initiatives as economic integration and mechanisms for regional independence based upon a logic of consequences. When compared to the EU's approach of combining the two approaches, differences between the two organisations become more easily understood. With ASEAN's clearer distinction between the two logics, it is potentially in a better position than the EU to pursue economic or normative policies without creating policy incoherence. This is because the distinction between the two logics is more clearly preserved than in the EU context. The EU's rule-based approach and substantial emphasis on legislation, compliance and policy harmonisation can, at least in part, be attributed to a concurrent focus on logics of appropriateness and consequences. ASEAN's emphasis on norms of peaceful interaction and regional stability, consensus decision-making and informality can be accredited to its original focus on actions of appropriateness. Its current initiatives to create its three communities, and the developments as a consequence of the ASEAN Charter, which has seen ASEAN gradually move towards more rule-based interactions, are evidence of its inclusion of a logic of consequences in its institutional development now that the initial impetus for the Association has changed with time.

The EU's promotion of institutionalisation to ASEAN

With regard to the EU's promotion of institutionalisation to ASEAN, the main areas in which promotion has been evident or suggested include the creation of ASEAN's CPR, EPG visits to Europe, the drafting and content of the ASEAN Charter, and ASEAN Secretariat capacity building under programmes such as APRIS and READI.

Survey and interview responses have attested to the fact that neither those working in the EU nor those in ASEAN view the EU as a perfect model or prototype which ASEAN can reproduce. A large number of interview and survey respondents referred to former ASEAN Secretary General, Surin Pitsuwan's, comment that ASEAN views the EU as an inspiration rather than a model. Therefore, apart from certain cases such as the READI initiative, it is more appropriate to analyse areas in which ASEAN has developed institutionally which reflect EU structures rather than areas in which the EU has actively promoted institutionalisation *per se*.

The EU has expressed that it is willing to provide information to ASEAN but simultaneously recognises that it is ASEAN which should, or does, take the initiative in this regard. The latest guidelines released by the Council of the EU, *Guidelines on the EU's Foreign and Security Policy in East Asia* (2012), indicate this position of the EU in its repeated emphasis that it is willing to share its experience and knowledge to ASEAN, when it is requested.

> The EU should be willing, *if requested*, to share lessons drawn from its own experience in post-war reconciliation, and in confidence-building, preventive diplomacy and conflict resolution. (Council of the EU, 2012a: 11, emphasis added)

Therefore, to begin with the areas in which the EU has been actively promoting and supporting ASEAN's institutionalisation, READI is a programme which is being run from 2011–2015 and has a budget of 4 million euro. It is open to any non-trade area of regional integration and its four main expected results are

> (i) the development of concrete action plans for integration and contribution to the ASEAN Secretariat and ASEAN member state initiatives to further education, (ii) improved institutional capacity of ASEAN including the ASEAN Secretariat, ASEAN collegial bodies, ASEAN chair countries and ASEAN member states, and (iii) extended and strengthened ASEAN–EU networks in areas of relevance to ASEAN's priorities, leading to effective learning processes through an exchange of experience between EU and ASEAN. (EEAS, 2011)

The four non-trade areas which have been included in the READI programme are Information and Communication Technology (ICT), which aims to support ASEAN's development of a transparent and harmonised ICT regulatory framework; energy, which involves supporting the implementation of the ASEAN Plan of Action on Energy Cooperation (APAEC) 2010–2015; science and technology, which involves the implementation of the ASEAN Plan of Action on Science and Technology (APAST); and disaster management, which involves supporting the creation of an ASEAN Agreement on Disaster Management and Emergency Response (AADMER) monitoring and evaluation system (Landell-Mills, 2013). READI has also involved expert consultations and a number of visits to the EU by ASEAN officials and experts on policy areas including the trafficking of persons, air transport and climate change.

Previous READI initiatives were designed to address the more political aspects of regionalism in ASEAN, including the strengthening of the ASEAN Secretariat and the capacity of ASEAN member states to formulate and implement regional policies. Policy areas that were covered under READI included conflict prevention, the environment and the sustainable management of natural resources, governance, democracy, human rights and support for economic institutional reforms, human development, infrastructure, communications and development, social cohesion and employment, trade and regional integration, water and energy (Delegation of the EU to Indonesia and Brunei Darussalam, 2011).

Whilst data on the implementation, impact and results of READI are currently not available due to the ongoing nature of the programme, from reports on READI activities which have been undertaken, a focus on dialogue, experience sharing and knowledge exchange is apparent, presenting READI as a collaborative programme as opposed to a training programme for ASEAN run by the EU. As READI is at a stage of policy sharing and learning, it is difficult to determine the impact the EU has had on ASEAN's development in these policy sectors and to what extent they have developed in accordance with EU initiatives or as a result of learning from the EU experience. Such a study is a future fruitful research project to be conducted in coming years.

Developments as a consequence of the ASEAN Charter appear to reflect structures present within the EU. However, on closer inspection it becomes apparent that ASEAN's institutional structure reflects the institutions of the EU but in composition is distinct in its role and functioning. As mentioned in Chapter 4, in order to draft the ASEAN Charter, an EPG was set up whose purpose was to make recommendations for the Charter. The EPG created a list of recommendations that focused on substantial changes to ASEAN which required a revision of the Association's main norms (ASEAN EPG, 2006).

The EPG visited Brussels in 2006 in order to study the EU's 'integration experience problems', and the EPG report on the ASEAN Charter stated that the visit gave the EPG a greater understanding of the issues the EU has faced and is facing in the context of ASEAN's own integration path (ASEAN EPG, 2006: 9). It was the report of the EPG which suggested creating a CPR for ASEAN, conferring upon ASEAN a legal identity, strengthening the capacity and organisational function of the ASEAN Secretariat and providing the Secretary General with a greater role (ASEAN EPG, 2006).

Although not explicitly stated by the EPG, or mentioned in their report, these suggestions do reflect institutional components of the EU. The report also referred to decision-making and stated that although ASEAN's process of consultation and consensus has served ASEAN well and should be preserved, ASEAN should also consider voting and other, more flexible decision-making mechanisms for less-sensitive issues. The report also called for dispute-settlement mechanisms for all areas of ASEAN policy as well as enforcement and compliance mechanisms. The eventual content of the ASEAN Charter did not match the recommendations of the EPG, and criticisms, especially among civil society organisations (CSOs), were raised as to the discrepancies between the EPG report and the final content of the ASEAN Charter. In short, the rule-based entity which the EPG report recommended was not fully realised within the ASEAN Charter, despite the fact that some suggestions were implemented.

Of note within the ASEAN Charter is the creation of the CPR. Reflecting the EU's *Comité des représentants permanents* (Coreper) in name, ASEAN's CPR has the same general function as Coreper, which is to have a representative from each member state permanently posted to their respective organisations. However, their roles, mandates and decision-making processes differ considerably. Coreper consists of Coreper I, which comprises the deputy permanent representatives, and Coreper II, which is made up of the permanent representatives to the EU. According to Article 240 of the Lisbon Treaty, Coreper prepares the work of the Council of the EU, with Coreper I responsible for technical matters and Coreper II dealing with political, commercial, external, economic or institutional issues (EU, 2009: Article 240; Europa, 2012c). Coreper present the Council with A and B items, with A items to be approved by the Council with no need for further discussion and B items requiring discussion and decision by the Council. Coreper is supported and assisted by a large number of working groups and committees which are permanent but can also be created on an *ad hoc* basis if necessary.

Although the general role of ASEAN's CPR is similar, it is not as established as Coreper or an intrinsic decision-making body as Coreper is in the EU. This is despite the fact that one interview respondent stated that ASEAN's CPR was 'copied and pasted from the EU's Coreper' (I9 EO, 2011). Unlike Coreper, its decisions and positions are non-binding, and it serves currently as a consultative body whose mandate is to give suggestions. Furthermore, due to its relatively recent introduction in 2009 under the ASEAN Charter, it is yet to develop a similar level of entrenched and distinguishable negotiation style as Coreper (Blankert, 2010; Lewis, 2000). The ASEAN Annual Report of 2009–2010 (ASEAN, 2010a: 17) explains that the CPR's mandate includes

> Supporting the work of the ASEAN Coordinating Council (ACC), coordinating with ASEAN National Secretariats and other ASEAN sectoral ministerial bodies, liasing with the Secretary-General of ASEAN and the ASEAN Secretariat on all subjects relevant to its work, facilitating ASEAN development cooperation with external partners, and performing such other functions as may be determined by the ACC.

This mandate is in fact wider than Coreper's in that the CPR is responsible for supporting all sectors within ASEAN's capacity (Blankert, 2010). However, decisions in ASEAN are still, to a large extent, prepared by sectoral bodies which report to the ASEAN Ministers rather than the CPR, which differs from the relationship between the committees and working groups and Coreper in the EU (Blankert, 2010). In addition, just when ASEAN has implemented its CPR, there have been observations in the EU that with the most recent enlargements and the tendency for EU capitals to make 'direct deals' among themselves as opposed to through EU institutional channels, the role of the Coreper in being the 'central dealmaker is becoming less prominent' (Blankert, 2010: 2). It may be that as Coreper's role potentially declines, ASEAN's CPR role develops.

An example of where the EU has offered ASEAN access to its experience and knowledge in institutionalisation was in 2009 when a former EU Commissioner, Ferrero-Waldner, suggested a visit to the EU to former ASEAN Secretary General Surin Pitsuwan. The suggestion was well received, and in 2010 the ASEAN CPR visited Brussels and Berlin. A statement by ASEAN explained that the aim of the visit was

> To gain firsthand experience of the EU institutions, its decision-making processes and its success stories. They (the ASEAN CPR) also took the opportunity to examine the roles and functions of its European counterpart, the EU's Permanent Representatives Committee (Coreper). (ASEAN, 2010b)

According to the report on the visit by the EU delegation in Jakarta, the CPR engaged in meetings with officials from the Council Secretariat in order to understand the functioning and role of the EU's institutions, those working in policy centres in Brussels, as well as Belgian governmental officials who explained how Belgium coordinates its national policies with EU policies and also how it manages being a host state to the majority of European institutions. In Belgium, the CPR also met with officials from Directorate General (DG) EuropeAid, DG Regional Policy and the Asia-Oceania Working Party (COASI) for Coreper. During the DG EuropeAid meeting the discussion focused on the capacity of the ASEAN Secretariat and the role of the CPR in managing donor coordination, especially in the context of EU donor programmes. The DG Regional Policy meeting was of interest to the CPR as they were referred to the EU Regional Policy, the European Regional Development Fund and Cohesion Policy as possible inspirations for an approach to 'bridge the development gap' within ASEAN (Blankert, 2010: 4). The meeting with COASI primarily covered the development of EU and ASEAN future engagement.

In Berlin, the CPR was given a presentation on the German position on engagement and relations with ASEAN. Their schedule included meeting with the Deputy Director General for European Affairs and the Deputy Director General for Europe in the Federal Chancellery, who both stressed the weakened role of Coreper as a consequence of the Lisbon Treaty and the move within member states to address EU policies 'in the prime minister's office' as opposed to 'the foreign minister's office' (Blankert, 2010: 6). In the case of Germany, the German Coreper representative, 'received instruction as to which position to take, according to the position agreed within the government, in writing' (Blankert, 2010: 6).

Both the EU and ASEAN have, at differing times, recognised the multi-faceted nature of regional organisations and created three 'pillars' to define the areas under which integration occurs. In the Maastricht Treaty of 1993, the EU established the Community pillar, the CFSP pillar and the Police and Judicial Cooperation in Criminal Matters pillar, which was also known as the Justice and Home Affairs pillar. The Lisbon Treaty of 2009 abolished the pillar system but still retained a system of competence divisions between the EU and EU member states depending on policy area. These included exclusive competences (Article 3, TFEU), in which the EU alone can legislate, shared competences (Article 4, TFEU), in which the EU and member states can adopt binding legislation and supporting competences (Article 6, TFEU), whereby the EU can only support or complement the legislative role of the member states.

In 2003, ASEAN also embarked upon the creation of an economic community, a security community and a socio-cultural community. Whilst they appear to reflect the tri-pillar system initiated with the Maastricht Treaty and the EU's system of a division of competences, ASEAN's three communities do not possess the same competence segregation as the EU and are rather organisational tools for ASEAN's regional integration development. As Henry (2007: 872) states, 'where the European Parliament speaks of common policies, ASEAN speaks of economic integration'. Organising competence between the supranational level and European member states is, within ASEAN, substituted for integration progress and development. This is especially evident in economic integration matters, where the EU has moved towards policy harmonisation and the creation of common policies, which has not been the approach of ASEAN to the same extent.

With regard to ASEAN's socio-cultural pillar, Henry (2007) argues that its initiation was a reaction to the social impact of the AFC in the late 1990s and potentially a lesson learnt from the EU to create a 'people-oriented ASEAN' and a sense of community among the citizens of ASEAN. Finally, the political-security community 'is designed to complement, rather than compete with, national or bilateral defence policies' (Henry, 2007: 874). All of these pillars retain the ASEAN decision-making process of consensus and consultation, and there is no segregation or balance of supranational and intergovernmental competences à *la* the EU. It is therefore difficult to suggest that ASEAN's development of three communities is a reflection of the European process of dividing competences between three groups of policy areas, as was initiated in the pillar system of the Maastricht Treaty and retained in a modified form within the Lisbon Treaty.

Responses to the EU's promotion of institutionalisation

Interview and survey responses have shed much light on the prevalent perceptions of the EU's role in promoting institutionalisation to ASEAN. According to survey responses, institutionalisation is considered the second most useful aspect of the EU's experience to ASEAN. Figure 5.1 below shows that after 'economic integration among other states', the next three most prominent responses, namely, 'regional governance practices', 'legal developments and frameworks', and 'political integration among member states' all refer to support for institutionalisation. The response rate to the question was 73%, and the respondents were allowed to choose more than one response.

Additionally, Figure 5.2 below demonstrates that the EU's support of 'economic integration and cooperation' and the 'development of business networks and investment mechanisms' are the aspects considered the most important, yet these are closely followed by EU support for 'institutional reform and development' and 'development of political and legal systems'. For this question there was a response rate of 91%.

According to the survey responses presented in Figures 5.1 and 5.2, the EU's institutionalisation experience is considered useful by the respondents, yet when the development of ASEAN's institutionalisation is analysed, what is apparent is that it is difficult to establish where the EU has, in fact, actively promoted institutionalisation and where it has been ASEAN which has taken the initiative to refer to the EU in order to make decisions on its own developmental path. In addition, institutional developments which can potentially be viewed as a result of inspiration or encouragement from the EU can also be attributed

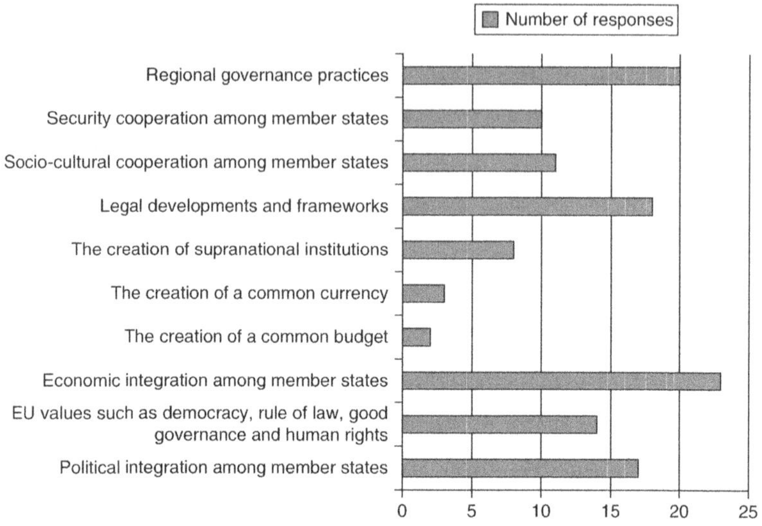

Figure 5.1 Which areas of the EU's regional integration experience are useful to ASEAN?

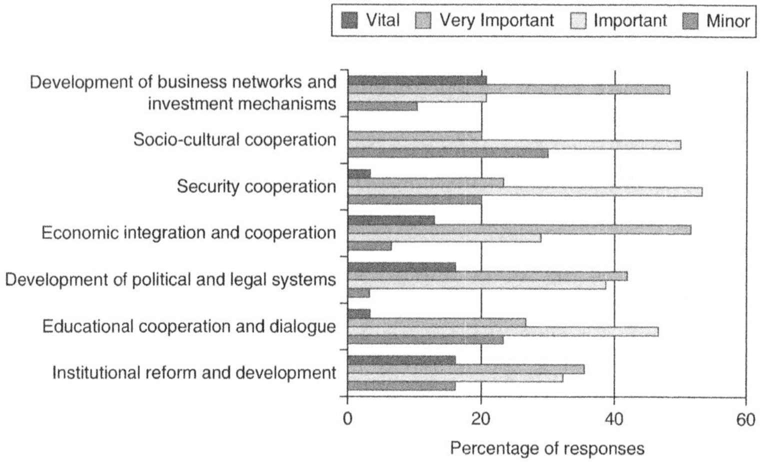

Figure 5.2 How important is it for the EU to promote the following aspects of regional integration to Southeast Asia?

to other sources. For example, the ASEAN Charter can be seen to have parallels with the Lisbon Treaty, as they both confer legal personality to their respective organisations, and the Charter's establishment of three distinct pillars of policy competence are similar to those established with the Maastricht Treaty, as discussed previously. However, interview respondents also explained that other regional organisations were reference points for ASEAN. For example,

> In the case of SAARC, the South Asian Association for Regional Cooperation, where India and Pakistan dominate most of the proceedings, we also see some positive things. For example, from a starting point, they have a constitution. It's relatively short, three or four pages or something. So that's why when we say, 'maybe we should also do a charter.' Then we say, 'What can we look at?' So we look at SAARC, SAARC only had three or four pages, so we ourselves, here, are we better run by a constitution or charter, that goes into thousands of pages like the European Union? (I1 AO, 2011)

One example of an initiative by the EU to support ASEAN institutionalisation was the invitation for ASEAN's CPR to visit Brussels and Berlin. The visit by the CPR to Brussels was deemed successful, with lessons learnt on both sides (Blankert, 2010). On the EU side, it was very clear that those in the EU did not want to be viewed as imposing their model on ASEAN. However, it was noted that the CPR visit to Brussels in 2010 demonstrated a disparity between discourse and reality. One respondent working at an academic institution in Europe said that:

> We have to be very careful, the EU is not a model for them, the EU is not a model for ASEAN ... but when you started talking with these people, it struck me, they were so eager to know more about the mechanisms and they wanted to learn everything about the EU. And they were almost obsessed by it. We walked from one building to another, they wanted to have pictures before the Berlaymont building. There was even one who said, 'look, this is the Taj Mahal of regional integration'. And again, this was quite a surprise for me. I said, 'these people look at the EU from a different perspective than academics'. Academics always say, 'no, we are not a model etc. etc'. For them, yes, the EU is a model.' (I5 EA, 2011)

Nevertheless, despite this recognition of the EU as a model by the CPR, according to the report on the visit complied by the EU Delegation in

Jakarta, and interview responses in Southeast Asia, there was also a sense of 'information overload' (Blankert, 2010). As one interview respondent stated, 'their reaction was, "do we really want this?" and the answer was "we probably don't want this"' (I8 EOA, 2011). This was especially noticeable when the CPR visited government officials from Belgium who discussed how they coordinate EU and national policies and function as a host state to the majority of EU institutions. The report on the visit states that the CPR 'participants were no doubt impressed, some of them perplexed, seeing what lies ahead for ASEAN, and some perhaps wondering if this was what they want' (Blankert, 2010).

Aspects of the visit that were of interest to the CPR were the institutional mechanisms, learning how EU member states negotiate, how they convey common positions and voting matters. One respondent mentioned that the smaller ASEAN states were interested in hearing from the smaller states of the EU such as Luxembourg and Latvia and were happy to hear that their voices are not lost within the EU and that they do not feel overawed as members of the Union (I9 EO, 2011).

Respondents generally commended the concept of a permanent body within a regional organisation, and Coreper was referred to as being a positive and essential element of the EU decision-making process.

> By having that intermediate level, you have a kind of permanent dialogue, and that makes it much easier for member states to agree with what comes out from the Commission and it is only if you have that kind of mechanism that you can really come to wide, or deep, integration. (I5 EA, 2011)

Respondents from the EU mentioned that the CPR is important because it is permanent and provides a full-time position that works exclusively on ASEAN matters and on issues that are difficult to reach an agreement on. Having such a permanent body helps the creation of opinions from an ASEAN perspective and therefore strengthens the position and presence of ASEAN.

Overall, one of the main messages given to the CPR as a result of the visit, according to the report on the visit, was that the EU has relied heavily on strong institutions and enforcement mechanisms such as the ECJ to move integration forward (Blankert, 2010). Among EU officials, there was a sense that further integration in ASEAN is not possible without further institutionalisation. As one EEAS official noted, 'I would say the ASEAN construction is far behind the EU construction, and there is one central element that is completely missing in the ASEAN construction, which is the Court of Justice' (I4 EO, 2011). Another EEAS official stated that 'ASEAN does not have the institutions to set up what they hope to achieve'. Furthermore, with reference to a more rule-based, institutionalised organisation, it was stated in the EEAS that, 'they are not at the stage psychologically to go there, eventually they will go there because they will have no other choice'. 'It will look like the EU more than it does now' (I7 EO, 2011). This official expressed frustration with the institutionalisation of ASEAN and the capacity of the ASEAN Secretariat in particular.

The ASEAN officials, however, explained that the institutional development of ASEAN is moving in a different direction from that of the EU, which to a certain extent explains the differences between the ASEAN Secretariat and the European institutions. An official working at the ASEAN Secretariat stated that:

> The Secretariat's role is very much facilitative, facilitating, acting as a resource person, and so on. So our institution building is a bit different ... We don't have any enforcement authority like the Commission. So we are silent on the enforcement part of it ... So in a sense, we are not a commission because we don't have that kind of authority. So institution-building wise, ASEAN is taking a different approach. (I2 AO, 2011)

In response to the EU's efforts to support ASEAN's institutionalisation, a difference in approach by the EU and ASEAN was noted.

> In terms of institution building, I think it is the reverse in ASEAN. Because I think that in the EU, there is this strong institutional building approach. That is, before they cooperated they built these institutions. Whereas ASEAN is the other way around. Where they look at cooperation first, and if the cooperation is substantive, then they build an institution. (I2 AO, 2011)

With reference to the EU's support for ASEAN's institutionalisation and integration more generally, an ASEAN official expressed the opinion that at times the EU is too rule-oriented in its approach. 'Now on the ASEAN side, we sometimes feel that the EU cooperation package, or technical assistance programme, is just too focused on the rules and the institutions, and when we in ASEAN don't have these institutions or rules, it is not very beneficial.' (I1 AO, 2011)

Responses to the EU's promotion of institutionalisation have indicated that there are significant gaps concerning how the EU wishes to be perceived with regard to its support of ASEAN's institutional development and how ASEAN perceives the EU. This is evident in the range of perceptions on whether the EU is a model, whether the EU's support is benign or imposing, the level of relevance the EU's institutional experience has for ASEAN, the recognition of ASEAN as distinct from the EU and whether developments in ASEAN can be attributed to the EU or to other sources. In addition, opinions have varied as to the state of ASEAN's institutionalisation and whether it is sufficient, proceeds at an adequate pace and how it should progress. A number of interview and survey responses have referred to the fact that there is inadequate knowledge within the EU of ASEAN and ASEAN's requirements. Figure 5.3 below shows that in response to the survey question, 'what are the challenges facing the EU in its relationship with Southeast Asia?', 'inadequate knowledge of the Southeast Asian region' was the dominant response. The response rate for this question was 97%, with respondents able to choose more than one option.

In addition, one survey respondent in response to the question presented in Figure 5.3 stated that, 'the lack of understanding and

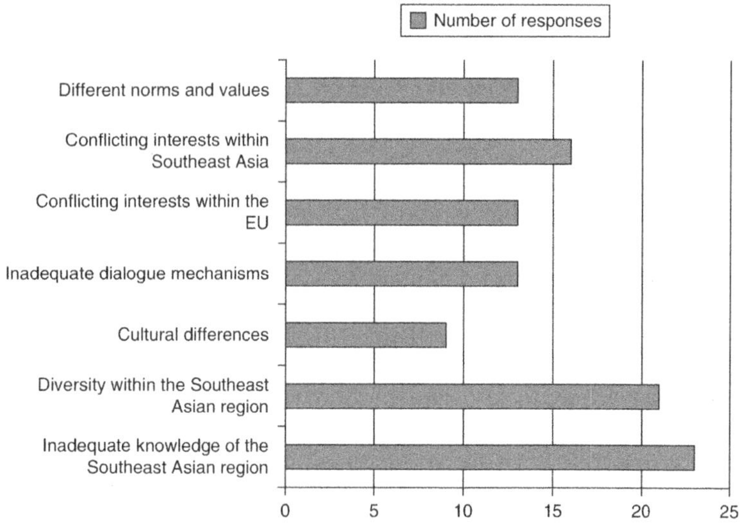

Figure 5.3 What are the challenges facing the EU in its relationship with Southeast Asia?

misperceptions are both ways' (S28 EA, 2012). Another survey respondent stated that, 'the general knowledge of ASEAN is low' (S11 AA, 2012). The EU's support for further institutionalisation of ASEAN is demonstrating how this lack of understanding and knowledge is manifesting itself in the frustrations expressed by officials in the EU and ASEAN regarding ASEAN's institutional structure and development and the support provided by the EU.

Institutionalisation and the EU as an international actor

The EU's actorness has had limited realisation with regard to its promotion of institutionalisation to ASEAN. This has, to a large extent, been because the EU has only been able to transform the target environment in an indirect manner and ASEAN has been discerning in determining which aspects of the EU's experience are of relevance to ASEAN. Furthermore, the differences in the normative frameworks of the EU and ASEAN as a result of their historical contexts have made it difficult for the EU to positively demonstrate that its distinct norms of institutionalisation are suitable for the ASEAN context. The EU's reluctance to be an obvious promoter of its institutional experience, however, has also contributed to its limited actorness in this regard. This, unfortunately for the EU, has not meant that it has evaded criticism for being a rigid interlocutor in some instances.

Regarding the EU's self-understanding and self-image, statements in the Commission's *A New Partnership with South-East Asia* (2003) and the Council of the EU's *Guidelines on the EU's Foreign and Security Policy in East Asia* (2012) explain that support will be offered if requested by ASEAN. These statements demonstrate that there is a perceived capacity in the EU to promote its institutionalisation experience, but the responsibility to do so is not evident in the form of a policy of active promotion.

It has been determined in this chapter that the EU has been deemed relevant with regard to its institutionalisation experience as a source of inspiration rather than as an active promoter or driver of ASEAN institutionalisation. This has been demonstrated by instances where the EU has been an inspiration for ASEAN institutional developments, such as the creation of the CPR, with results being distinct from the EU experience and unique to ASEAN. As a survey respondent stated,

> The EU has very little leverage over countries that do not necessarily aspire closer relations with the EU, not to mention membership. As a reference model, however, the EU is important, but that does not mean that it is fully followed. (S10 EA, 2012)

Similarly, a Deputy Secretary General of ASEAN stated that the EU is one of the main, but not the only, relevant source of inspiration for ASEAN.

> We try to take the best practices from all institutions, we have the Gulf Cooperation Council, for example, Mercosur is another good example, we have several in the Latin American region. So we are open to looking at other institutions, how they look at specific issues. But I think, of course, one of the key models will still be the EU. But we cannot take directly from the EU everything. We need to modify to our needs. The scorecard is a good example. The EU has a scoreboard, but it is a very detailed scoreboard, and ... they have a very big staff to manage this scoreboard. In our case we don't have this staffing. (I2 AO, 2011)

The CPR and EPG visits to Brussels were tangible instances where the EU was able to utilise its resources by hosting these groups. Whilst the EU is willing to use its resources in this regard, it is also aware of its limitations. As an interview respondent stated with regard to the EPG visit, the 'EU tried to present an image to ASEAN but realised that ASEAN would never make it' (I11 EO, 2011). A survey respondent explained the active role ASEAN plays in selecting which aspects of EU institutionalisation are of relevance to ASEAN. This respondent stated that the EU is considered 'more as a passive reference – ASEAN picks and chooses from the EU menu and translates the EU institutions it emulates into its own regional context' (S10 EA, 2012).

An interview respondent gave an example of an instance where the EU's institutional structure and concept of interregional dialogue did not necessarily fit with that of ASEAN's. The interviewee referred to the ASEM 8 meeting during which there had been conflict over who was to chair the meeting in Brussels. The respondent explained that,

> ... at that point, Van Rompuy[5] was already in office, and from the European side, it was obvious that Van Rompuy should chair the meeting, and the Asians didn't want that, they wanted Belgium to chair the meeting because Belgium was then having the presidency of the EU. (I5 EA, 2011)

This interview respondent explained that whilst the EU is more inclined to talk with one voice in ASEM, their Asian counterparts preferred the meetings to be chaired by individual member states. This respondent stated that during ASEM 8 members of ASEAN did not want Van

Rompuy to chair the meeting because that could imply that something similar should happen in the following ASEM meeting in Vietnam (I5 EA, 2011). This example provides an insight into the different approaches towards institutionalisation in the EU and ASEAN and how this is affecting interregional fora such as the ASEM meeting. Despite the instances where ASEAN has referred to the EU for inspiration, ASEAN is also simultaneously exerting its preferences for institutional, and also interregional, development.

Another factor related to the EU's institutional structure and its impact on the EU's promotion of institutionalisation is EU visibility in ASEAN member states. Better coordination and synergy between the EU's regional and bilateral initiatives in ASEAN were often mentioned in interviews (I2 AO, 2011). The evaluation on EU–ASEAN cooperation commissioned by the European Commission noted that visibility should be enhanced via the EU Delegations. The evaluation states that, 'the main instrument of improving broad EU visibility must be EC Delegations which should redouble their efforts to reach out to populations at large in their respective countries' (Particip GmbH, 2009). The EU delegations, therefore, have the potential to further facilitate initiatives at the ASEAN member state level and therefore enhance the coordination of regional and national initiatives.

With regard to institutional developments in ASEAN, the EU has only been able to transform ASEAN in an indirect manner. As a survey respondent noted, where the EU has been a source of inspiration for ASEAN, the framework may resemble aspects of the EU experience, but the results are ultimately unique to ASEAN. The respondent commented by stating,

> I consider the EU either as a formal model or an empirical experiment upon which other regional organisations like ASEAN can look and from which they may get inspiration. But it cannot be an institutional construct to be emulated even if ASEAN would wish so. Due to different conditions even the exact emulation of the 'model EU' would lead to different institutional and policy outcomes. (S29 EA, 2012)

By virtue of the fact that ASEAN has taken an assertive role in referring to the EU's institutionalisation, from an ASEAN perspective, the results have thus far been successful in terms of meeting the needs of ASEAN. Officials within the EU continue, however, to criticise the institutional capacity of ASEAN and often blame a lack of institutions, enforcement mechanisms and rule-based procedures on ASEAN's perceived slow progress in terms of regionalism. The preference for strong institutional design was stated by one EU official who expressed the opinion that, 'in the long term, to give some stability and to really move forward, you need a framework. People come and go, coalitions come and go, but institutions prevail' (I4 EO, 2011). It is, therefore, primarily the divergence of perceptions, priorities and expectations between the EU and ASEAN which limits the EU's actorness regarding institutional norm diffusion and promotion.

Institutionalisation and the EU as a norm entrepreneur

The EU's norm entrepreneur role is limited due to ASEAN's appraisal of the EU's relevance regarding institutionalisation. Moreover, the historical context and pre-existing normative framework of ASEAN have influenced the EU's ability to promote institutionalisation to ASEAN and guided ASEAN's distinct institutional structure. Therefore, Manners's norm diffusion processes have not had the same amount of impact as the EU's efforts to promote economic integration, discussed in Chapter 4.

Attempts have been made at norm transference, in the form of study tours and visits of the CPR and the EPG to draft the ASEAN Charter, for example, yet the results of such norm promotion have not often produced comparable institutional structures. Similarly, overt diffusion in the form of EU officials conducting workshops, training programmes and policy-sharing seminars, especially under the READI programme, has often had similar results to transference efforts.

Instead, contagion, in the sense that some developments have to a certain extent reflected EU structures such as the pillar system developed within the ASEAN Charter, is evidenced, whereby similarities between the EU have occurred by mere coincidence as opposed to active promotion by the EU. Functional necessity in many cases has been a stronger driver of institutional development than norm promotion by the EU. These similarities are limited, however, to the extent to which they are appropriate to the ASEAN context. For example, the ASEAN pillar system, as discussed previously, is organisationally similar to the EU yet does not have the same division of competence as the EU pillars had under the Maastricht Treaty.

Informational and procedural diffusion mechanisms regarding institutionalisation are present within the EU–ASEAN relationship. Informational diffusion in the form of statements in EU policy documents refers to the EU's position that it will support ASEAN's regionalism processes when and if requested by ASEAN. Procedural diffusion mechanisms, such as the ASEAN–EU Ministerial Meetings (AEMM), the ASEAN Post-Ministerial Conference with the EU (PMC) + 1 and the

ASEAN–EU Joint Cooperation Committee (JCC) often include statements on the EU's interest and willingness to support ASEAN integration and institutionalisation. These diffusion mechanisms, however, have not resulted in the diffusion of EU norms of institutionalisation to ASEAN but have rather fostered a cooperative relationship between the two actors. The press statement for the 20th JCC meeting in 2013 stated that:

> While welcoming the progress made in ASEAN integration, connectivity and Community-building, the EU reaffirmed its assistance to ASEAN's efforts in furthering the above-mentioned processes as well as its continued support to the centrality of ASEAN in the evolving regional architecture. (ASEAN, 2013h)

The cultural filter has played a crucial role in the diffusion of EU norms of institutionalisation to ASEAN. The EU's willingness to promote its norms of institutionalisation has led to a large amount of adaption as a consequence of the normative context in which ASEAN is situated. Normative learning by ASEAN has resulted in an institutional structure which has elements of the EU's institutionalisation experience, but there is limited evidence of normative diffusion which has not been influenced by ASEAN's role as a norm recipient.

Regarding norm resonance, the EU's norms of institutionalisation do not have a high level of resonance with ASEAN's existing norms. The analysis in this chapter has demonstrated that the different historical backgrounds and resultant normative frameworks have produced two distinct approaches to institutionalisation. It is not the fact that one is institutionalised and the other is not; it is rather that the styles and objectives differ. As one survey respondent stated:

> (The EU's promotion of regionalism) runs up against sovereignty-related norms like non-interference and consensus decision-making; (the) legacy of colonialism; many Asians believe there should be a different path to development than the one chosen by Europe. (S19 EA, 2012)

Norm resonance only exists in as much as ASEAN also requires a certain form of regional governance, yet the specifics of its governance structure do not resonate with the EU's institutional norms. One interview respondent explained that in certain instances, the EU's institutional and organisational norms were not considered appropriate for ASEAN.

> We (ASEAN) also learnt from the EU the use of language. We chose English, one single language; the European Union has several languages. In meetings, all our documents are in English. So that is something we learnt from the EU. Sometimes the EU experience is good for us because we learn what not to do. (I2 AO, 2011)

However, there have been instances where actors within ASEAN have seen the benefit of referring to EU norms of institutionalisation. The instances presented in this chapter refer to visits by certain ASEAN groups to Europe for workshops and knowledge sharing. Nevertheless, survey results have suggested that ASEAN does not solely consider institutional norms of the EU of benefit, or that the EU is the only reference from which to learn. In response to the survey question, 'are any other regional organisations useful as a model of regionalism in Southeast Asia?' 54% of respondents answered the question, with the African Union being the most prominent choice. Respondents we able to choose as many options as they believed were appropriate. The results of the survey question are provided in Figure 5.4 below.

With reference to the African Union, one respondent stated that 'ASEAN interlocutors refer sometimes to the African Union, especially the fact that to an extent it (the African Union) is politically more integrated than ASEAN' (S16 EOA, 2012).

According to interview and survey data, there is a strong sense that the institutional structure and capacity of the ASEAN Secretariat

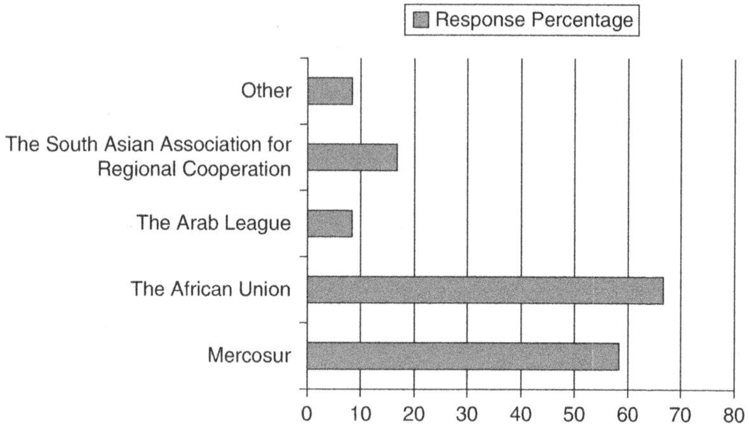

Figure 5.4 Are any other regions useful as a model of regionalism for ASEAN?

requires improvement. This is one instance where existing institutional norms are considered inadequate. However, in terms of ASEAN's core norms of informality and consensus decision-making, the articles of the ASEAN Charter, which reinforce these existing norms, demonstrate that these norms are still regarded as adequate and appropriate for the ASEAN context. This is despite the recommendations for the ASEAN Charter made by the EPG which suggested a more drastic revision of these norms. Whilst ASEAN rhetoric refers to the evolution of ASEAN into a more rule-based organisation, at this stage at least it is apparent that any rule-based developments are still implemented within the existing normative framework.

Furthermore, there is no evidence to suggest that the EU's promotion of its institutionalisation norms would have an impact on ASEAN's legitimacy and authority, which is one of the main reasons why examples of EU institutional norms in ASEAN are limited. I contend that instead legitimacy and authority for ASEAN is a result of ASEAN's functioning as an economically integrated region and the role it can play with regard to security in the region and also increasingly, non-traditional security threats such as its management of natural disasters, food security, terrorism and health security. The contribution institutional norms make to ASEAN's legitimacy and authority is only secondary to these aforementioned aspects.

ASEAN's profile is not necessarily linked to its institutional structure, and therefore, institutional norms are not necessarily seen to enhance ASEAN's profile or contribute to its aims or objectives. Its normative framework, in contrast, based upon local norms as espoused through the 'ASEAN Way', is intrinsic to its profile. ASEAN's profile is enhanced more through its consistent and effective adherence and execution of its existing norms rather than through the possible development of institutional norms which would reflect the EU's experience. It is for this reason that institutional structures such as ASEAN's CPR and the three-pillar structure of ASEAN do not have strong similarities to the EU's institutional organisation.

Moreover, institutional development in ASEAN is not a reaction to the need to replace existing norms. It is rather a response to the changing demands, priorities and expectations of the Association. Institutionalisation in ASEAN, therefore, as discussed in this chapter with reference to historical institutionalism, has built upon the existing normative, contextual and institutional framework which is in place. In addition, there is potential for institutionalisation norms of the EU to be seen as threatening to ASEAN's identity and norms. It is for this reason that there is limited similarity between the EU's and ASEAN's institutional structures and also why in instances where the EU has been able to promote its institutionalisation experience, the results have shown evidence of a high level of adaption. ASEAN's reluctance to introduce an institution comparable to the ECJ is evidence of this fact.

Whilst there is no evidence to suggest that the EU's promotion of institutionalisation or the adoption of EU-style institutions would cause instability, they would not increase stability in Southeast Asia. This is mainly due to the fact that stability in the region is more reliant upon the established norms of interaction, as evidenced by the TAC and economic development and also the increasing recognition of ASEAN as a reference point for other regional organisations.

Finally, the continued recognition of the 'ASEAN Way' and the resultant unique institutional structure of ASEAN are examples of challenging and resisting behaviours in the sense that ASEAN has created distinctive norms which have enhanced its autonomy. These norms have also been exported outside of the ASEAN region through the signing of the TAC by a large number of external actors. Some institutional elements of ASEAN have supported external and global norms of regional governance, such as the CPR, but this chapter has shown that these supportive elements are only superficial with a significant amount of design emanating from ASEAN's priorities and objectives with regard to regionalism. In the context of institutional development, challenging and resisting behaviours have been more evident than supportive and strengthening behaviours.

Conclusion

Hobson (2004) makes an observation on Eurocentrism which parallels fittingly with the findings of this chapter. He describes Eurocentrism as encompassing the idea that:

> The East has been a passive bystander in the story of world historical development as well as a victim or bearer of western power, and that accordingly it can be legitimately marginalised from the progressive story of world history. (Hobson, 2004: 4)

Comparative studies on Europe and Asia, as well as processes of norm diffusion, can easily become discourses framed around active and passive actor dynamics, and benefactor–recipient arrangements, reflecting

Hobson's remarks on Eurocentrism. These processes and frameworks are largely redundant when it comes to the EU's promotion of institutionalisation to ASEAN. This is due to the significant amount of initiative shown by ASEAN in gathering information from external sources on what path of institutional development it should take. In addition, when ASEAN has sought support from the EU, there is often evidence of EU influence in the results, yet these results are noticeably specific and unique to the ASEAN experience.

The discussion presented on the role of institutions and historical contexts within a theoretical framework focusing on historical institutionalism has explained why the EU and ASEAN have taken different approaches to institutionalisation. It has also allowed for the realisation that a major distinction between the two is that their approaches have differed – the EU rationale for institutional development has often been driven simultaneously by a logic of consequences and appropriateness, and ASEAN's rationale has tended to alternate between the two logics, with its initial focus being on creating and entrenching agreed-upon norms of interaction among its members.

Based on the analysis of areas in which the EU has promoted institutionalisation to ASEAN, for example through the READI programme, and also aspects of ASEAN's institutionalisation which reflect structures within the EU, such as the CPR, ASEAN's pillar system and certain contents of the ASEAN Charter, I have presented assessments on the EU's international actorness. With regard to the EU's promotion of institutionalisation to ASEAN contributing to the EU's international actorness, the results have been somewhat limited. This is due to the fact that ASEAN is seen to be the determining factor of whether any promotion will take place, and also on what the results of such promotion will be. The EU's actorness in this regard is also limited by the continued expectation and understanding gap between what level and style of institutionalisation is most appropriate for ASEAN. This was emphasised in interview responses in which EU officials, especially those working in the EEAS in Brussels, expressed frustration regarding the capacity and functioning of the ASEAN Secretariat and the opinion of ASEAN officials that those working in the EU did not always fully understand the processes ASEAN follows in order to develop institutionally. Nevertheless, the EU's recognition as a legitimate regional organisation with lessons, information and suggestions relevant to other actors such as ASEAN is reinforced and evident in such actions as the EPG's and CPR's visits to Europe, as well as the continued dialogue and information sharing among the two organisations.

Regarding norm diffusion and localisation, certain institutional norms of the EU have been localised in the ASEAN context. External norms have been considerably altered and customised in order to merge with, and accommodate, the pre-existing norms of ASEAN. In this respect, ASEAN's development of institutionalisation fully demonstrates the activeness of norm diffusion recipients in norm diffusion processes.

6
The EU, ASEAN and Political Norms

> We must develop true habits of cooperation. We must be bold and realistic in defining our common goals and committed in achieving them. We must lead by force of our own example, being diligent in applying the same standards to ourselves as we do to others. Our 'soft power' and credibility in the world – which as much as any economic power can draw the respect and encourage the human rights compliance of third countries – depend on it.
>
> Stavros Lambrinidis, EU Special Representative for Human Rights, speech at the European Parliament, 3 September, 2012.

> I will continue to work with ASEAN and its Member States as well as civil society organisations to promote human rights nationally, regionally and globally on the basis of internationally-agreed human rights standards.
>
> Catherine Ashton, former European Union High Representative for Foreign Affairs and Security Policy, statement on the adoption of the ASEAN Human Rights Declaration, 2012.

Constructivism and the normative underpinnings of the EU and ASEAN

Although the aim to promote values such as human rights is seen as an important element of the EU's normative framework and an integral part of its foreign policies and relations with other actors,[1] in the context of ASEAN, economic interests have taken priority. Furthermore, the EU's promotion of economic integration has experienced more results than its promotion of political norms, which has had relatively less recognition. In Chapter 4 I argued that the EU's distinctiveness affected ASEAN's ability to view the EU's efforts to promote economic integration as relevant to the Southeast Asian region. Again, in the context of political norms, the EU's distinctiveness plays a role in its ability to promote the political norm of human rights. However, although the EU views the promotion and protection of human rights as essential norms upon which its policies are based, because human rights is not necessarily a norm specific to the EU, the EU's relevance in respect of this norm is not strong enough for it to have a robust norm entrepreneurship role in the area of political norm promotion.

Further to this, Tan (2011) explains the importance of recognising the context specificity of ASEAN from which a human rights framework is emerging and which is not always in line with external actors' aims and approaches to human rights promotion. There are three considerations which Tan (2011: 6–7) believes to be essential to understanding ASEAN's approach to human rights. Firstly, 'the need to accept the justifiable demands of cultural particularities with respect to human rights and discount those which are merely excuses for continued violations' is important. In other words, awareness and evaluation of any existent 'Asian values' must occur simultaneously and rigorously. Secondly, an understanding of the continuing prominence of sovereignty among the states of Southeast Asia is an important consideration. Finally, an awareness of the contribution and 'transformative power of regional and domestic rights movements' is essential. These considerations are discussed within this chapter and contribute to an understanding of how and why the EU has been largely perceived to be of limited relevance with regard to human rights norm promotion in Southeast Asia.

The conceptual distinction between first and second-generation human rights also makes a useful contribution to an understanding of the EU's role in human rights promotion to ASEAN. Whilst it has recently become recognised that placing human rights into two categories is neither useful nor accurate (Tan, 2011), this chapter will reveal that these distinctions remain reflected in the instances of human rights promotion which have been accepted or resisted by ASEAN and its member states. Since the end of World War II, first-generation human rights, civil-political rights, were often favoured by capitalist, Western states. Developing and socialist states, on the other hand, were more in favour of supporting economic, social and cultural rights. Due to the hegemonic influence of capitalist powers in the years following the war, civil and political rights were perceived as valid, and economic, cultural and social rights were relegated to what has been referred to as second-generation human rights (Tan, 2011). The gap between the two groups decreased after the fall of communism, when second-generation rights gained recognition and importance. This segregation between the two generations was reduced in the 1980s when the right to development became recognised by the UN General Assembly and sought to encompass economic, social, cultural, civil and political rights (Tan, 2011).

Reflecting the split between first and second-generation rights, it has often been the case that ASEAN has been more willing to cooperate with the EU on second-generation rights as opposed to first-generation rights. Economic development, reduction of poverty and cultural and educational exchange have been areas of concern for ASEAN, and assistance provided by the EU in these respects has been appreciated. In contrast, insistence on democracy promotion and political rights, especially when they have been linked to the trade or aid policies of the EU, has often been met with resistance. The primacy of first-generation rights in Western states as mentioned above and discussed in further detail below with regard to the World Conference in Vienna in 1993 is one such explanation for this resistance. This is due to the underlying perception of a universality of human rights which does not take into account contextual differences and the presumption that liberal democratic qualities will lead to an increased protection of human rights which has not always resonated with the states of Southeast Asia, despite democratic developments within the region. The states of ASEAN have shown that believing in the benefits of a liberal democracy or economic growth does not necessarily need to be attached to, or preclude, human rights promotion and protection.

The Lisbon Treaty (EU, 2009) refers to the political norms to which the EU subscribes. Article 3 (5) of the Lisbon Treaty states that,

> In its relations with the wider world, the Union shall uphold and promote its values and interests and contribute to the protection of its citizens. It shall contribute to peace, security, the sustainable development of the Earth, solidarity and mutual respect among peoples, free and fair trade, eradication of poverty and the protection of human rights, in particular the rights of the child, as well as the strict observance and the development of international law, including respect for the principles of the United Nations Charter. (EU, 2009)

The values identified within Article 3 are also present in the EU's formulation of its policies towards ASEAN and the Southeast Asian region. Not only the European Commission, but also the EP has referred to these norms whilst preparing and evaluating policies relating to the EU's relations with ASEAN and Asia more generally. The EU's policy document, *A New Partnership with South-East Asia* (2003), repeatedly refers to human rights and states,

> Human rights, democratic principles and good governance should be promoted in all aspects of EC (European Commission) policy dialogue and development cooperation, through building constructive partnerships with ASEAN and national governments based on dialogue, encouragement and effective support. (European Commission, 2003)

Similarly, the EP has also made recurrent reference to the importance of including human rights promotion and protection into EU policies towards ASEAN. At the 32nd ASEAN Inter-Parliamentary General Assembly (AIPA) in 2011, Werner Langen, the Head of the EP Observer Delegation to the ASEAN Inter-Parliamentary Assembly, referred to the importance the EP places on the inclusion of human rights promotion and protection in EU policies and relations with ASEAN (Langen, 2011). This is supported by resolutions adopted by the EP on issues of importance to the promotion and protection of human rights in ASEAN member states, as well as EP studies done on human rights (EP, 2012).

In promoting regionalism to ASEAN, the EU has also actively sought to support and promote ASEAN norms which are in accordance with EU political norms, such as the promotion and protection of human rights and democracy. The way in which the EU has done this is presented in section three of this chapter and includes hosting a study tour for representatives from the AICHR, various statements which have been agreed upon at ASEAN–EU Ministerial Meetings and specific efforts to support human rights in Myanmar.[2]

However, even though the EU has aimed to promote political integration and norms which it deems to be necessary for the successful functioning of a regional organisation such as ASEAN, this area of regionalism promotion has been the weakest for the EU in comparison with the promotion of economic integration and institutionalisation, which are examined in Chapters 4 and 5 of this book. Results of interview and survey analysis have shown that recognition of the EU's political norms by ASEAN has been low, and when ASEAN has been seen to acknowledge the relevance of EU political norms, it is often that those norms have been universal in nature and not specific to the EU. It is therefore difficult to determine if the EU has been the specific actor which has prompted change or if it has come from other sources within ASEAN or from other external actors.

This assessment of the EU as an international actor and a norm entrepreneur with regard to political integration has found utility in a discussion and application of a constructivist framework. Constructivism's premise that there are intrinsic links between human behaviour, and the behaviour of states, and their social environment is reflected in the integration of human rights concerns in the EU and ASEAN. The two-way process that constructivism suggests, whereby norms, values and ideas have the power to influence and construct political structures and *vice versa*, is pertinent to understanding two foci of this chapter (Wiener and Diez, 2009). The first is that the EU and ASEAN have integrated human rights and have viewed how to improve human rights in different ways as a consequence of their divergent normative structures. Furthermore, the recognised need to address human rights has simultaneously altered, or at minimum challenged, their political structures and, especially in the case of ASEAN, their normative values.

Wendt's (1999) observations that structures contain both normative and material elements, that normative structures can create agents and that agents can, in turn, create and transform structures are utilised as a way to conceptualise the relationship between the EU and Southeast Asia. Constructivism can be used to analyse how an actor's political norms affect its political identity, reputation, legitimacy and the external perceptions of the actor. The EU's incorporation of human rights into its external policies and its policy of promoting this norm to ASEAN are evidence of internal and external pressure making this political norm an important component of the EU's political identity. When analysing specifically the way in which the EU has attempted to promote its political norms to ASEAN, it becomes apparent that Wendt's constructivist propositions assist in explaining why the EU has struggled to promote its political norms to ASEAN even though this is expressed as an objective in its policy documents. Following a constructivist logic, it is recognised that not only do material concerns such as political structures and systems determine the nature of the relationship, but also that normative considerations play a major role. Constructivism allows the possibility to analyse and understand the processes and results of political norms and how they affect, shape and determine identities and interests (Wiener and Diez, 2004).

Constructivism provides a theoretical explanation that allows for the recognition that the interests, identities and normative underpinnings of regional organisations such as the EU and ASEAN are neither static nor unchangeable and influence, and are influenced by, political structures. As March and Olsen (1998) state,

> Human actors are imagined to follow rules that associate particular identities to particular situations, approaching individual opportunities for action by assessing similarities between current identities and choice dilemmas and more general concepts of self and situations.

Constructivism has also been credited with providing an understanding of how regional institutions such as ASEAN and the EU can contribute to influencing the expectations and interests of other actors such as governments, NGOs and CSOs (Wiessala, 2006) and also how pressure from these external actors can influence the norms and values the EU and ASEAN deem to be priorities and essential to their normative or political identity.

The EU's political norms and human rights

Human rights protection and promotion, as EU political norms, were not explicitly stated in its founding treaties and documents. Nevertheless, they have had implicit presence since the Treaty of Rome in 1957 with its references to prosperity, peace and economic growth (EEC, 1957). The 1948 *United Nations Declaration of Human Rights* demonstrated a global recognition and concern for human rights and was closely followed by the *European Convention on Human Rights* (ECHR) in 1950, a convention signed by the member states of the Council of Europe and to which all EU member states have since acceded (Europa, 2013e).[3] Such a convention began an 'incremental' path towards incorporating the promotion and protection of human rights into EU law and EU competence (Wiessala, 2006: 55).

The *Copenhagen Declaration on European Identity* (European Council, 1973) introduced human rights to the EU's external relations. The declaration stated that a determination 'to defend the principles of representative democracy, of the rule of law, of social justice – which is the ultimate goal of economic progress – and of respect for human rights' was a 'fundamental element' of the EU's identity which was to be reflected in its external relations (European Council, 1973: 1). A Joint Declaration by the European Parliament, Commission and Council, *Concerning the Protection of Fundamental Rights and the European*

Convention for the Protection of Human Rights and Fundamental Freedoms in 1977, further consolidated the fact that human rights were to become increasingly incorporated into EU policy and law. The joint declaration precipitated the inclusion of human rights explicitly into the Single European Act (SEA) (1986). The preamble of the SEA states that the EU is

> Aware of the responsibility incumbent upon Europe to aim at speaking ever increasingly with one voice and to act with consistency and solidarity in order more effectively to protect its common interests and independence, in particular to display the principles of democracy and compliance with the law and with human rights to which they are attached, so that together they may make their own contribution to the preservation of international peace and security in accordance with the undertaking entered into by them within the framework of the United Nations Charter (European Community, 1986).

In 1986 a *Declaration on Human Rights* was issued by the European Political Cooperation (EPC), and in 1987 a working party on human rights within the framework of the EPC, the Human Rights Working Group (COHOM), was established (King, 1999). However, up until this point, although there had been increasing mention of human rights as a fundamental principle guiding EU foreign relations and policies, observers made reference to the vagueness of statements concerning human rights which lacked any tangible steps or actions to concretely promote human rights (King, 1999). Smith (2004) states that in the early 1980s the EU did not have an active human rights policy, and one only eventuated in the 1990s. Examples of this strengthening of a human rights agenda include the EP Resolution of 1991 which stated, *inter alia*, the need to link development aid and human rights (EP, 1991).

The EP has actively promoted human rights and produced an annual report and numerous resolutions on human rights since 1983 (Smith 2004). It has promoted and influenced the European Commission and Council to include human rights considerations and conditions in aid and development programmes (Smith, 2004) and to include human rights in the foreign policies of the EU. Pressure from the EP contributed to the pooling of funds designated for the promotion and protection of human rights and democracy into the European Initiative for Democracy and Human Rights (EIDHR), and the EP has continuously pushed for an increase of funds for this initiative.

The Maastricht Treaty (1993) further integrated human rights into EU law with Article 6.2. It stated that,

> The Union shall respect fundamental rights, as guaranteed by the European Convention for the Protection of Human Rights and Fundamental Freedoms signed in Rome on 4 November 1950 and as they result from the constitutional traditions common to the Member States, as principles of community law. (EU, 1993: Article 6.2)

In addition, the CFSP established under the Maastricht Treaty included the protection and promotion of human rights as principal aims (EU, 1993). Future treaties gave more space and provisions to human rights within EU legislation as well as intensified references to the core ideals and principles which defined the EU. For example, the Treaty of Amsterdam (1999) stated that the EU 'is founded upon the principles of liberty, democracy, respect for human rights and fundamental freedoms, and the rule of law, principles which are common to the Member States' (EU, 1999: Article F (1)). Article 7 of the 1999 treaty makes it possible to sanction member states that violate the EU's principles (EU, 1999) and, with regard to external relations, Article 177 stated that development policies would contribute to the general objective of respecting human rights, along with other principles such as supporting democracy and the rule of law (EU, 1999). The Nice Treaty (2003) again expanded what had been established in the Treaty of Amsterdam by amending Article 301 to allow for economic sanctions on external actors and made provisions for the EU to suspend the voting rights of member states if they were seen to breach, or potentially breach, EU principles (EU, 2003).

In 2000, the *EU Charter of Human Rights and Fundamental Freedoms* was signed by the European Commission, Council and Parliament. With the ratification of the Lisbon Treaty in 2009, this Charter became enforceable by EU law (EU, 2009). The Lisbon Treaty also allowed for the EU to become a signatory of the ECHR, the aim of which is to ensure that the EU's legal system is controlled by an external mechanism (EU, 2009). Negotiations are currently taking place in order for this to occur (Europa, 2013e).

The Lisbon Treaty (2009) expressed the EU's objective of promoting human rights and its political norms more generally in other parts of the world.

> The Union's action on the international scene shall be guided by the principles which have inspired its own creation, development

> and enlargement, and which it seeks to advance in the wider world: democracy, the rule of law, the universality and indivisibility of human rights and fundamental freedoms, respect for human dignity, the principles of equality and solidarity, and respect for the principles of the United Nations Charter and international law. (EU, 2009: Article 21)

In 2012, the Council of the EU adopted a *Strategic Framework on Human Rights and Democracy* and an *Action Plan* to implement the framework. The strategic framework aims to improve the effectiveness and consistency of EU policy, to increase cooperation between EU member states and EU institutions and to develop a strong relationship with civil society (Council of the EU, 2012c). The strategic framework builds upon the communication *Human Rights and Democracy at the Heart of EU External Action* (European Commission, 2011b). The significance of the strategic framework is that it is the first unified strategic document – previous policies had tended to focus on specific issues or countries (Council of the EU, 2012c).

The EU's gradual path towards incorporating human rights as a key principle and a defining element of its external policies has seen the gradual strengthening of statements and decisions linking the promotion and protection of human rights to development, trade and external relations more generally. Catherine Ashton, the former EU High Representative for Foreign Affairs and Security Policy, stated at the Foreign Affairs Council Meeting in 2012 that 'human rights are one of my top priorities and a silver thread that runs through everything that we do in external relations' (Council of the EU, 2012c). This, however, is coupled with the assessment by the EP, among others (Robles, 2008; Farrell, 2009), that the EU must continue to ensure that its policies and actions are in line with its rhetoric.

ASEAN's political norms and human rights

In contrast to the EU's recognition of human rights as a core normative principle, and the gradual increased inclusion of human rights protection into EU law and external relations, ASEAN's approach to human rights has been steered and influenced by the norms and principles underpinning ASEAN. Due to ASEAN's adherence to the principles of non-interference and respect of sovereignty, human rights have, until recently, been the responsibility and concern of member states. The ASEAN Charter (2008) has demonstrated a shift in this approach and has incorporated human rights as an ASEAN norm to be addressed and protected. Article 1 (7) of the Charter states that one of the purposes of ASEAN is to

> Strengthen democracy, enhance good governance and the rule of law, and to promote and protect human rights and fundamental freedoms, with due regard to the rights and responsibilities of the Member States of ASEAN. (ASEAN, 2008)

In addition, Article 14 of the Charter states that ASEAN will establish a human rights body and that the terms of reference are to be determined by the ASEAN Foreign Ministers Meeting (ASEAN, 2008). This commission, the AICHR, which was launched a year after the Charter, has been the most recent and significant development within ASEAN regarding human rights.

Up until this point the protection and promotion of human rights within the ASEAN member states had been, and to some extent continues to be, a contentious issue due to the difficulty in reconciling ASEAN norms with addressing human rights. In the founding documents and declarations of ASEAN, including the Bangkok Declaration of 1967, there was no explicit mention of human rights but rather statements and objectives which aimed at the stability of the region and economic development and integration (Ginbar, 2010). The Bangkok Declaration (ASEAN, 1967) expressed the motivation of ASEAN's creation by stating that:

> Conscious that in an increasingly interdependent world, the cherished ideals of peace, freedom, social justice and economic well-being are best attained by fostering good understanding, good neighbourliness and meaningful cooperation among the countries of the region already bound together by ties of history and culture. (ASEAN, 1967)

In the 1990s, however, external criticism on human rights abuses within ASEAN member states and also pressure from within ASEAN member states themselves brought attention to ASEAN's placement of human rights onto its agenda (Ciorciari, 2012). Ciorciari (2012) states that the imprisonment of Aung San Suu Kyi and the rejection of national election results by the military junta in Myanmar in 1990, the massacre of Timorese protesters in Dili in 1991 and the 'Black May' military retaliation against pro-democracy protesters in Thailand in 1992 were all incidents which brought attention to ASEAN's role as a protector of human rights. These events caused national governments and ASEAN to receive a large amount of criticism and reaction from the international community and from groups within ASEAN member states. Included in these reactions was the ASEAN Institute of Strategic and International Studies's (ASEAN ISIS) recommendation in 1992 for ASEAN to consider the creation of a human rights mechanism (Ciorciari, 2012).

In the March of the following year, ASEAN ministers attended a pan-Asian meeting on human rights in Bangkok, which was in preparation for the World Conference on Human Rights held in Vienna three months later. The result of this meeting was the *Bangkok Declaration* which emphasised 'the significance of the World Conference on Human Rights' and recognised 'the contribution that can be made to the World Conference by Asian countries with their diverse and rich cultures and traditions' and welcomed 'the increased attention being paid to human rights in the international community' (Asian Ministers, 1993: 1).

The declaration, however, also made clear that the participants continued to place importance on the established norms of interaction fundamental to the Asian region and to ASEAN. The declaration stated that, 'the principles of respect for national sovereignty, territorial integrity and non-interference in the internal affairs of states' were of continued meaning and importance (Asian Ministers, 1993: 1). Ciorciari (2012) has argued that the *Bangkok Declaration* was also a response to the Western critics of Asia's approach to human rights and the declaration also alluded to the position of many member states which did not approve of the promotion of human rights through force or imposition nor the application of 'double standards' – potentially assertions aimed at Western governments and human rights groups. The declaration stated the importance of acknowledging 'the universality, objectivity and non-selectivity of all human rights and the need to avoid the application of double standards in the implementation of human rights and its politicisation' and 'that the promotion of human rights should be encouraged by cooperation and consensus, and not through confrontation and the imposition of incompatible values' (Asian Ministers, 1993: 1).

The context of the *Bangkok Declaration* was one where the debate on 'Asian Values' was at the fore. Significantly, Malaysia's Prime Minister, Mahathir Mohamad, Lee Kuan Yew, Singapore's leader, and Indonesian President Suharto were advocates of an Asian approach to human rights whereby community rights and a stable and organised society were prioritised over the rights of the individual. These leaders denounced the perceived imposition of a Western conception of human rights onto their societies (Thio, 1999; Ciorciari, 2012). For leaders such as Mahathir, Lee and Suharto, human rights were contextualised to the extent that it was governmental elites who determined how and when individual human rights should be protected within their states. This, according to Thio (1999) and Ciorciari (2012), often served the purpose of legitimising and securing the political circumstances which could maintain and protect leadership roles as opposed to enabling improved human rights conditions, which in some cases included authoritarian regimes.

Nevertheless, despite the presence of the 'Asian Values' debate in the early 1990s, the inclusion of human rights considerations within ASEAN states continued to increase. ASEAN's recognition of human rights more explicitly occurred after the World Conference on Human Rights in Vienna in 1993. The 26th ASEAN Ministerial Meeting (AMM), which took place after this conference, issued a joint communiqué on the Declaration and Programme of Action which resulted from the Vienna conference. Similar to the *Bangkok Declaration* of 1993, this communiqué demonstrated ASEAN's support for what had been decided upon in Vienna but was also released in order to reassert ASEAN's position on human rights protection and promotion based on its intrinsic norms of interaction.

Whilst recognising that 'ASEAN should coordinate a common approach on human rights and actively participate and contribute to the application, promotion and protection of human rights', the foreign ministers made reference to ASEAN principles and norms by stating that these rights should be addressed with 'regard for specific cultural, social, (and) economic circumstances' (AMM, 1993: 3). The foreign ministers also stated that 'the promotion of human rights in the international community should take cognizance of the principles of respect for national sovereignty, territorial integrity and non-interference in the internal affairs of states' (AMM, 1993: 3). The communiqué also made reference to an ASEAN human rights mechanism stating that the establishment of such a body should be considered.

Between 1993 and the inauguration of the AICHR in 2009, initiatives were taken to increase ASEAN's attention to the promotion and protection of human rights. Within the ASEAN member states, such initiatives included the first annual ASEAN ISIS Colloquium on Human Rights by the Institute for Strategic and Development Studies in 1994 and a Working Group for an ASEAN Human Rights Mechanism set up by the Law Association for Asia and the Pacific (LAWASIA) in 1995 (Ciorciari, 2012). In 2000 this Working Group submitted a *Draft Agreement for the Establishment of the ASEAN Human Rights Commission*. From 2000 onwards, the working group began holding workshops on an ASEAN human rights mechanism which incorporated government representatives and increasingly active CSOs (Working Group for an ASEAN Human Rights Mechanism, 2012). In addition, in 1995 the ASEAN ISIS established the ASEAN People's Assembly (APA) which developed an ASEAN Human Rights Scorecard and advocated for a regional human rights mechanism.

Simultaneously, developments within individual ASEAN member states demonstrated a shift towards greater human rights protection and promotion. In 1998, the then foreign minister of Thailand, Surin Pitsuwan, proposed a revision of the 'constructive engagement' policy of ASEAN and suggested a policy of 'flexible engagement'. 'Flexible engagement' is an approach that seeks greater political openness among states and includes a revision of the Westphalian notion of sovereignty by advocating for collective action, and also recognises the significance of humanitarian intervention (Acharya, 2004). The proposal suggested that 'constructive engagement', a policy which does not advocate sanctions or political isolation of a state seen to be in breach of international norms such as human rights abuses and which provides a certain amount of autonomy to a state to conduct its own affairs, was not always sufficient. 'Flexible engagement' allowed for ASEAN member states to take a more assertive and vocal stance against member states such as Myanmar in certain circumstances. This proposal, however, was only supported by the Philippines and rejected at the subsequent 31st AMM held in July 1998.

Other developments, which demonstrated increasing attention to human rights protection and promotion, included the growing number of member states which established human rights commissions. Following the ousting of Ferdinand Marcos in the Philippines, a human rights commission was established in 1986. The Philippines was the only member state with a national human rights commission until 1993, when Indonesia created a national commission on human rights. Malaysia also created a commission in 1999, in part a result of when pressure and criticism was directed towards Mahathir's human rights record by Anwar Ibrahim and the US (Ciorciari, 2012). In 2001 Thailand also established a national human rights commission. Whilst these commissions are primarily mandated with functions such as offering recommendations to the government, disseminating information and creating awareness and do not possess any enforcement capabilities, they have demonstrated the individual paths towards human rights protection and promotion by certain ASEAN member states. Changes in domestic politics including democratic reforms in Indonesia after

Suharto have also facilitated revised approaches towards human rights protection and promotion within ASEAN.

ASEAN's *Vientiane Action Plan* (VAP) of 2004 reiterated ASEAN's aspirations to promote human rights (ASEAN, 2004).[4] Subsequently, a Working Group was requested to enable the realisation of the objectives set out in the VAP, which organised and managed a number of workshops and meetings in order to achieve these goals. Following on from the VAP, the *Kuala Lumpur Declaration on the Establishment of the ASEAN Charter* (ASEAN, 2005) established the EPG, discussed in previous chapters, to make recommendations on the creation of the ASEAN Charter. The report by the EPG stated that 'respect for human rights and fundamental freedoms' should be a principle of ASEAN and that 'the EPG discussed the possibility of setting up an ASEAN human rights mechanism, and noted that this worthy idea should be pursued further ...' (ASEAN EPG, 2006: 22). However, no concrete proposal was recommended by the EPG, and the organisational chart they suggested for ASEAN did not include a human rights organ.

Furthermore, the inclusion of the AICHR created tension among the ASEAN member states and only eventuated through a compromise between ASEAN's inclusion of human rights onto its agenda and its pre-existing norms, resulting in processes of localisation. The initial proposal to include a human rights mechanism into the Charter was rejected by Myanmar and met with hesitation by Vietnam, Cambodia and Lao PDR (Yen, 2011). These members of ASEAN only changed their position under the condition that the proposed majority-rule decision-making proposal, a suggestion that was very much in contrast to ASEAN's established norms of consultation and consensus decision-making, be rejected (Yen, 2011). Consequently, Article 6.1 of the Terms of Reference (ToR) of the AICHR states that decision-making within the AICHR is based on these pre-existing norms.

In 2007, the National Human Rights Commissions (NHRCs) of Indonesia, Malaysia, the Philippines and Thailand signed a *Declaration of Cooperation* within which they agreed to 'advise their respective governments to take necessary steps to establish an appropriate ASEAN human rights mechanism and/or any organ in the ASEAN Charter' (ASEAN NHRC, 2007: 1). Support for an ASEAN human rights mechanism by the EPG for the ASEAN Charter, various national human rights commissions, support and pressure from CSOs and the inclusion of Article 14 into the final draft of the ASEAN Charter led to the creation of a High Level Panel (HLP) to draft the Terms of Reference (ToR) for the AICHR. The ToR outlines the purpose of the AICHR, which is to promote and protect human rights and allow those in ASEAN member states to live in peace and prosperity and to promote stability and harmony in the region (ASEAN, 2009a). The ToR refers to international human rights standards as set out in the *Universal Declaration of Human Rights*, the *Vienna Declaration and Programme of Action* and the international human rights instruments to which ASEAN member states are parties. The acknowledgement of the presence of universal and internationally agreed-upon human rights standards, however, were set in the context of ASEAN's desire to address human rights while 'bearing in mind national and regional particularities and mutual respect for different historical, cultural and religious backgrounds, and taking into account the balance between rights and responsibilities' (ASEAN, 2009a). The ToR also states that the AICHR will work with respect for ASEAN's principles of sovereignty, territorial integrity and non-interference (ASEAN, 2009a).

The creation and content of the AICHR and the ToR have not been without their debates or critiques. The AICHR has been viewed as a consultative body as opposed to an enforcement mechanism, which, as a result, has received some criticism from CSOs that it lacks any real substance regarding the promotion and protection of human rights (Kelsall, 2009). With members of the Commission remaining accountable to their national governments, the independence of the AICHR has also been questioned by CSOs (Yen, 2011). In addition, due to its role in supporting coherent strategies within ASEAN, the AICHR may result in weakening the positions of more vocal ministers as opposed to bolstering them (Kelsall, 2009). The lack of transparency of the drafting processes of the ToR was another critique, with scepticism, especially from CSOs, on how seriously their suggestions were taken into consideration. This was due to their inability to access earlier drafts of the ToR and the fact that only CSOs from certain member states[5] were consulted during the process (Yen, 2011; Ginbar, 2010).

As well as the establishment of the AICHR, another development in the promotion and protection of human rights was the ASEAN Commission on the Promotion and Protection of the Rights of Women and Children (ACWC). The objectives of such a commission were first mentioned in the VAP and restated in the *Roadmap for the ASEAN Community (2009–2015)* (ASEAN, 2012c). The drafting of the ToR of the ACWC was assigned to a purpose-created working group who collaborated closely with CSOs, resulting in the establishment of the ACWC in 2010.[6] In addition to the AICHR and the ACWC, ASEAN has also adopted declarations on human rights such as the *Declaration on the Elimination of Violence Against Women in the ASEAN Region* (2004), the *ASEAN Declaration Against Trafficking in Persons Particularly Women and Children* (2004) and the *ASEAN Declaration on the Protection and Promotion of the Rights of Migrant Workers* (2007).

The EU's promotion of its political norms to ASEAN

The EU's relationship with ASEAN regarding human rights has seen a number of developments. The EU has supported the creation of the AICHR and the *Co-Chair's Statement of the 19th ASEAN–EU Ministerial Meeting* stated that,

> The Ministers agreed to strengthen mutual cooperation in promoting and protecting human rights, in particular by supporting the work of the ASEAN Inter-Governmental Commission on Human Rights (AICHR) with emphasis on capacity building. (ASEAN–EU, 2012b: 2)

The *Co-Chair's Statement of the 19th ASEAN–EU Ministerial Meeting* (2012b) also made reference to the rights of women stating, 'the Ministers also agreed on the need to promote gender equality, women's empowerment and improving the lives of girls and women' (ASEAN–EU, 2012b: 3).

In 2011, a group of representatives from the AICHR visited Brussels, Strasbourg and Vienna in order to observe how the EU manages its human rights bodies. The purpose of the study tour was to share the EU experience in the promotion and protection of human rights and was organised by the EEAS and funded by the European Instrument for Democracy and Human Rights. Informational sessions during the study tour included providing information on the EU's human rights policies in order to potentially contribute to an ASEAN Declaration on Human Rights, the drafting of an ASEAN thematic study on migration as well as explaining the EU's cooperation between NGOs and CSOs. In addition, the representatives from the AICHR visited the Council of Europe and the ECHR. Representatives were also given the opportunity to meet with those working at the Fundamental Rights Agency (FRA) and the Organization for Security and Co-operation in Europe (OSCE).

In 2013, the ACWC visited Brussels to 'exchange experience in promoting and protecting women's and children's rights in Europe and Southeast Asia and explore cooperation in areas of mutual interest' (ASEAN 2013i: 1). It also provided the opportunity for the ACWC to 'better understand the EU institutions, mechanisms, instruments and policy priorities on a broad spectrum of issues relating to women's and children's rights' (ASEAN, 2013i: 1).

Until recently, the EU's policy towards Myanmar has primarily been based on the imposition of sanctions due to the human rights conditions within this ASEAN member state. A year after Myanmar's accession to ASEAN, the EU reached a common position which provided for visa bans on senior members of the State Peace and Development Council of Myanmar (SPDC),[7] and senior members of the military. This resulted in Myanmar officials being unable to attend EU–ASEAN meetings in Europe (Alecu de Fleurs, 2010). During the 1990s, the EU's approach towards Myanmar differed greatly from that of ASEAN's, who pursued the policy of 'constructive engagement' as opposed to the EU's use of sanctions. In 1990, the European Commission imposed an arms embargo on Myanmar, and in 1991 defence and security cooperation was stopped (Egreteau, 2010). An EU common position on Myanmar was adopted in 1996, and in 1997 the EU withdrew the Generalised System of Preferences (GSP) for agricultural and industrial products (Egreteau, 2010).

For ASEAN, Myanmar's political situation and human rights abuses were internal and ASEAN's norm of respecting sovereignty enabled Myanmar's accession to ASEAN. It also meant that the Association could engage with Myanmar despite the human rights concerns within this state. As mentioned earlier in the chapter, not all ASEAN member states agreed to maintain ASEAN's policy of 'constructive engagement' and proposed the policy of 'flexible engagement'. As this proposal was not adopted by the ASEAN ministers, differences between EU and ASEAN approaches persisted in the late 1990s and resulted in EU–ASEAN meetings being suspended for more than two years and ministerial meetings for almost three years (Alecu de Fleurs, 2010). Despite these tensions, however, the EU managed to remain engaged with ASEAN by focusing on economic interests and avoiding or softening discussions on values where possible (I6 EO, 2011).

In 2000, a number of developments led to the resumption of ministerial meetings. According to Rüland (2010), the AFC of 1997–98 caused ASEAN to lose some of its bargaining power and credibility. In addition, Myanmar agreed to lift some restrictions on the National League for Democracy (NLD) and accepted a visit by the EU Troika.

In the 2000s, whilst the EU and ASEAN approaches towards Myanmar did not align, they did begin to converge slightly. In 2003, following the violence in Depayin and the reintroduced house arrest of Aung San Suu Kyi, ASEAN and its member states increasingly voiced their disapproval and criticism of the situation. In 2004, an ASEAN Intergovernmental Caucus on Burma/Myanmar (AIPMC) was established and placed increased pressure on Myanmar. A result of the caucus was to restrict Myanmar from assuming the ASEAN chair which was scheduled for 2006/2007.

Simultaneously, the EU increased and strengthened the sanctions packages on Myanmar through a number of common positions and decisions.[8] In 2004, the EU issued another common position which strengthened its sanctions but also allowed Myanmar to join ASEM meetings as a way in which to engage the state and possibly improve human rights and democracy within the country.[9] In 2005 the EU opened the European Commission Humanitarian Office (ECHO) in Yangon which aimed to increase humanitarian aid to Myanmar. In 2006, however, the EU renewed sanctions, which were further renewed in 2009 when Aung San Suu Kyi's house arrest was extended.[10] This development also saw ASEAN diverge from its usual stance of non-interference through a statement given by the ASEAN Chairman who stated that,

> The Government of the Union of Myanmar, as a responsible member of ASEAN, has the responsibility to protect and promote human rights. It is therefore called upon to provide timely and adequate medical care to Daw Aung San Suu Kyi as well as to accord her humane treatment with dignity. With the eyes of the international community on Myanmar at present, the honour and the credibility of the Government of the Union of Myanmar are at stake. (ASEAN, 2009b)

ASEAN's increased willingness to address the internal concerns of Myanmar was once again demonstrated during the aftermath of Cyclone Nargis in 2008. It managed to successfully mediate between the SPDC and the UN to convince the SPDC to allow foreign aid workers into Myanmar and managed the international humanitarian efforts employed to address the disaster (Cook, 2010).

Whilst Council of the EU Decisions in 2011 reinforced sanctions on Myanmar, developments in the relationship between the EU and Myanmar changed once again in 2012 when the EU opened an EU delegation in Yangon and suspended all sanctions on Myanmar apart from the arms embargo (Council of the EU, 2012d). Catherine Ashton, the former High Representative for Foreign Affairs and Security Policy, stated that,

> The European Union welcomes the remarkable changes in Burma/Myanmar and has decided to open a new chapter in our relations.

> Now that the sanctions will be effectively suspended, we encourage trade and investment in the country. (Council of the EU, 2012d)

Responses to the EU's promotion of its political norms

An analysis of interviews and surveys suggests that human rights promotion to ASEAN is supported by the EU but is not a main priority. Scholars have discovered similar findings. Robles (2008), for example, explains that the EU's negotiations surrounding an FTA with ASEAN is an example of the EU's inability to act coherently at the international level. This is because the EU desires to be economically competitive in the Southeast Asian region whilst simultaneously attempting to adhere to the human rights principles that it claims to be part of its development policy and identity as an international actor (Robles, 2008).

The fact that the EU and ASEAN commenced negotiations on an FTA before EU preconditions were met,[11] and during EU sanctions on Myanmar over human rights violations, demonstrates that economic interests potentially play a larger role than the political ideals of the EU when it comes to relations with third parties. It appears that although human rights, democracy and the rule of law are rhetorically important issues regarding the EU's external relations and development policy, when it comes to trade, economic benefits take precedence (Robles, 2008).

The issue here is that the EU also claims that development and trade are interlinked, yet human rights principles do not appear to be equally important across policy areas or, in fact, with all external partners of the EU. For example, the Cotonou Agreement between the EU and the African, Caribbean and Pacific (ACP) countries focuses significantly on human rights and democracy. Agreements between the EU and ASEAN and between the EU and individual member states of ASEAN do not have the same amount of emphasis on these issues (Reiterer, 2006). One EU official working in the Southeast Asian region stated that 'ASEAN does say that the EU–ASEAN relationship is influenced by Myanmar, but it is not true' and that 'you sometimes hear from ASEAN, or at least the people outside the EU that the EU–ASEAN FTA would be possible without Myanmar' but that this is also not true and that the stalling of the FTA negotiations were based on other obstacles (I10 EOA, 2011). This official mentioned that the EU is ready to engage Myanmar and that the sentiment that the EU is not ready and that the Myanmar situation affects the EU–ASEAN relationship is 'an idea we are trying to get rid of because it is no longer true' (I10 EOA, 2011).

The EU did not consider ASEAN's human rights record and democratic standards at any time when deciding to enter into FTA negotiations (Robles, 2008). For example, the fact that ASEAN did not have any human rights mechanisms, that most ASEAN member states did not have human rights commissions and, most significantly, the presence of Myanmar in ASEAN at the time negotiations commenced were all, theoretically, concerns for the EU (Robles, 2008). Prior to May 2007 the situation in Myanmar had been of great concern to the EU and had caused disagreement between the EU and ASEAN; however, this date saw the EU's decision to enter into FTA negotiations with ASEAN even though they still did not approve of the situation in Myanmar (Robles, 2008).

Up until this point, the EU had been determined to conduct negotiations in the WTO and to attempt to convince ASEAN to modify its trade regulations to conform to those of the EU. In 2002–2003, some ASEAN members suggested EU–ASEAN FTA negotiations take place; however, this was refused by the EU as what ASEAN was offering did not match the EU's aspirations (I11 EO, 2011). Instead, the European Commission proposed TREATI, which was to inform the two parties on regulatory systems but, in essence, required ASEAN to conform to EU-style regulations (Robles, 2008).

This leads to the question as to why the EU changed its approach to an EU–ASEAN FTA regardless of the fact that ASEAN did not meet EU standards for partnership. Robles (2008) claims that this was because WTO negotiations were suspended and that ASEAN member states had signed FTAs with Japan.[12] The issue of an EU–ASEAN FTA is by no means resolved, as focus has now moved to establishing bilateral agreements between the EU and individual member states, demonstrating yet another change in the direction of EU trade policy with the Southeast Asian region. This change in approach also illustrates the EU's desire to be economically involved in the Southeast Asian region even if its actions do not align with its values. Although the EU would prefer to interact on a region-to-region level, the importance of trade has overridden this so as to allow for the justification of bilateral agreements. This opportunistic approach to relations with Southeast Asia is something which Rüland (2002) warns against. He states that 'opportunism ... is a bad guide if it is Europe's interest to build stronger international institutions. It revolts against predictability – a key principle of institutionalism' (Rüland, 2002: 5). In other words, purely interest-driven and opportunistic policies are prone to change as quickly as the political context, which, rather than creating desired patterns of international relations lead to unreliability and instability.

Another finding has been that the EU's promotion of its political norms has not experienced the same amount of concrete results as support for economic integration or institutionalisation of ASEAN. In addition, ASEAN's initiatives to incorporate the promotion and protection of human rights have come from external pressure that is not exclusively or principally emanating from the EU. An interview participant made reference to the fact that as ASEAN's dialogue partners generally, and not just the EU, refer to human rights, there has been external pressure on ASEAN to incorporate this norm into the ASEAN Charter and to create a body such as the AICHR (I1 AO, 2011).

Furthermore, interview responses have revealed that there is acknowledgement that the EU is limited in its capacity to support human rights protection in ASEAN and that ASEAN will ultimately act in its own interest and within its capabilities in this regard. ASEAN acknowledges that it is at a stage of human rights promotion rather than protection. This was mentioned by interview participants in the EEAS and ASEAN Secretariat. As an official from ASEAN stated, 'currently, we are more focused on promoting human rights rather than protecting human rights, but then, this is for the future. We systematically must move towards that, the two ps, both promotion as well as protection' (I1 AO, 2011). The EU's approach to human rights concerns is not the same as ASEAN's, at least at this stage, and this therefore has an impact on the relevance of the EU to ASEAN. One official from an EU delegation in Southeast Asia stated that the EU would have liked ASEAN's human rights agenda to be more developed than it is, even though it appreciates the developments which have occurred (I10 EOA, 2011).

Farrell (2009) also refers to the dilemma of the EU's desire to maintain and enhance relations with Asia and the importance placed on human rights, stating that although the EU has attempted to include a human rights agenda in its relations with Asian countries, it has not been accepted readily. ASEAN now presents the promotion and protection of human rights as defining principles of ASEAN, yet economic concerns take precedence over such conditionality in the EU-ASEAN context and ASEAN still maintains its core principles of consensus, non-interference and respect for sovereignty (ASEAN, 2008).

Finally, regarding the promotion of political norms to ASEAN, and referring to norms such as human rights promotion and protection in EU policies, it is evident that issues regarding ASEAN and issues regarding ASEAN member states are seen as two distinct areas. One official working at the EEAS stated that when it comes to upholding political norms and pursuing economic interests within ASEAN and its member states, ASEAN is considered a 'force for good', and therefore any problems of a normative nature are not related to the EU's engagement with ASEAN (I9 EO, 2011). A 2012 speech by Karel De Gucht, the European Commissioner for Trade, also emphasised this point. With reference to Myanmar he stated that, 'these contacts with individual ASEAN Member States are important. But Europe's ambitions for our relations with ASEAN do go beyond dealing with each country one by one' (De Gucht, 2012c: 1).

Political norms and the EU as an international actor

Through an assessment of the qualitative data presented in the previous section against the criteria developed in Chapter 2 to determine the EU's actorness regarding the promotion of regionalism, it can be concluded that the EU's promotion of political norms as a component of its regionalism support policy is lacking in substance and coherence. It is evident that the EU is not an international actor with regard to the promotion of political norms. It has attempted to be an actor in this respect, yet in the context of ASEAN this objective has had limited realisation.

Within the official documents released by the EU there is continual reference to the EU objective to promote and protect human rights within and beyond its borders. The quote at the beginning of this chapter from the EU Special Representative for Human Rights explains that the EU's credibility and respect is reliant upon its adherence to human rights values. The *Europe and Asia: A Strategic Framework for Enhanced Partnerships* document states that the EU should 'contribute to the protection of human rights (in Asia)' and that to do this the EU should 'work together with Asia to uphold the universality and indivisibility of human rights' and 'mainstream human rights and governance issues' in their activities with Asia (European Commission, 2001: 3, 18). The document also makes reference to the EU's relations with ASEAN specifically and states that the EU should give attention to human rights issues in its dialogue with ASEAN (European Commission, 2001). Additionally, the Commission document, *A New Partnership with South-East Asia*, called for bilateral agreements with countries within Southeast Asia to contain the 'essential element' clause, which requires human rights and democratic principles to form the basis of such agreements and for human rights to be promoted across all policy dialogues between the EU and the Southeast Asian region (European Commission, 2003). These documents therefore suggest that the EU does consider itself to have the responsibility and capacity to promote its political norms.

However, based on an analysis of the incremental inclusion of the promotion, and to some extent, the protection, of human rights in ASEAN, there is limited evidence to suggest that the EU has been seen as relevant with regard to its political norms. An example of this has been the EU's response to Myanmar. The EU's reaction to states that have experienced human rights abuses has principally been to impose sanctions. Such a policy has not been deemed of relevance to ASEAN, who has not supported policies based on sanctions but maintained the position that approaches involving some form of engagement are preferable. Data collected in interviews and surveys have also been lacking in references to the EU's relevance with regard to its political norms.

Furthermore, survey responses have also suggested that the EU's political values are not as important to ASEAN's integration experience as its norms of economic integration or institutional structures and processes. Figure 6.1 below shows that in response to the question 'which areas of the EU's regional integration experience are useful to ASEAN?', the response 'EU values such as democracy, rule of law, good governance and human rights' was the fifth most predominant response after responses related to economic integration and political integration

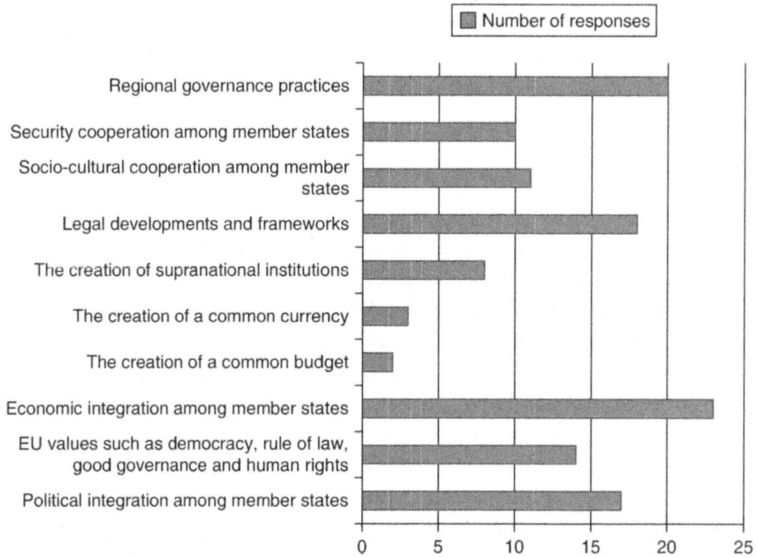

Figure 6.1 Which areas of the EU's regional integration experience are useful to ASEAN?

among member states and legal and governance practices. The response rate for this question was 73%, with respondents given the opportunity to choose as many options as they felt were appropriate.

One example of where the EU has utilised its resources with regard to the promotion of its political norms has been the extension of invitations to the AICHR and the ACWC to visit Europe. The hosting of such events has demonstrated willingness on the side of the EU to engage with these ASEAN commissions and offer funds, personnel and knowledge to ASEAN. These visits, however, have often been framed as information-sharing opportunities and opportunities to enhance greater cooperation between the EU and ASEAN as opposed to a situation whereby the EU promotes its political norms to ASEAN.

As the Deputy Secretary General for the ASEAN Socio-Cultural Community stated after the ACWC visit in 2013:

> ... the study visit has provided the opportunity for sharing experiences and good practices and paved the way for the strengthening of the partnership and identifying possible areas of cooperation and collaboration in the promotion and protection of the rights of women and children. (ASEAN, 2013i)

The inclusion of human rights into the EU's foreign policy agenda has been strongly supported by the EP. There has been general agreement across the European institutions as to the importance of including human rights principles into its policies with third parties. This agreement has become manifest in such joint declarations as the *Declaration of Human Rights* in 1977 and the *EU Charter of Human Rights and Fundamental Freedoms* in 2000. However, the actual execution of external policies has not always aligned with EU aspirations, as the case of Myanmar has shown. Bilateral relations and the continuation of trade negotiations despite concerns for human rights have demonstrated a lack of adherence to, and coherence of, EU policy.

Evidence to suggest that the EU has transformed ASEAN with regard to political norms is scarce. As I discussed earlier in the chapter, other factors, such as the World Conference in Vienna in 1993, the end of the Suharto regime in Indonesia and the political developments towards democratisation in a number of ASEAN member states have had a greater impact on ASEAN's human rights agenda than the EU's policies. ASEAN has also included human rights into its agenda whilst still retaining the core ASEAN norms of interaction, which has resulted in a different institutional design than that of the EU's. The AICHR is one such example as it is not comparable to the EU's internal structure which allows for actions such as the suspension of voting rights for members which do not comply with EU values and the incorporation of external mechanisms such as the ECHR to which the EU and its members are accountable.

Finally, whether approaches and results have been deemed successful, statements related to initiatives such as the study tours to Brussels by the AICHR and the ACWC have been positive. On the ACWC visit, the chair of the ACWC stated that:

> It is very interesting to see how initiatives and projects related to women's and children's rights are being implemented in the EU. I am confident that our visit will only be the beginning of a long and fruitful partnership between ASEAN and the EU to protect the rights and raise the status of women and children in our two regions. (ASEAN, 2013i)

However, when survey respondents were asked how well the EU's current policy for Southeast Asia, set out in the European Commission's *A New Partnership with South-East Asia*, was meeting the EU's political and economic priorities, the response suggests that it is meeting the EU's economic priorities to a greater extent than its political policies. In addition, the majority of responses indicated that the EU's policy was only meeting EU political and economic priorities 'moderately well' on a scale which included the responses 'poorly', 'moderately well', 'well' and 'very well'. With no participants responding that the EU was meeting economic or political priorities 'very well'. The results of this survey question are set out in Figure 6.2 below.

The EU's policy of imposing sanctions on Myanmar and the inclusion of human rights and democratic principles within its agreements with external actors have not been viewed favourably by officials within ASEAN and ASEAN member states. This has, at times, caused tension between the two actors. Similarly, the EU has received wide criticism for not consistently adhering to its policies of considering the protection and promotion of human rights, especially in conjunction with trade agreements and relations with ASEAN and its member states, as discussed earlier in this chapter. The perception of the EU's successful promotion of its political norms is varied, and at times, absent. The absence of perceptions of successful promotion of political norms is also linked to the fact that there has been low recognition of the EU's relevance in this regard. The inclusion of human rights protection and

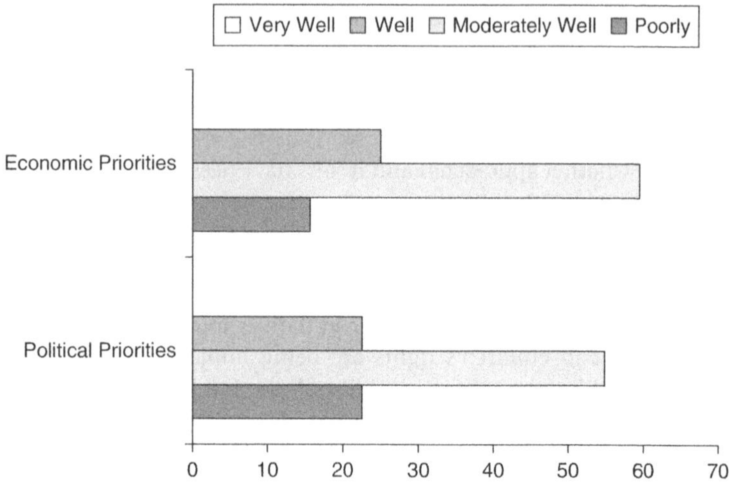

Figure 6.2 How well do you think the EU's current policy towards Southeast Asia, outlined in the European Commission's *A New Partnership with South-East Asia* document of 2003 is meeting the EU's political and economic priorities?

promotion in the EU's policies towards ASEAN has mainly served to maintain and consolidate the EU's political narrative of prioritising human rights concerns and ensuring a rhetoric based on its principles. External perceptions of the EU as a successful promoter of human rights to ASEAN have been minimal.

The analysis of the EU's actorness above results in the finding that the EU is not an international actor with regard to the promotion of its political norms to ASEAN. Whilst it does include the principles of protection and promotion of human rights into its dialogue with ASEAN and there are cooperative initiatives between the two actors, the promotion of human rights principles to ASEAN does not have a significant impact on the EU's actorness.

Political norms and the EU as a norm entrepreneur

Based on Manners's (2002) norm diffusion processes, in the realm of political norms, the EU has had limited success in promoting and diffusing its political norms to ASEAN. Due to the fact that ASEAN has developed its human rights agenda without extensive support from the EU, evidence of Manners's diffusion processes, which focus primarily on the norm entrepreneur, is limited. Based on the data collected and an analysis of the EU's cooperation with ASEAN regarding human rights, contagion has only occurred when the EU's approach to the protection and promotion of human rights has converged with international human rights norms. This has been evident in both the EU and ASEAN acknowledging the importance of international declarations on human rights, for example. More distinct EU approaches, such as the inclusion of human rights clauses into cooperation agreements and the use of sanctions have not been subject to unintentional diffusion processes.

Informational diffusion, procedural diffusion and transference have not been present in the sense that EU human rights norms have been diffused to ASEAN. Instead, these processes have occurred more as agreements on the need to acknowledge and tackle human rights concerns and support the EU's and ASEAN's approaches to do so. Informational diffusion has principally been in the form of the EU's declaratory support for human rights developments within ASEAN and the incorporation of human rights dialogues between the two organisations. For example, the EU's former High Representative for Foreign Affairs and Security Policy stated that,

> Democratic and human rights values are a vital adjunct to the EU–ASEAN relationship. There is no single model. But just as the EU has expanded human rights protection and promotion in our domestic and foreign policies – including through a Charter of Fundamental Rights and the creation of a Fundamental Rights Agency – so the advent of the ASEAN Intergovernmental Commission on Human Rights provides a new basis for collaboration in this important field (Ashton, 2012c).

Additionally, the *A New Partnership with South-East Asia* document expresses the importance of ensuring respect for human rights and the negative consequences of a lack of human rights protection.

> ... terrorism, organised crime and illegal migration undermine the rule of law, discourage investment, and hinder development. Similarly economic and trade development can best flourish in countries that not only encourage economic freedom but also respect human rights and the rule of law, practice good governance and rule democratically. (European Commission, 2003: 10)

Procedural diffusion is primarily evidenced through dialogue mechanisms within ASEM. The Informal ASEM Seminars on Human Rights, which began in 1998 and are thematic seminars, are held annually and involve representatives from universities, NGOs, civil society, the European Commission and the ASEAN Secretariat. They are one example where human rights are discussed in a structured and institutionalised setting (Asia Europe Foundation, 2013). Another example is the ASEM Interfaith Dialogue, initiated in 2005, which involves dialogue on social, cultural and religious issues (ASEM, 2013).

Examples of transference with regard to EU human rights norms include the study tours organised for the AICHR and the ACWC to Europe. Through hosting these tours, the EU has provided assistance in the form of information and knowledge-sharing to the newly formed human rights mechanisms in ASEAN. Nevertheless, instances of informational diffusion, procedural diffusion and transference are all within the context of policy and information sharing and cooperative dialogue and are therefore not purely processes whereby the EU is diffusing its human rights norms to ASEAN in an asymmetrical sense. The cultural filter, in the context of the EU's promotion of political norms, has had the strongest impact due to ASEAN's incorporation of human rights norms in conjunction with its pre-existing normative framework. Processes of norm adaption and learning have occurred with ASEAN entering into cooperative dialogue with the EU whilst still developing its human rights norms along its own trajectory. This is further examined and explained using Acharya's (2004, 2011a) norm localisation and subsidiarity framework later in the chapter.

Overt diffusion, the final diffusion process presented by Manners as regards the promotion of human rights norms specifically is not evident. When the EU has been physically present in ASEAN member states with any connection to human rights, it has been through programmes which indirectly address human rights concerns rather than the promotion of human rights norms *per se*. They have been cooperative programmes and declarations as opposed to an overt diffusion of norms through the EU's physical presence. Overt diffusion has potentially been limited by the current approach of ASEAN towards human rights and insistence on progressing in the style and manner suited to its environment and member state preferences. As Tan (2011: 9) explains, 'ASEAN states have tended to prefer a systemic and "step-by-step" approach with proper consultation and consensus in building the regional human rights mechanism'. According to Tan (2011: 9), 'attempting to strong-arm them (ASEAN states) into institutions such as an AICHR with international standards of human rights protection by merit of their promises made in international declarations have not worked'. The growing understanding that this is the case may contribute to the EU's unwillingness to instigate overt diffusion practices when cooperating with and encouraging ASEAN with respect to human rights.

Manners's diffusion processes are not substantially evident with regard to the EU's promotion of human rights norms to ASEAN. This is due to ASEAN's initiative in designing and implementing unique mechanisms to address human rights concerns and the lack of relevance of the EU with regard to its political norms. More apparent have been the processes of norm localisation as a result of ASEAN's active role as a norm recipient.

Human rights norms are incorporated into the ASEAN Charter, and can therefore be considered ASEAN norms. In this regard, the EU's support for human rights and the inclusion of a human rights agenda into its dialogue with ASEAN, at a cursory glance, resonate with ASEAN's normative priorities. However, given that ASEAN's human rights agenda is tempered by the pre-existing ASEAN norms of respect for sovereignty and non-interference, the EU's approach to human rights protection and promotion does not resonate with ASEAN's concept of human rights. Instead, ASEAN's incorporation of human rights into its normative and political framework can be interpreted as an extension of ASEAN's aims of ensuring peace, stability and prosperity within its region.

Furthermore, Tan (2011) emphasises the need to incorporate contextual considerations.

> Even while universal human rights must take centre stage, distinct cultural traditions, social practices, and environments result in particular needs for each Asian country. A 'margin of appreciation' – to borrow the term from the Europeans – should, as far as possible and without making a travesty of human rights, be respected so as to encourage enculturation and ownership of the system. (Tan, 2011: 1–2)

Based on official statements and documents released by ASEAN, it appears that local actors see the benefit of human rights norms, especially in the sense that they enhance the external perceptions of ASEAN. In many cases, external pressure in the context of situations such as Myanmar has resulted in ASEAN realising the need for it to actively address human rights concerns within its region. Further examples of increased attention on human rights as presented in this chapter have included the creation of human rights commissions in numerous ASEAN member states and the recommendations by the EPG on the

ASEAN Charter to include human rights mechanisms within ASEAN. In comparison with the EU's experience with economic integration and institutionalisation, the recognition of benefit of the EU's experience with human rights protection and promotion is low, as has been found in interview and survey responses. Therefore, the benefit of human rights promotion and protection is acknowledged by ASEAN but not necessarily human rights promotion and protection as associated with the EU.

It was recognised by ASEAN officials in Southeast Asia that there was a need for ASEAN to begin to address human rights and include them in the ASEAN Charter. As a former ASEAN Secretary General stated, 'we cannot show that we have no concerns at all in the tension between human rights' (I1 AO, 2011). The tension between upholding the ASEAN norm of non-interference and adequate levels of engagement among ASEAN states has also demonstrated that whilst existing norms remain important to ASEAN, there is a need to reframe such norms to include greater attention to human rights.

In addition, whilst it has been recognised that ASEAN needed to begin to incorporate a human rights agenda into its normative framework (I1 AO, 2011), the approach has been to complement an ASEAN human rights agenda with pre-existing norms. This suggests that there is the perception that the pre-existing norms are adequate, yet the Association can benefit from increased attention on human rights. This focus on complementing pre-existing norms with the inclusion of human rights into the ASEAN normative agenda is also evident in the approach of encouraging ASEAN member states to first sign international conventions on human rights and then subsequently incorporating these measures to protect and promote human rights at the regional level. A former Secretary General of ASEAN explained:

> It is a national decision to sign on to any international convention, but when we meet together we always say, 'the majority of us are in this convention of the rights of children, the rights of women, why doesn't every one of us sign on, so that it is easier when we develop our own ASEAN programme for women and children?' So these are the kinds of things that we do. Most of the time looking at outside organisations, external bodies and what happens elsewhere in the region, and other parts of the world. (I1 AO, 2011)

Due to the international community's concern for the promotion and protection of human rights, ASEAN has recognised the positive effects on its legitimacy and authority by acknowledging human rights norms. This was evidenced by the positive response to the policies and mediation capacities ASEAN demonstrated in the aftermath of Cyclone Nargis in Myanmar in 2008. Furthermore, domestic political changes within a number of ASEAN member states, as discussed in this chapter, such as the democratisation of Indonesia and leadership change in Thailand and Malaysia, have also provided impetus for ASEAN to maintain a prominent and legitimate role alongside its member states.

Whether human rights norms are seen to enhance the profile of ASEAN and its beliefs, as an association which aims to increase the prosperity of its member states and citizens based on the ideals of 'peace, freedom, social justice and economic well-being' (ASEAN, 1967), the norms of human rights promotion and protection are intrinsically linked to such aims and principles. The inclusion of human rights concerns into the ASEAN agenda, therefore, does have the capacity to enhance the profile of ASEAN and its beliefs and also to allay a number of concerns and criticisms of ASEAN with regard to its meeting internal and external expectations and having a role of consequence in the well-being of its citizens.

Furthermore, there is no evidence to suggest that the norm of human rights is seeking to replace an existing ASEAN norm. On the contrary, human rights have been added to and conditioned by the existing normative structure of ASEAN. The creation of the AICHR, which does not replace any existing norms of ASEAN, is evidence of this. The ASEAN norm of 'constructive engagement' with Myanmar was challenged by the proposal of 'flexible engagement' and eventually had an impact on how ASEAN interacted with Myanmar. Nevertheless, there have been calls for ASEAN's core norms of interaction to, at best, be revised as opposed to potentially rejected and replaced.

To present a further example, in the same year that the Charter was signed, 2007, the UN General Assembly adopted a resolution that condemned the human rights violations enacted by Myanmar and implored Myanmar to cease politically motivated arrests and to free political prisoners. As the ASEAN Charter included some adoption of human rights norms but also reiterated ASEAN's pre-existing norms of interaction, these coinciding events demonstrate the incremental inclusion of human rights onto the ASEAN agenda, potentially in response to exogenous changes and pressure on the one hand, and the continued assertion of ASEAN's independent approach to human rights on the other.

As there may be difficulty in reconciling ASEAN's pre-existing norms with the promotion and protection of human rights, there is the potential for a human rights agenda to put ASEAN norms into question. Interview respondents in the EEAS expressed the opinion that ASEAN will eventually have to reconsider its principal norms in order for it to develop as a regional organisation and for it to address issues such as human rights concerns (I11 EO, 2011). One interviewee stated, 'these norms will need to be reviewed eventually, but it is difficult. It won't happen in the short term. This is because it would mean that certain countries would be overruled and that would not be acceptable' (I11 EO, 2011). Due to the fact that human rights protection and promotion will not always align with pre-existing ASEAN norms, instability may occur through the process of increasing efforts to protect, as well as to promote, human rights. To date, however, the process has been incremental and tensions have been present, such as the disagreement over the use of 'flexible engagement' with regard to Myanmar, yet these tensions have not resulted in substantial instability.

In instances where ASEAN member states have signed international conventions on human rights, supportive and strengthening behaviours have been evident in the sense that these states have supported global norms which contribute to their autonomy. At the regional level, the incorporation of human rights within the ASEAN Charter is embedded within the pre-existing norms of ASEAN, demonstrating that challenging and resisting behaviours are existent. This is because human rights have not replaced or undermined ASEAN's existing norms of non-interference, respect for sovereignty and peaceful interaction among its members but have in fact reinforced the validity of these established norms. Similarly, the creation of the AICHR, which differs in its structure and mandate from human rights mechanisms in other regional organisations such as the EU, has also demonstrated ASEAN's acknowledgement of international concern for human rights but also the assertion of ASEAN's unique approach to managing these norms.

ASEAN's emphasis on human rights promotion results in ASEAN deeming the EU's approach towards addressing human rights concerns as partially irrelevant and incompatible with ASEAN norms such as non-interference and respect of sovereignty, despite the ongoing revision of these norms by ASEAN. This irrelevance and incompatibility explains why the EU's political norms have only received a limited amount of attention in the ASEAN context. Human rights norms have been localised with a high level of adaption into ASEAN's normative context, yet this has been a result of efforts made by those within ASEAN as opposed to normative promotion by the EU.

The recognition of a need to establish legitimacy and authority at the international level is a recurring theme for ASEAN throughout this chapter. It becomes apparent that friction tends to occur when an actor strives for international legitimacy whilst also attempting to consolidate and maintain domestic integrity. This appears to be reconciled by ASEAN's attempts to strike a balance between complying with and strategically utilising internationally dominant or accepted norms and protecting those norms which are distinct to the Association.

Conclusion

The EU's ability to export and promote its political norms to ASEAN is primarily constrained by the normative foundations upon which each region has been established. The EU, with its foundation of democracy, human rights and freedom, the pooling of sovereignty and the presence of supranational institutions, is seen in contrast to Southeast Asian regionalism with its strong focus on the protection of sovereignty, the power of states and the norm of non-interference into the affairs of other states. Constructivism's focus on the interaction between norms, structures and agents helps to explain the processes the EU and ASEAN have experienced by pointing out that these components are not created in isolation from each other but in fact continuously influence the constitution of all three.

The EU's lack of influence in the area of political norm promotion, which has been recognised by the EP, has also been attributed to the fact that human rights have been viewed by ASEAN not as something distinct to the EU. The EP *Report on the Annual Report on Human Rights in the World and the European Union's policy on the matter, including implications for the EU's strategic human rights policy* (2012: 1), states that 'the enforcement of human rights clauses and human rights conditionality in partnership agreements between the EU and third countries entailing EU development aid remains unsatisfactory'. The EP (2012: 1) in this report also expressed

> its disappointment at the lack of progress achieved in a number of human rights dialogues (which now number over forty) and takes note of the view expressed in some quarters that, in certain cases, EU human rights consultations are being instrumentalised and have become a process rather than a means to achieve measurable, tangible results.

External pressure on ASEAN to address human rights concerns has stemmed from more universal sources such as the Vienna World

Conference in 1993. ASEAN is currently promoting rather than protecting human rights, which, at least at this stage, is not compatible with the EU's view on how to address human rights concerns. This is another reason presented as to why the EU has been of limited relevance to ASEAN in the realm of human rights.

In addition, even though the EU has stated that the promotion and protection of human rights is one of its principal aims and that it includes this norm in its external relations, evidence presented in this chapter has shown that economic interests, and the promotion of economic integration, have taken precedence over the EU's political agenda. The EU has been clear in stating that it views ASEAN human rights concerns as distinct from human rights concerns of the ASEAN member states (I10 EOA, 2011). Also, where the EU has attempted to support the inclusion of human rights protection and promotion in ASEAN it has often not gone beyond declaratory statements of support. The EP *Report on the Annual Report on Human Rights in the World and the European Union's policy on the matter, including implications for the EU's strategic human rights policy* (2012: 1), makes a similar observation as it 'stresses that participation in a structured human rights dialogue, while welcomed, is too often used as a pretext to avoid discussion of these issues at higher political levels including partner summits'.

In terms of international actorness and norm diffusion, the EU is not an international actor with regard to the promotion of political norms mainly due to the fact that it has not been able to transform the target environment significantly. Nor have its actions reflected its policies or had the desired results. In terms of norm diffusion, localisation has occurred, evidence of this being the inclusion of statements on human rights in the ASEAN Charter and the creation of the AICHR alongside reassertions of ASEAN's pre-existing norms. However, this has been due to efforts made by other actors than the EU.

7
The Implications of Regionalism Support and Norm Diffusion on EU Actorness

> It (the EU) tries to help other regions develop. This is perhaps done arrogantly, or Eurocentrically, but the EU believes that other regions should grow and develop ... it is in our nature to reproduce ourselves.
>
> Interview Respondent 9, Official at the EEAS in Brussels, 2011.

> EU discourse seems to emphasise a clear lack of insight into the ASEAN ... for example branding ASEAN itself as an institution which more or less has copied the EU.
>
> Survey Respondent 11, Academic in Southeast Asia, 2012.

Conceptualising the EU as a certain type of power does not provide an accurate conceptualisation of the EU's impact on international affairs. Rather than basing an assessment of EU actorness on principles supported by the EU and which frame its foreign policies, this book has primarily based its analysis on EU norm promotion and the evaluation of internal and external perceptions. By doing so, it has avoided an analysis excessively influenced by normative formulations of how EU foreign policy should be devised and implemented and instead relied principally on perception analysis.

I examined the hypothesis that *the EU has set itself up as a norms diffuser in its engagement with ASEAN. This diffusion is contingent upon ASEAN's receptiveness. It is therefore ASEAN which has the determining role in the realisation of the EU's regionalism promotion policies*. Based on the empirical analysis of the EU's policy of promoting its experience with regionalism, which included the examination of interview and survey responses, this hypothesis has been proven and supported by the central arguments and findings presented. This was done in a series of steps.

Firstly, in Chapter 2, 'Seeking to Reconceptualise the EU as a "Power"', I presented the arguments for the need to move beyond conceptions of the EU as a power. Through the empirical analysis of the EU's promotion of its regionalism experience to ASEAN, I determined that 'power' is an inappropriate term with which to describe the EU as an international actor. This is first and foremost due to the fact that the term 'power', as defined and developed by scholars such as Galtung (1973), Etzioni (1961) and Poggi (2001), has often relied on a triad of power types involving political, economic or normative power, or force, reward and ideational power (Manners, 2013), which cannot be applied to the EU's external policies towards ASEAN. This is primarily because the exercise of power and power transference often assume a degree of asymmetry in a relationship which is not present in the EU–ASEAN context (Galtung, 1973).

Furthermore, an examination of power dynamics involves a disproportionate focus on the processes of power transference and the employment of power, as opposed to a focus on results and impact. In addition, empirical analysis has shown that although the majority of conceptualisations of the EU have referred to the civilian, ethical and normative nature of the EU's external role, this markedly normative approach has not, in certain instances, sufficiently allowed for objective or accurate analysis. It has also been prone to neglecting the tension between pursuing a normative agenda and fulfilling strategic interests. I therefore refrained from linking conceptualisations of the EU's external action to the concept of power and instead assessed the EU's international actorness and influence against perceptions and outcomes of its capacity to promote regionalism to ASEAN. In order to do this, whilst acknowledging that all analysis is laden with a certain amount of normativity, I claimed that the relatively unbiased and normatively unburdened framework necessary to approach a study on EU actorness should involve processes of norm diffusion.

The approach I have taken has differed from earlier studies on EU actorness by including the analysis of norm diffusion in the conceptualisation process. As discussed in Chapter 2, scholarly analysis of norm diffusion has tended to focus on either the role of the norm entrepreneur or the norm recipient. Manners's (2002) norm diffusion framework, with its categorisation of processes into contagion, informational diffusion, procedural diffusion, transference, overt diffusion and the cultural filter, provides a strong basis for examining the role and impact of the norm entrepreneur. Acharya's (2004, 2011a) explanations of norm localisation and norm subsidiarity, on the other hand, provide a comprehensive analysis of norm recipients. It was important to utilise both of these frameworks, for if they had been addressed in isolation from one another, the role of either the norm recipient or the norm entrepreneur would not have been examined sufficiently. I therefore used the two frameworks simultaneously to analyse the processes of norm diffusion between the EU and ASEAN.

I also demonstrated that previous studies of the EU as an international actor have been introspective in their approach. Relatively little attention has been given to the EU's external interlocutors and the role they play in shaping the EU's actorness. The role of the EU's external partners and the impact the EU has had externally must be included into studies of EU actorness. One of the principal aims of this book has been to go beyond this introspectiveness and base a study on EU actorness which incorporates the analysis and role of one of the EU's dialogue partners, ASEAN. With the EU's promotion of regionalism to ASEAN as its basis, I have been able to include not only elements of this promotion which have been successful but also instances where EU policy has failed to match the policy aspirations that the EU has adopted and supported. For instance, a pertinent finding has been the fact that the EU has not been able to exert its actorness, or be considered an influential actor with regard to human rights, despite the fact that this is one of the central values espoused within its foreign policies and in relations with its external partners. Another principal finding has been that EU actorness is not consistent across these three areas. It is profoundly contingent upon the perception ASEAN has of the EU and the salience of EU norms of integration to ASEAN.

Chapter 3, 'Drivers of Interregionalism: EU-ASEAN Engagement', answered the research question as to why the EU considers itself to have the ability and responsibility to promote and diffuse its norms of regionalism to ASEAN. Central to the arguments in Chapter 3 was the assumption that the EU and ASEAN are drivers of regionalism in their own geographical and political contexts and supporters of regional integration elsewhere. This chapter argued that there are mainly economic and political motivations for the EU and ASEAN to remain partners and interlocutors. Economic motivations, especially, have contributed to the EU's determination to promote its regionalism experience to ASEAN. In addition, the objectives of one motivation can hinder the successful achievement of another, leading to policy incoherence and outcomes that do not always match objectives. Incoherence was analysed in this chapter, and

I argued that the tension created between pursuing economic goals and promoting normative values and norms often results in an incoherent actor. Additionally, data collected in interviews also demonstrated that ASEAN officials perceived the EU to be a fragmented and disjointed international actor. The opinion of ASEAN officials regarding who would represent the EU at the EAS, as discussed in Chapter 3, is one such example of this perception.

In Chapter 4, 'The EU, ASEAN and Economic Integration', I argued that the EU's promotion of its economic integration experience has had a substantial impact on the actorness of the EU. The results of the APRIS programme and the continuation of economic integration support to ASEAN with the ARISE programme demonstrate a structured and continued recognition of the importance of ASEAN economic integration by the EU and the contribution which can be made to ASEAN by the EU.

The distinctiveness of norms is a critical consideration when determining their diffusion from one actor to another. In the case of the EU's economic integration norms, the distinctiveness of the EU as an economic entity has had a favourable effect on the diffusion of norms to ASEAN. As the most highly integrated region in terms of economic integration, the EU has been considered an accepted and useful source of inspiration for ASEAN by both ASEAN officials and scholars in the fields of EU and ASEAN studies. Interview and survey responses have attested to this fact, yet they also revealed a sense of frustration and misunderstanding between the two actors. According to interview and survey responses, much of the discord has been a result of different expectations of the approaches taken, and the speed of implementation and development. For example, EU officials working in the EEAS expressed their frustration with the lack of capacity of the ASEAN Secretariat and the lack of resources available for implementing initiatives. Respondents who provided insight into the reactions of ASEAN officials to the EU's initiatives complained about the fact that the EU was often too rigid in requiring ASEAN to conform to its regulatory standards and too often based developments on the legal and bureaucratic capacities of ASEAN institutions.

To comprehend such friction, I used principles of neofunctionalism to determine why such a discrepancy between expectations exists. A neofunctional logic of integration is apparent in the EU and ASEAN, yet manifests in different ways. For example, ASEAN has been actively advancing the neofunctional concept of spillover rather than allowing it to have a deterministic momentum of its own, which has been the case in certain areas of EU economic integration. The EU and ASEAN have followed incremental paths of economic integration. However, the EU's *ad-hocism* with regard to the development of supranational institutions is markedly different from ASEAN's determination to maintain its intergovernmentalism whilst progressing towards a single market. The EU's approach has been more reactive, with a focus on outcomes, as opposed to the approach taken by ASEAN, which has had stronger emphasis on processes, initiating spillover effects and implementing preventative measures.

The neofunctional determinism inherent in EU developments and programmes such as APRIS and ARISE is not taken up by ASEAN which, at this stage, is demonstrating a more measured approach to the development of the AEC. This controlled approach taken by ASEAN was evident in interview responses from ASEAN officials who were clear in stating what ASEAN was and was not capable of currently achieving, and which aspects of economic integration were currently not viable or desirable, such as the implementation of a common currency. The stalled FTA negotiations were another example of this approach, and a Deputy Secretary General of ASEAN stated that one of the impediments of the FTA negotiations was that the EU included in the agreement certain conditions, such as government procurement, which ASEAN was not ready or able to implement (I2 AO, 2011). It was therefore determined that the EU is a significant actor with regard to its promotion of economic integration, and that it is regarded as an influential actor, even despite the current crisis within the EU. However, there are limitations to its actorness in this area, and the potency of the EU's actorness will only remain for as long as ASEAN deems the EU's economic integration experience to be of relevance and use.

In Chapter 5, 'The EU, ASEAN and Institutionalisation', I argued that ASEAN does not accord as much importance to norms of institutionalisation as it does to the EU's economic integration experience. The promotion of institutionalisation by the EU, in the form of decision-making processes, governance structures and legal and organisational processes, has influenced ASEAN, but a high level of norm localisation in conjunction with norm subsidiarity is evident, creating institutional structures whose initiation can be attributed to the EU. Yet the presence of localisation and subsidiarity has resulted in institutional developments distinct from the EU and unique to ASEAN. ASEAN's CPR was presented as an example of an institution which in nomenclature is similar to the EU's Coreper yet differs in role, function and mandate. Similarly, the establishment of the AICHR, at this stage a dispute settlement mechanism, cannot be compared to the ECJ or the ECHR of the

Council of Europe in terms of role or enforcement capabilities. Another example was the EPG report on the drafting of the ASEAN Charter. As part of the drafting process of the report, the EPG visited Brussels in 2006. Nevertheless, the EU is only mentioned briefly in the final version of the report, and whilst suggestions within the report included the creation of the CPR and the strengthening of ASEAN institutions such as the Secretariat, the ultimate contents of the Charter did not comprehensively reflect the recommendations of the EPG report, nor could they be necessarily attributed to norm promotion by the EU.

Distinctiveness of the EU's norms has been a factor in determining the extent to which ASEAN deems the EU's norms of institutionalisation relevant. Central to Chapter 4 was the argument that ASEAN actively evaluates which aspects of EU institutionalisation are of relevance. The EU has been willing to provide ASEAN with support, but interview and survey responses have revealed that there are limits as to the applicability of EU institutional structures and processes. Historical institutionalism was utilised to comprehend these limitations and the divergent institutional paths of ASEAN and the EU. Based on their different historical contexts, preferences for institutional development have emerged which differ between the two organisations.

The promotion of institutionalisation to ASEAN has demonstrated that discourses framed around active and passive actor dynamics, and benefactor–recipient arrangements are largely redundant. This has been determined by the amount of initiative shown by ASEAN in gathering information from external sources on the path its institutional development should take.

In addition, the EU's actorness with regard to institutionalisation is limited, and when EU norms have been incorporated into ASEAN's institutional structure, they have been extremely customised to complement ASEAN's pre-existing norms. In comparison with the EU's promotion of economic integration, the EU is not as willing to present itself as an active force in the promotion of institutionalisation. This is in order to avoid an overassertive and domineering presence in the ASEAN region, which, according to interview and survey responses, it often fails to achieve.

Chapter 6, 'The EU, ASEAN and Political Norms', presented the case that the EU does not have a strong norm entrepreneurship role, nor is it an international actor, with regard to the promotion of human rights to ASEAN. The promotion of human rights by the EU has, in fact, exacerbated the EU's own policy incoherence discussed in Chapters 2 and 3. In this chapter I put forward the case that the EU's promotion of human rights to ASEAN is lacking in substance and that interview and survey responses suggest that it is supported but not a priority. In recent years, the EU has stated its support for the creation of the AICHR and hosted representatives from the AICHR and ACWC. However, the EU's economic engagement with ASEAN has often created incoherence between its normative ideals, economic interests and development assistance. Its past policies with Myanmar and simultaneous pursuit of an EU–ASEAN FTA, followed by the negotiation of bilateral trade agreements once these negotiations stalled, present examples of where economic imperatives have taken precedence over normative values.

Although ASEAN has begun to include human rights into its political agenda, there is little hard evidence to suggest that this has been a result of norm promotion by the EU. Such developments within ASEAN can be better explained by efforts of the wider international community and organisations such as the UN. As human rights protection and promotion are not norms that are specific to the EU, the EU's relevance to ASEAN with regard to these norms is not strong enough for the EU to have substantial presence or relevance. ASEAN first mentioned the importance of a concern for human rights after the 1993 World Conference on Human Rights, which demonstrated the influence the wider global community has had on ASEAN's path towards incorporating human rights into its agenda. In addition, the increasing pressure put on ASEAN by its member states to promote and protect human rights was another example of influence arising from sources other than the EU. Human rights promotion and protection are norms connected to the EU but not unique to the EU, and therefore, ASEAN has numerous sources of inspiration and pressure on which to draw other than the EU.

Through an analysis of the EU's promotion of regionalism to ASEAN, a major finding has been that although the EU aspires to be an international actor whose actions are largely based on its normative values, it is inaccurate to conceptualise the EU as a power connected to its normative or ethical ideals. The results of its policies of regionalism promotion to ASEAN, as well as internal and external perceptions of the EU, do not suit such a conceptualisation. Although the EU's engagement with ASEAN is rhetorically focused on its normative principles, in practice, the EU's success and priorities lie in its trade and economic policies and their alignment with those of ASEAN. Furthermore, external perceptions by ASEAN officials of the EU are also based on the EU's economic integration experience rather than on its political, institutional or normative foundations. Also, ASEAN has referred to the EU as a reference most prominently with regard to its economic integration experience.

Nevertheless, assuming that the EU is an international actor at least with regard to some policy areas, as has been determined by some scholars (Smith, 2011; Wunderlich, 2012; Bendiek and Kramer, 2010), the question remains, then, as to how the EU should be conceptualised (Nunes, 2011). The findings presented in this book suggest that due to the fact that perceptions and results of the EU's actorness are so varied according to the policy areas which have been examined – economic integration, institutionalisation and political norms – there are challenges to the conceptualisation of the EU as an actor. Furthermore, the perception of the EU's interlocutor must be taken into account when considering the EU's policies and actorness. In the context of EU–ASEAN dialogue, the EU's actorness is largely determined not so much by whether the EU attempts to be an influential actor, as this is evident in statements provided by EU officials and in EU policy documents, but rather by whether ASEAN perceives it as such.

The determination of actorness in this book has relied on questions pertaining to ASEAN's perception of the EU as an actor, why or why not the EU is considered an actor and what has contributed to such perceptions. Based on the research conducted, I find that the EU is an opportunistic actor. This is attributed to the fact that the EU's actorness is often determined by its desire to fulfil economic interests beyond all else, even if they are in contradiction to other EU external policy aims. As statements and documents relating to the EU emphasise the normative principles underlying the EU's external action, the results are often unclear and incoherent policy outcomes. If the EU were conceptualised less as a consistent and uniform international actor, a more comprehensive and accurate assessment of the EU would be possible to achieve. Future studies which focus on the nuances of the EU's external action, including the divisions within the EU's institutional structure and the priorities and interests of its member states, will contribute to a thorough examination of EU actorness.

I have sought to make a valuable contribution to the existing research on EU actorness and EU–ASEAN relations by reassessing the methods through which the EU is conceptualised as an actor and the criteria employed to establish such conceptualisations. By moving beyond conceptualisations of the EU as a power, and especially a power related to its normative composition, aspirations and ambitions, this book has sought to provide an innovative framework for future research. I have argued that processes of norm diffusion are a useful basis of examination for EU actorness. This is under the condition, however, that the norm entrepreneur and the norm recipient are both taken into consideration. I have sought to establish a basis for future studies of EU foreign policy with a framework based on a comprehensive analysis of the processes of norm diffusion and the roles of norm entrepreneurs and norm recipients. I have also aimed to provide an original contribution by developing an analysis of in-depth interview and survey responses. The perception analysis facilitated by such data has added a nuanced and comprehensive examination of EU–ASEAN relations in the context of regionalism development.

This book provides a basis for areas of study which would benefit from further research and development. Firstly, as I have focused exclusively on the EU's promotion of regionalism to ASEAN, there are substantial opportunities for further research to be undertaken following a similar methodology and design which analyses the EU's promotion of its regionalism experience to regional organisations other than ASEAN. Such research agendas would then make it possible to assess whether the findings of this study are specific to the EU–ASEAN relationship or are consistent among interregional dynamics in which the EU is engaged.

Secondly, I examined the EU's actorness and norm entrepreneurship capabilities in three specific areas – economic integration, institutionalisation and political norms. These three areas have been identified as the main areas of regionalism promotion in which the EU is involved. However, there is still opportunity for expansion on, and analysis of, regionalism promotion which is not covered in this book. For example, although human rights were analysed, it would also be valuable to investigate other political norms such as promotion of democracy, sustainable development or rule of law. Similarly, social or cultural regional networks and business networks, such as NGOs or CSOs, as well as broader processes such as ASEM, could be other areas which may contribute to an understanding of the EU's actorness with regard to ASEAN or other regional organisations.

In addition, the subject of this book has been the international actorness of the EU as a result of its efforts to promote regionalism to ASEAN. In order to broaden the research agenda on regional organisations and interregionalism, the literature in this field could also begin to examine regional organisations other than the EU as the central actor and examine and assess the degree to which other regional organisations, such as ASEAN, attempt to promote their experience, or are viewed by external interlocutors as reference points, and how this impacts on their international actorness.

Finally, this book has provided a framework to assess actorness in conjunction with, and as a consequence of, norm diffusion. This framework has been generated by utilising criteria to assess actorness which includes an examination of the perceptions, capabilities and resources of the actor under investigation without neglecting the crucial incorporation of an analysis of the perceptions of the actor's interlocutors. Rather than focusing on the power of an actor, norm diffusion frameworks have provided the opportunity to assess the contribution the norm entrepreneur and the norm recipient have in determining actorness. As current norm diffusion frameworks have tended to focus on either the norm entrepreneur or the norm recipient, I utilised a number of existing frameworks so that a comprehensive study could be undertaken. Further research may indeed be beneficial to determine other factors besides norm diffusion which may be used to assess the international actorness of regional organisations.

Based on the rhetoric of the EU's leaders and statements and policies released by its institutions, it is not likely that the EU will abandon its ambitions to be an international actor of influence in the near future. Nor is it likely that it will renounce the strategy of reproducing itself in other parts of the world (I4 EO, 2011). Based on the results of the research conducted for this study, it is predicted, however, that such ambitions will only be realised if the EU firstly affords greater importance to its relationship with ASEAN and, secondly, demonstrates a greater understanding and acceptance of the distinct path of ASEAN's regionalism development. The majority of survey respondents referred to inadequate knowledge of the Southeast Asian region as the main challenge facing the EU in its relationship with ASEAN. ASEAN has by no means 'copied the EU' (S11 AA, 2012), and unless EU efforts to support regionalism to ASEAN meet the objectives and fulfil the interests of ASEAN, the EU will continue to remain frustrated with the pace and style of ASEAN's development. This is despite increasing inclusions in EU rhetoric that it understands that ASEAN's context, priorities and design are different from the EU's. As ASEAN strives to have a more defined and central role within its own region, and be a predominant architect of interregional arrangements and trade relations, the EU will need to demonstrate that it acknowledges the increasing influence and actorness of ASEAN within its own region. The EU's signing of the TAC is one step in this direction, yet an enhanced understanding of ASEAN perceptions of the EU, such as the concern of over-representation if the EU were to join the EAS, will also be necessary for the interregional relationship to continue with adequate intensity.

As ASEAN matures, an EU policy of promoting its own norms of regionalism will continually lose potency. As discussed in Chapter 3, results of the survey conducted for this study reflect the prediction that the EU will need to enhance its relationship with ASEAN in the future. 96.9% of respondents agreed to the statement that 'the importance of ASEAN to the EU will steadily increase'. This is in contrast to a lower percentage, 65.6% of respondents, who agreed to the statement that 'the importance of the EU to ASEAN will steadily increase'. In addition, only 28.1% of respondents agreed to the statement that 'the EU is an influential actor in the Southeast Asian region'. Not only has the relationship moved beyond a donor–recipient asymmetrical relationship, but no longer can the EU be considered a regionalism project exemplar of which there is no alternative. Only with this recognition can EU support to ASEAN's development be sufficiently and successfully implemented, and this can contribute to the international actorness of the EU and the development of a more symmetrical relationship between the EU and ASEAN.

Notes

Prelims

1. The then EU Commissioner for Enlargement, speech at the Centre for European Policy Studies Annual Conference 'Europe's Role in the World', 2008.

1 Ambitions of Actorness

1. Similar to the categories used to code interview and survey respondents in this book, Southeast Asia here refers to the member states of ASEAN – Brunei Darussalam, Cambodia, Indonesia, Lao PDR, Malaysia, Myanmar, the Philippines, Singapore, Thailand and Vietnam. Oceania refers to Australia and New Zealand. East Asia refers to Japan, China and South Korea.

2 Seeking to Reconceptualise the EU as a 'Power'

1. According to Smith (2011), the power instruments available to the EU include economic power, civilian power, ethical power, power of attraction, light military power and heavy military power.
2. At the time of the speech, Benita Ferrero-Waldner was the European Commissioner for External Relations and Neighbourhood Policy.
3. At the time of the speech, Hugh Richardson was the Head of the Delegation of the European Commission to Japan.

3 Drivers of Interregionalism: EU–ASEAN Engagement

1. Referenced in *Towards a New Asia Strategy* (European Commission, 1994) from Le Commerce Mondial au XXI Siècle, Institut Francais des Relations Internationales, 2002.
2. Examples include the importance placed on diversity, the preference for a rule-based multi-polar world with strong multilateral organisations and the recognition of the value of regional integration (European Commission, 2003).
3. The conclusion to Chaban, Elgström and Holland's 2006 article also argues a similar point, claiming that a more coherent approach to public diplomacy would increase the EU's role as an international actor and its legitimation.
4. Both the *East Asia Policy Guidelines* (Council of the EU, 2007) and the *Guidelines on the EU's Foreign and Security Policy in East Asia* (Council of the EU, 2012a) mention the promotion of regionalism as one of the EU's key objectives.

5. In addition to the ASEAN member states, non-ASEAN members which have signed the treaty are Papua New Guinea, China, India, Japan, Pakistan, South Korea, Russia, New Zealand, Australia, France, East Timor, Bangladesh, Sri Lanka, North Korea, the US, the UK and the EU.
6. The study discussed here was based on interviews with state representatives from three different multilateral meetings; the United Nations Forum on Forestry's (UNFF) fourth session in Geneva in May 2004, the Convention on International Trade in Wild Fauna and Flora's (CITES) 13th Conference of the Parties in Bangkok in October 2004 and the World Trade Organization (WTO) meeting in Geneva in May 2005 (Chaban, Elgström and Holland, 2006).
7. ASEAN member states which participated in the intervention in East Timor included Thailand, Singapore, Malaysia and the Philippines (Caballero-Anthony and Haywood, 2011).
8. The example given in this regard were protests held in Italy against the import of shoes from Vietnam.
9. The two EU member states which have signed the TAC are the UK and France.
10. The IAI (Initiative for ASEAN Integration) was a programme initiated at the 2000 ASEAN summit meeting which aimed to provide 'a framework for regional cooperation through which the more developed ASEAN members could help those member countries that most need it'. It was followed by the *Ha Noi Declaration on Narrowing the Development Gap for Closer ASEAN Integration* in 2003, which set out the areas which the IAI would concentrate on (Severino, 2007b). These areas were infrastructure, human resources development, information and communications technology and regional economic integration.
11. Chaban, Elgström and Holland (2006: 248) make a similar point stating that, 'outsiders' expectations and perceptions influence the impact of EU foreign policy role performance'.

4 The EU, ASEAN and Economic Integration

1. The other areas which are covered in this book are the promotion of institutional structures (see Chapter 5 for more details) and the EU's political norms (see Chapter 6 for more details).
2. This includes functional, political and cultivated spillover as presented by Haas (1968).
3. As discussed in greater detail in Chapter 5, the EU's approach of ensuring peace and stability primarily through economic integration from the outset of the European integration project has differed from ASEAN's approach of initially emphasising the consolidation of peaceful interaction among its member states with economic integration entering the ASEAN agenda at a later stage.
4. To expand on these four freedoms, moves to allow the free movement of goods include the removal of tariff and non-tariff barriers. The free movement of capital largely includes allowing the freedom of investment in any member state. One of the main components of the free movement of

services is the right of establishment for industrial and commercial activity and the free movement of labour aims to eliminate restrictions on worker mobility which includes the recognition of qualifications and experience (Cini and Borrogán, 2010).

5. Harmonisation refers to the process of aligning standards, practices and regulations throughout the members of the EU.
6. The ERT (European Roundtable of Industrialists) was a group consisting of the heads of the major multinational corporations in Europe whose aim was to advocate for the completion of the single market (Wallace and Young, 1996).
7. The three pillars introduced by the Maastricht Treaty were the European Communities. The first pillar covered economic, social and environmental policies, the second pillar was the CFSP (Common Foreign and Security Policy) and the third pillar covered Justice and Home Affairs (Europa, 2012a).
8. Also referred to as the Convergence Criteria.
9. The five criteria are price stability, 'the inflation rate should be no more than 1.5 percentage points above the rate for the three EU countries with the lowest inflation over the previous year'; budget deficit, 'the budget deficit should be below 3% of gross domestic product (GDP)'; debt, 'the national debt should not exceed 60% of GDP, but a country with a higher level of debt can still adopt the Euro provided its debt level is falling steadily'; interest rates, 'the long-term interest rate should be no more than two percentage points above the rate in three EU countries with the lowest inflation over the previous year'; and, exchange rate stability, 'the national currency's exchange rate should have stayed within certain pre-set margins of fluctuation for two years' (Europa, 2012b: 1).
10. In 2004, Cyprus, Czech Republic, Estonia, Hungary, Latvia, Lithuania, Malta, Poland, Slovakia and Slovenia joined the EU. This was followed by the accession of Bulgaria and Romania in 2007. In 2013 Croatia became the newest member of the EU (Europa, 2013c).
11. Ordinary legislative procedure 'gives the same weight to the European Parliament and the Council of the European Union on a wide range of areas' (European Parliament (EP), 2013: 1). The policy areas include economic governance, transportation and consumer protection. The process involves the Commission sending a proposal to the Parliament and the Council. The proposal is then discussed by the Council and the Parliament. If they both agree to the proposal, it is adopted as law. If they cannot agree, the proposal is sent to a Conciliation Committee, which consists of members of the Council and Parliament, and representatives of the Commission. Once they have reached a decision, the proposal is sent back to the Parliament and Council and a final decision is made (EP, 2013).
12. The APT (ASEAN +3) process was also initiated in response to ASEM which was inaugurated in 1996 as a way to bolster the strength of the Asian side of ASEM. ASEAN invited China, Japan and South Korea to be a part of the ASEM process (Morada, 2008).
13. In 1996 ASEAN signed the Protocol on Dispute Settlement Mechanism. It covered economic agreements of ASEAN and set out the methods of dispute settlement which involved consultation, conciliation or mediation.

If a result was not achieved via these methods the issue was referred to the Senior Economic Officials Meeting (SEOM) who deliberated and provided a decision and outcome. This protocol was replaced by the ASEAN Protocol on Enhanced Dispute Settlement Mechanism in 2004, which continued to include consultation and consensus as primary methods of settlement.

14. As READI (Regional EU-ASEAN Dialogue Instrument) has had a political and institutional focus rather than economic focus, it will be discussed in more depth in Chapter 5.
15. As discussed earlier in this chapter, ASEAN has recognised the need to address NTBs (non-tariff barriers) to trade by harmonising product standards and regulations. The cosmetics sector has experienced the most progress in this area to date. An Agreement on the ASEAN Harmonised Cosmetic Regulatory Scheme was signed in 2003 which aimed to promote increased trade facilitation of cosmetic goods. The Agreement covers the ASEAN Mutual Recognition Arrangements of Product Registration Approvals for Cosmetics and the ASEAN Cosmetics Directive (APRIS II, 2012a).
16. If producers can prove that their products have at least 40% ASEAN value content, tariff duties on intra-regional trade are zero for the majority of ASEAN member states. Cambodia, Lao PDR, Myanmar and Vietnam are expected to reduce their tariffs to zero by 2015 (APRIS II, 2012b).
17. In 1998 ASEAN signed a Framework Agreement for the Facilitation of Goods in Transit. However, the protocols necessary to fulfil the agreement were not active until APRIS II officials, together with ASEAN officials, agreed on a work plan to implement the protocols (APRIS II, 2012d).
18. The EDSM (Enhanced ASEAN Dispute Settlement Mechanism) manages economic and trade disputes and helps to enforce commitments under the AEC. It does so through informal advisory mechanisms, consultative mechanisms and adjudicatory mechanisms (APRIS II, 2012e).
19. Three other initiatives of significance which have seen EU support for ASEAN's economic integration have been the ASEAN-EC Programme on Intellectual Property Rights (ECAP III), the EU-ASEAN Statistical Capacity Building Programme (EASCAB) and the ASEAN-EC Programme on Air Transport Integration (AATIP).
20. Whilst ASEAN intra-FDI flows are increasing, in the period 2009–2010 there was a 127.3% increase in intra-FDI flows and in the period 2010–2011 an 83.4% increase, the overall share of intra-ASEAN FDI for the period 2009–2011 was 18.5%. This was the largest share of FDI flows to ASEAN, yet it was only 1.4% above the second biggest share, which came from the EU and was at 17.1% (ASEAN, 2013g).

5 The EU, ASEAN and Institutionalisation

1. The *aquis communautaire* of the EU encompasses the legal frameworks of the EU, including international treaties and agreements, declarations, resolutions and the rights and obligations of its member states (Europa, 2013d).
2. The other major institutional development which has occurred as a consequence of the Lisbon Treaty is the creation of the EEAS (European External Action Service) and the role of the High Representative.

3. Indonesia's *Konfrontasi* policy primarily focused on challenging the legitimacy of the Malaysian Federation. Following the end of the policy, Suharto replaced Sukarno which was a transition that has been seen to greatly facilitate the establishment of ASEAN (Webber, 2001).
4. Diplomatic initiatives by France and Japan resulting in the Paris Peace Agreement in 1991, the withdrawal of Vietnamese troops from 1989 on due to a reduction in military assistance from the Soviet Union and the collapse of the Soviet Union in 1991 were also major factors that led to the resolution of the conflict (Morada, 2008).
5. Herman Van Rompuy is the former President of the European Council.

6 The EU, ASEAN and Political Norms

1. This aim is mentioned in official EU documents such as *Europe and Asia: A Strategic Framework for Enhanced Partnerships* (European Commission, 2001) and *A New Partnership with South-East Asia* (European Commission, 2003).
2. Myanmar has been chosen as a specific example in this chapter as it has been the ASEAN member state with the greatest need to improve its human rights conditions.
3. In 1950, the European Convention on Human Rights established a commission for the examination of applications from states or individuals, a European Court of Human Rights (ECHR) and a Committee of Ministers of the Council of Europe which 'acted as guardians of the ECHR' (Europa, 2013e). In 1998, these bodies were replaced by the ECHR.
4. Proposals to promote human rights under the VAP (Vientiane Action Plan) included establishing 'a network among existing human rights mechanisms', promoting 'education and public awareness on human rights', an 'elaboration of an ASEAN instrument on the protection and promotion of the rights of migrant workers' and the 'establishment of an ASEAN commission on the promotion and protection of the rights of women and children' (ASEAN, 2004: 29–30).
5. Namely member states with more established civil society organisations (CSOs).
6. The establishment of the ACWC complemented the signing of the UN Convention on the Elimination of All Forms of Discrimination against Women (1979) and the UN Convention on the Rights of the Child (1989) by all ASEAN member states.
7. The SPDC (State Peace and Development Council) is the military junta which seized power of Myanmar in 1988.
8. Common Position (2003/297/CFSP) (Council of the EU, 2003a) and Council Decision (2003/461/CFSP) (Council of the EU, 2003b).
9. Common Position (2004/423/CFSP) (Council of the EU, 2004).
10. Common Position (2006/318/CFSP) (Council of the EU, 2006) and Common Position (2009/615/CFSP) (Council of the EU, 2009). However, as explained in the following section in more detail, these developments did not restrict the EU from continuing and increasing its economic relations with ASEAN. The initiation of negotiations for an EU-ASEAN FTA in 2007 is one such example.

11. Preconditions included the requirement of ASEAN regulations to converge with EU regulations, and the successful completion of a new WTO round, as the EU preferred to bargain in the WTO rather than bilaterally (Robles, 2008).
12. The decision by ASEAN member states to sign FTAs with Japan has been attributed to the inflexibility of the EU in WTO negotiations and its reluctance to consider the demands and concerns of ASEAN member states in the WTO forum (Robles, 2008).

References

Acharya, A. (2004) 'How Ideas Spread: Whose Norms Matter? Norm Localisation and Institutional Change in Asian Regionalism'. *International Organisation,* Vol. 58, No. 2, pp. 239–275.

Acharya, A. (2005) *Why is there no NATO in Asia?: the Normative Origins of Asian Multilateralism.* Weatherhead Center for International Affairs, Harvard University.

Acharya, A. (2009) 'Arguing about ASEAN: What Do We Disagree about?'. *Cambridge Review of International Affairs,* Vol. 22, No. 3, pp. 493–499.

Acharya, A. (2011a) 'Norm Subsidiarity and Regional Orders: Sovereignty, Regionalism, and Rule-Making in the Third World'. *International Studies Quarterly,* Vol. 55, pp. 95–123.

Acharya, A. (2011b) 'Dialogue and Discovery: In Search of International Relations Theories beyond the West'. *Millennium,* Vol. 39, No. 3, pp. 619–637.

Acharya, A. and Buzan, B. (2007) 'Why Is There No Non-Western International Relations Theory?'. *International Relations of the Asia Pacific,* Vol. 7, No. 3, pp. 267–312.

Acharya, A. and Tan, S. S. (2006) 'Betwixt Balance and Community: America, ASEAN and the Security of Southeast Asia'. *International Relations of the Asia Pacific,* Vol. 6, No. 1, pp. 37–59.

Acheson, D. (1949) *Telegram from Dean Acheson to the US Embassy in Paris.* Washington, 19 October. Available at: <http://www.cvce.eu/obj/telegram_from_dean_acheson_to_the_us_embassy_in_paris_washington_19_october_1949-en-ef456d4c-b0cc-4a98-a496-586b8ccb19b5.html>.

Aggestam, L. (2008) 'Introduction: Ethical Power Europe?'. *International Affairs,* Vol. 81, No. 1, pp. 1–11.

Alecu de Fleurs, N. (2010). 'EU-ASEAN Relations: The Importance of Values, Norms and Culture'. *Working Paper No. 1.* June (Singapore: EU Centre).

Allen, D. and Smith, M. (1990) 'Western Europe's Presence in the Contemporary International Arena'. *Review of International Studies,* Vol. 16, No. 1, pp. 19–37.

Allen, D. and Smith, M. (1991) 'Western Europe's Presence in the Contemporary International Arena'. In Holland, M. (ed.) *The Future of European Political Cooperation* (New York: St Martin's Press).

Andreosso-O'Callaghan, B. and Nicolas, F. (2007) 'Are the Economies of ASEAN and the EU Complementary?'. *ASEAN Economic Bulletin,* Vol. 24, No. 2, pp. 205–224.

Andreosso-O'Callaghan, B. and Nicolas, F. (2008) 'What Scope for an EU-ASEAN Free Trade Agreement'. *Journal of World Trade,* Vol. 42, No. 1, pp. 105–128.

APRIS II. (2012a) *Towards a Single ASEAN Cosmetics Market: APRIS II and the ACD.*

APRIS II. (2012b) *APRIS II Helps ASEAN Member States Reap AFTA Benefits through ROO Self Certification Scheme.*

APRIS II. (2012c) *Harmonising Customs Clearance Procedures: The ASEAN Customs Declaration Document.*

APRIS II. (2012d) *A Modern Regional Transit System: ASEAN Customs Transit System (ACTS) to Ensure AEC Trade Facilitation.*
APRIS II. (2012e) *Managing Trade Rules Via the Enhanced ASEAN Dispute Settlement Mechanism.*
APRIS II. (2012f) *Promoting Mutual Understanding through Enhanced Dialogue: APRIS Support for TREATI and READI.*
ASEAN. (1967) *ASEAN Bangkok Declaration.*
ASEAN. (1971) *Kuala Lumpur Declaration on the Zone of Peace, Freedom and Neutrality.*
ASEAN. (1976) *Treaty of Amity and Cooperation.*
ASEAN. (1997) *ASEAN Vision 2020.*
ASEAN. (1998) *Ha Noi Plan of Action.*
ASEAN. (2003) *Bali Concord II.*
ASEAN. (2004) *Vientiane Action Plan.*
ASEAN. (2005) *Kuala Lumpur Declaration on the Establishment of the ASEAN Charter.*
ASEAN. (2007a) *ASEAN Economic Community Blueprint.*
ASEAN. (2007b) *ASEAN Consultation to Solve Trade and Investment Issues Factsheet.* 13 April.
ASEAN. (2008) *The ASEAN Charter.*
ASEAN. (2009a) *Terms of Reference of the AICHR.*
ASEAN. (2009b) ASEAN Chairman's Statement on Myanmar. *Ministry of Foreign Affairs of Thailand.* Bangkok, 18 May. Available at: <http://euro-burma.eu/doc/ASEAN%20Chairmans%20Statement%20on%20Myanmar%20-%2018.05.09.pdf>.
ASEAN. (2010a) 'Bridging Markets, Connecting Peoples'. *ASEAN Annual Report 2009–2010.*
ASEAN. (2010b) 'EU Reaffirms Support to ASEAN'. Press Statement, 12 July.
ASEAN. (2012a) *ASEAN Annual Report 2011–2012.*
ASEAN. (2012b) *ASEAN Economic Community Scorecard.*
ASEAN. (2012c) *Roadmap for the ASEAN Community (2009–2015).*
ASEAN. (2013a) *ASEAN-German Cooperation in Narrowing the Development Gap: Towards a Strategic Alliance.* Available at: <http://www.asean.org/news/asean-secretariat-news/item/asean-german-cooperation-in-narrowing-the-development-gap-towards-a-strategic-alliance>.
ASEAN. (2013b) *Protocol Governing the Implementation of the ASEAN Harmonised Tariff Nomenclature.* Available at: <http://www.asean.org/resources/document-archives/item/protocol-governing-the-implementation-of-the-asean-harmonised-tariff-nomenclature>.
ASEAN. (2013c) *ASEAN Framework Agreement for the Integration of Priority Sectors.* Available at: <http://www.asean.org/news/item/asean-framework-agreement-for-the-integration-of-priority-sectors-vientiane-29th-november-2004>.
ASEAN. (2013d) *Joint Statement of the Twelfth AEM EU Trade Commissioner Consultations.* Available at: <http://www.asean.org/news/asean-statement-communiques/item/joint-media-statement-of-the-twelfth-aem-eu-trade-commissioner-consultations>.
ASEAN. (2013e) *Inaugural Speech by HE Le Luong Minh Secretary-General of ASEAN at the Transfer Office Ceremony.* Available at: <http://www.asean.org/news/

item/inaugural-speech-by-he-le-luong-minh-secretary-general-of-asean-at-the-transfer-of-office-ceremony-2>.

ASEAN. (2013f) *Welcome Remarks by Surin Pitsuwan, Secretary-General of ASEAN, at the Workshop on Benchmarking an Monitoring Progress of the ASEAN Economic Community.* Available at: <http://www.asean.org/resources/2012-02-10-08-47-56/speeches-statements-of-the-former-secretaries-general-of-asean/item/welcome-remarks-by-dr-surin-pitsuwan-secretary-general-of-asean-at-the-workshop-on-benchmarking-and-monitoring-progress-of-the-asean-economic-community?category_id=51>.

ASEAN. (2013g) *Foreign Direct Investments.* Available at: <http://www.asean.org/news/item/foreign-direct-investment-statistics>.

ASEAN. (2013h) *20th ASEAN-EU JCC Meeting Convenes in Jakarta.* Available at: <http://www.asean.org/news/asean-secretariat-news/item/20th-asean-eu-joint-cooperation-committee-jcc-meeting-convenes-in-jakarta>.

ASEAN. (2013i) *ASEAN Commission on the Promotion and Protection of the Rights of Women and children (ACWC) concludes successful visit to the EU.* Available at: <http://www.asean.org/news/asean-secretariat-news/item/asean-commission-on-the-promotion-and-protection-of-the-rights-of-women-and-children-acwc-concludes-successful-visit-to-the-eu>.

ASEAN Eminent Persons Group (EPG). (2006) *Eminent Persons Group Report on the ASEAN Charter.*

ASEAN-EU. (1980) *Cooperation Agreement between the Member Countries of ASEAN and the European Community.*7 March. Available at: <http://www.asean.org/news/item/external-relations-european-union-nuremberg-declaration-on-an-eu-asean-enhanced-partnership-nuremberg-germany-15-march-2007>.

ASEAN-EU. (2007a) *Nuremberg Declaration of an ASEAN-EU Enhanced Partnership* (2007–2012).

ASEAN-EU. (2007b) *Plan of Action to Implement the Nuremberg Declaration on an EU-ASEAN Enhanced Partnership.*

ASEAN-EU. (2009) *Phnom Penh Agenda for the Implementation of the ASEAN-EU Plan of Action (2009–2010).*

ASEAN-EU. (2012a) *Bandar Seri Begawan Plan of Action to Strengthen the EU-ASEAN Enhanced Partnership (2013–2017).* Available at: <http://www.consilium.europa.eu/uedocs/cms_Data/docs/pressdata/EN/foraff/129884.pdf>.

ASEAN-EU. (2012b) *Co-Chair's Statement of the 19th ASEAN-EU Ministerial Meeting.*

ASEAN Finance Ministers. (1998) *Terms of Understanding on the Establishment of the Surveillance Process.* Available at: < http://www.aseansec.org/739.htm>.

ASEAN Ministerial Meeting (AMM). (1993) *Joint Communiqué of the 26th AMM on the Declaration of Human Rights and Programme of Action.*

ASEAN National Human Rights Commissions (NHRC). (2007) *Declaration of Cooperation.*

ASEAN +3 Finance Ministers (APT). (2000) *Joint Ministerial Statement of the ASEAN +3 Finance Ministers Meeting.* 6 May. Available at: <http://www.mof.go.jp/english/international_policy/convention/asean_plus_3/20000506.htm>.

ASEAN +3 Macroeconomic Research Office (AMRO). (2013) *AMRO Website.* Available at: < http://www.amro-asia.org/>.

Ashton, C. (2012a) *Remarks by the European Union High Representative for Foreign Affairs and Security Policy, Catherine Ashton, at the opening of the EU-ASEAN*

Post-Ministerial Conference. Phnom Penh, 11 July. Available at: <http://www.eu-un.europa.eu/articles/en/article_12412_en.htm>.

Ashton, C. (2012b) *Statement at the Adoption of the ASEAN Human Rights Declaration*. Available at: <http://www.consilium.europa.eu/uedocs/cms_Data/docs/pressdata/EN/foraff/133682.pdf>.

Ashton, C. (2012c) 'ASEAN and the EU: An Expanding Partnership with Global Reach'. *The Jakarta Post*. 26 April.

Asia Europe Foundation (ASEF). (2013) *ASEF Website*. Available at: <www.asef.org>.

Asia Europe Meeting (ASEM). (2013) *ASEM Website*. Available at: <www.aseminfoboard.org>.

Asian Ministers. (1993) *Bangkok Declaration on Human Rights: Final Declaration of the Regional Meeting for Asia of the World Conference on Human Rights*.

Balassa, B. (1967) *Studies in Trade Liberalisation*. (Maryland: The John Hopkins Press).

Barnett, M. and Finnemore, M. (2004) *Rules for the World: International Organisations in Global Politics*. (Ithaca, Cornell University Press).

Barroso, J. M. (2007) 'Europe and the Challenges of Globalisation'. *St Anthony's College Lecture*. Oxford, 11 October. Available at: < http://europa.eu/rapid/press-release_SPEECH-07-620_en.htm>.

Barroso, J. M. (2012a) *Statement by José Manuel Barroso, President of the European Commission, at the Press Conference following the 9th ASEM Summit*. 6 November, Vientiane. Available at: <http://www.eu-un.europa.eu/articles/en/article_12806_en.htm>.

Barroso, J. M. (2012b) *State of the Union 2012 Address Plenary Session of the European Parliament*. 12 September. Available at: <http://europa.eu/rapid/press-release_SPEECH-12-596_en.htm>.

Beeson, M. (2004) *Contemporary Southeast Asia: Regional Dynamics, National Differences*. (New York: Palgrave Macmillan).

Beeson, M. (2009) 'ASEAN's Ways: Still Fit for Purpose?'. *Cambridge Review of International Affairs*, Vol. 22, No. 3, pp. 333–343.

Bendiek, A. and Kramer, H. (2010) 'The EU as a 'Strategic' International Actor: Substantial and Analytical Ambiguities'. *European Foreign Affairs Review*, Vol. 15, pp. 453–474.

Bersick, S. (2010) 'Perceptions of Asia in Europe'. *Asia Europe Journal*, Vol. 8, pp. 245–255.

Bersick, S. and Pasch, P. (2007) 'Germany in International Relations: Aims, Instruments and Prospects'. *Compass 2020*, Friedrich Ebert Stiftung.

Bicci, F. (2006) "Our Size Fits All': Normative Power Europe and the Mediterranean'. *Journal of European Public Policy*, Vol. 13, No. 2, pp. 286–303.

Blankert, J. W. (2010) *Report on the Visit of ASEAN Committee of Permanent Representatives (CPR) to Brussels and Berlin, 5–9 July, 2010*.

Bloomberg. (2013) 'EU, Singapore Trade Tax-Free Oil Deal May Start End 2014'. January 31.

Borrás, S. (2009) 'The Politics of the Lisbon Strategy: The Changing Role of the Commission'. *West Politics*, Vol. 32, No. 1, pp. 97–118.

Borrás, S. and Peters, G. (2011) 'The Lisbon Strategy's Empowerment of Core Executives: Centralizing and Politicizing EU National Co-Ordination'. *Journal of European Public Policy*, Vol. 18, No. 4, pp. 525–545.

Borrás, S. and Radaelli, C. (2011) 'The Politics of Governance Architectures: Creation, Change and Effects of the Lisbon Treaty'. *Journal of European Public Policy*, Vol. 18, No. 4, pp. 463–484.

Boulding, K. (1989) *Three Faces of Power* (London: Sage).

British Broadcasting Cooperation. (2013) 'Italy election: Results point to impasse'. 25 February. Available at: <http://www.bbc.co.uk/news/world-europe-21574116>.

Browne, J. (2012) 'The UK in Southeast Asia'. *Speech to the Office of the Council of Minister in Phnom Penh*. 3 July.

Bull, H. (1982) 'Civilian Power Europe: A Contradiction in Terms?'. *Journal of Common Market Studies*, Vol. 21, No. 1–2.

Buller, J. and Gamble, A. (2002) 'Conceptualising Europeanisation'. *Public Policy and Administration*, Vol. 17, No. 4, pp. 4–24.

Buzek, J. (2011) 'State of the Union: Three Cheers for the Lisbon Treaty and Two Warnings for Political Parties'. *Journal of Common Market Studies*, Vol. 49, pp. 7–18.

Börzel, T. and Risse, T. (2012) 'When Europeanisation Meets Diffusion: Exploring New Territory'. *West European Politics*, Vol. 35, No. 1, pp. 192–207.

Caballero-Anthony, M. and Haywood, H. (2011) 'Defining ASEAN's Role in Peace Operations: Helping to Bring Peacebuilding 'Upstream'?'. *Civil-Military Working Papers 3/2010*. (Canberra: Australian Government, Asia-Pacific Civil-Military Centre of Excellence).

Cameron, F. (2007) *An Introduction to European Foreign Policy*. (New York: Routledge).

Camroux, D. (2010) 'Interregionalism or Merely a Fourth-Level Game? An Examination of the EU-ASEAN Relationship'. *East Asia*, Vol. 27, pp. 57–77.

Camroux, D. (2012) 'Commentary on Arif Havis Oegroseno's article: And there are other ways, too, the EU must raise its game'. *Europe's World Website*. Autumn. Available at: <http://www.europesworld.org/NewEnglish/Home_old/Article/tabid/191/ArticleType/ArticleView/ArticleID/22050/language/en-US/Default.aspx>.

Carolan, B. (2008) 'The Birth of the European Union: US and UK Roles in the Creation of a Unified European Community'. *Tulsa Journal of Comparative and International Law*, Vol. 16, No. 1, pp. 51–65.

Center for Strategic and International Studies. (2007) *CSIS Commission on Smart Power: A Smarter, More Secure America*. (Washington: CSIS Commission on Smart Power).

Chaban, N., Elgström, O. and Holland, M. (2006) 'The European Union As Others See It'. *European Foreign Affairs Review*, Vol. 11, pp. 245–262.

Chaban, N. and Holland, M. (2008) (eds) *The European Union and the Asia-Pacific: Media, Public and Elite Perceptions of the EU*. (Singapore: Asia-Europe Foundation).

Chaban, N. and Holland, M. (2010) 'The EU in the Eyes of Asia: Motivation and Methodology'. *Asia Europe Journal*, Vol. 8, pp. 127–131.

Chia, S. Y. (2011) 'Association of Southeast Asian Nations and Economic Integration: Development and Challenges'. *Asian Economic Policy Review*, Vol. 6, pp. 43–63.

Christiansen, T., Kirchner, E. and Murray, P. (2013) (eds) *The Palgrave Handbook of EU-Asia Relations*. (Basingstoke: Palgrave Macmillan).

Cini, M. and Borrogán, N. (2010) (eds) *European Union Politics*. (Oxford: Oxford University Press).

Ciorciari, J. (2012) 'Institutionalising Human Rights in Southeast Asia'. *Human Rights Quarterly,* Vol. 34, pp. 695–725.

Cook, A. (2010) 'Positions of Responsibility: A Comparison of ASEAN and EU Approaches towards Myanmar'. *International Politics,* Vol. 47, No. 3/4.

Cosgrove, C. and Twitchett, K. (1970) *The New International Actors: The United Nations and the European Economic Community.* (Michigan: Macmillan).

Council of the European Union. (2003a) Common Position on Burma/Myanmar. Common position 2003/297/CFSP.

Council of the European Union. (2003b) Implementing Common Position 2003/297/CFSP on Burma/Myanmar. Decision 2003/461/CFSP.

Council of the European Union. (2004) *Renewing Restrictive Measures on Burma/ Myanmar.* Common position 2004/423/CFSP.

Council of the European Union. (2006) *Renewing Restrictive Measures against Burma/Myanmar.* Common position 2006/318/CFSP.

Council of the European Union. (2007) *East Asia Policy Guidelines.*

Council of the European Union. (2009) *Notice for the Attention of the Persons and Entities Added to the Lists Provided for in Articles 11 and 15 of Council Regulation (EC) No 194/2008 Renewing and Strengthening the Restrictive Measures in Respect of Burma/Myanmar, by virtue of Commission Regulation (EC) No 747/2009.* Common position 2009/615/CFSP.

Council of the European Union. (2010) *18th ASEAN-EU Ministerial Meeting Co-Chair's Statement.* Madrid, 26 May 2010.

Council of the European Union. (2012a) *Guidelines on the EU's Foreign and Security Policy in East Asia.*

Council of the European Union. (2012b) *Joint Press Release: 19th ASEAN-EU Ministerial Meeting, Bandar Seri Begawan, 26–27 April 2012, 35 Years of Friendship and Cooperation.*

Council of the European Union. (2012c) EU Strategic Framework and Action Plan for Human Rights and Democracy. 11855/12.

Council of the European Union. (2012d) *Burma/Myanmar: EU Sanctions Suspended.* 9626/12. 14 May.

Damro, C. (2012) 'Market Power Europe'. *Journal of European Public Policy,* Vol. 19, No. 5, pp. 682–699.

Davies, M. (2012) 'The Perils of Incoherence: ASEAN, Myanmar and the Avoidable Failures of Human Rights Socialization?'. *Contemporary Southeast Asia,* Vol. 34, No. 1, pp. 1–22.

De Gucht, K. (2012a) 'EU-ASEAN Trade and Investment'. *Speech at the 2nd EU-ASEAN Business Summit.* Phnom Penh, 1 April.

De Gucht, K. (2012b) 'Statement on the EU-Singapore FTA'. In European Commission. *EU and Singapore Agree on Landmark Trade Deal.* Press Release, 16 December.

De Gucht, K. (2012c) 'EU-ASEAN: An Efficient Machine for the Next 45 Years'. *Speech at the Friends of Europe Policy Summit: ASEAN at 45: Regional Hopes, Global Clout.* 19 June.

Delegation of the European Union to Indonesia and Brunei Darussalam. (2011) *List of Projects.* Available at: <http://eeas.europa.eu/delegations/indonesia/projects/list_of_projects/projects_en.htm>.

Delegation of the European Union to Singapore. (2010) *EU-Singapore Trade and Investment 2010*. (Singapore: EU).
Dent, C. (2004) 'The Asia-Europe Meeting and Inter-Regionalism: Toward a Theory of Multilateral Utility'. *Asian Survey*, Vol. 44, No. 2, pp. 213–236.
Denzin, N. (1978) *The Research Act: A Theoretical Introduction to Sociological Methods 2e*. (New York: McGraw Hill).
DeRosa, D. (1995) 'Regional Trading Arrangements among Developing Countries: The ASEAN Example'. *Research Report 103*. (Washington: International Food Policy Research Institute).
Deutsche Welle. (2013) *Italian Election Leaves only Uncertainty*. 26 February. Available at: <http://www.dw.de/italian-election-leaves-only-uncertainty/a-16628165>.
Devex. (2012) *ARISE Job Position*. Available at: <http://www.devex.com/en/jobs/key-expert-5-institutional-strengthening-specialist-intermittent-part-time-project-ta-for-the-asean-regional-integration-support-by-the-european-union>.
Diez, T. (2005) 'Constructing the Self and Changing Others: Reconsidering "Normative Power Europe"'. *Millennium-Journal of International Studies*, Vol. 33, pp. 613–636.
Dimier, V. (2006) 'Constructing Conditionality: The Bureaucratization of EC Development Aid'. *European Foreign Affairs Review*, Vol. 11, pp. 263–280.
Dinan, D. (2010) 'Institutions and Governance: A New Treaty, a Newly Elected Parliament and a New Commission'. *Journal of Common Market Studies*, Vol. 48, pp. 95–118.
Dinan, D. (2011) 'Governance and Institutions: Implementing the Lisbon Treaty in the Shadow of the Euro Crisis'. *Journal of Common Market Studies*, Vol. 49, pp. 103–121.
Doidge, M. (2007) 'Joined at the Hip: Regionalism and Interregionalism'. *European Integration*, Vol. 29, No. 2, pp. 229–248.
Dooge, J. (1985) *Report of the Ad Hoc Committee for Institutional Affairs to the European Council*. Brussels, 29–30 March. Available at: <http://www.cvce.eu/content/publication/2001/10/19/17c22ae3-480a-4637-ad28-e152d86105b7/publishable_en.pdf>.
Doyle, M. (1983) 'Kant, Liberal Legacies and Foreign Affairs'. Part 1, *Philosophy and Public Affairs*, Vol. 12.
Doyle, M. (1986) 'Liberalism and World Politics'. *The American Political Science Review*, Vol. 80, No. 4, pp. 1151–1169.
Duchêne, F. (1972) 'Europe's Role in World Peace'. In Mayne, R. (ed.) *Europe Tomorrow: Sixteen Europeans Look Ahead*. (London: Fontana).
Eaton, S. and Stubbs, R. (2006) 'Is ASEAN Powerful? Neo-realist versus Constructivist Approaches to Power in Southeast Asia'. *The Pacific Review*, Vol. 19, No. 2, pp. 135–155.
Eisenhardt, K. (1989) 'Building Theories from Case Study Research'. *The Academy of Management Review*, Vol. 14, No. 4, pp. 532–550.
Egreteau, R. (2010) 'Intra-European Bargaining and the "Tower of Babel" EU Approach to the Burmese Conundrum'. *East Asia*, Vol. 27, pp. 15–33.
Eliassen, K. and Arnesen, C. (2007) 'Comparison of European and Southeast Asian Integration'. In Telò, M. (ed.) *European Union and New Regionalism: Regional Actors and Global Governance in a Post-Hegemonic Era*. (Aldershot: Ashgate).
Etzioni, A. (1961) *A Comparative Analysis of Complex Organizations* (Glencoe, Ill: Free Press).

Europa. (2012a) *Treaty of Maastricht on European Union*. Available at: <http://europa.eu/legislation_summaries/institutional_affairs/treaties/treaties_maastricht_en.htm>.

Europa. (2012b) *A Plain Language Guide to Eurojargon*. Available at: <http://europa.eu/abc/eurojargon/index_en.htm>.

Europa. (2012c) *Coreper*. Available at: <http://europa.eu/scadplus/glossary/coreper_en.htm>.

Europa. (2013a) *Countries and Regions, the Association of South East Asian Nations (ASEAN)*. Available at: <http://ec.europa.eu/trade/creating-opportunities/bilateral-relations/regions/asean/>.

Europa. (2013b) *The Single European Act*. Available at: <http://europa.eu/legislation_summaries/institutional_affairs/treaties/treaties_singleact_en.htm>.

Europa. (2013c) *From 6 to 27 Members*. Available at: <http://ec.europa.eu/enlargement/policy/from-6-to-27-members/index_en.htm>.

Europa. (2013d) *Eurojargon*. Available at: < http://europa.eu/abc/eurojargon/>.

Europa. (2013e) *European Convention on Human Rights*. Available at: <http://europa.eu/legislation_summaries/glossary/eu_human_rights_convention_en.htm>.

European Coal and Steel Community (ECSC). (1951) *Treaty Establishing the European Coal and Steel Community, the Treaty of Paris*.

European Commission. (1985) *Completing the Internal Market. White Paper from the Commission to the European Council*, COM (85) 310 Final.

European Commission. (1988) *Europe 1992: The Overall Challenge (Summary of the Cecchini Report)*. Brussels.

European Commission. (1994) *Towards a New Asia Strategy*.

European Commission. (1995) *Free Trade Areas: An Appraisal*.

European Commission. (1997a) *Action Plan for the Single Market: Communication of the Commission to the European Council*, CSE (97) 1 Final.

European Commission. (1997b) *Single Market Scoreboard*.

European Commission. (2001) *Europe and Asia: A Strategic Framework for Enhanced Partnerships*.

European Commission. (2003) *A New Partnership with South-East Asia*.

European Commission. (2009a) *Eurobarometer 71*. Available at: <http://ec.europa.eu/public_opinion/archives/eb/eb71/eb71_std_part1.pdf>.

European Commission. (2009b) *Eurobarometer 72*. Available at: <72.http://ec.europa.eu/public_opinion/archives/eb/eb72/eb72_first_en.pdf>.

European Commission. (2011a) *Single Market Act*. Brussels.

European Commission. (2011b) *Human Rights and Democracy at the Heart of EU External Action*. Brussels.

European Commission. (2012a) *Simpler Community Legislation*. Available at: <http://ec.europa.eu/internal_market/simplification/index_en.htm#slim>.

European Commission. (2012b) *Stability and Growth Pact*. Available at: <http://ec.europa.eu/economy_finance/economic_governance/sgp/index_en.htm>.

European Commission. (2012c) *Ordinary Legislative Procedure 'Step By Step'*. Available at: <http://ec.europa.eu/codecision/stepbystep/text/index_en.htm>.

European Commission. (2012d) *Delivering the Single Market: State of Play*.

European Commission. (2013) *Memo: The EU-Singapore Free Trade Agreement*. 20 September. Memo 13/805.

European Commission Directorate-General for Trade. (2007) *TREATI-Work Programme and Progress Report*. Brussels, December. Available at: <http://trade.ec.europa.eu/doclib/docs/2007/december/tradoc_137414.pdf>.

European Community. (1986) *The Single European Act.*

European Council. (1973) *Copenhagen Declaration on European Identity.*

European Council. (1984) *Conclusions of the Fontainebleau European Council.*

European Council. (1997) *European Council Meeting Conclusions, Amsterdam, 16–17 June.*

European Council. (2001) *Presidency Conclusions European Council Meeting in Laeken 14 and 15 December 2001.*

European Council. (2008) *Report on the Implementation of the European Security Strategy: Providing Security in a Changing World.*

European Council. (2010) *European Council Conclusions 16 September 2010.*

European Court of Justice (ECJ). (1974) *Procureur du Roi v Benoit and Gustave Dassonville.* Case 8/74. Available at: <http://eurlex.europa.eu/smartapi/cgi/sga_doc?smartapi!celexplus!prod!CELEXnumdoc&lg=en&numdoc=61974J0008>.

European Court of Justice (ECJ). (1979) *Rewe-Zentral AG v Bundesmonopolverwaltung für Branntwein.* Case 120/78. Available at: <http://eurlex.europa.eu/smartapi/cgi/sga_doc?smartapi!celexplus!prod!CELEXnumdoc&lg=en&numdoc=61978J0120>.

European Economic Community (EEC). (1957) *Treaty Establishing the European Union (TEEU), Treaty of Rome.*

European Economic and Social Committee (EESC). (2011) *Opinion on 'The Treaty of Lisbon and the Functioning of the Single Market'* (own-initiative opinion). Official Journal C 044 , 11/02/2011 P. 0068 – 0074.

European External Action Service (EEAS). (2011) *READI Presentation.* Available at: <http://ec.europa.eu/research/iscp/pdf/workshop-june-2011/presentation_antoniou.pdf>.

European Parliament. (1991) Resolution of 22 November. B3-1783/91: PV44II. PE155.084/Ann. In *Official Journal of the European Communities No. C 326/227*: 16 December, 1991.

European Parliament. (2012) *Report on the Annual Report on Human Rights in the World and the European Union's policy on the matter, including implications for the EU's strategic human rights policy* (2011/2185(INI)). Available at: <http://www.europarl.europa.eu/sides/getDoc.do?type=REPORT&reference=A7-2012-0086&language=EN>.

European Parliament. (2013) *Ordinary Legislative Behaviour.* Available at: <http://www.europarl.europa.eu/aboutparliament/en/0080a6d3d8/Ordinary-legislative-procedure.html>.

European Union (EU). (1993) *Treaty of Maastricht, Treaty on European Union (TEU).*

European Union (EU). (1999) *Treaty of Amsterdam.*

European Union (EU). (2003) *Treaty of Nice.*

European Union (EU). (2009) *Treaty of Lisbon Amending the Treaty on European Union and the Treaty Establishing the European Community.*

European Union Institute for Security Studies. (2010) *A Strategy for EU Foreign Policy,* Report No. 7, June.

Farrell, M. (2009) 'EU Policy Towards other Regions: Policy Learning in the External Promotion of Regional Integration'. *Journal of European Public Policy,* Vol. 16, No. 8, pp. 1165–1184.

Fenn, R. (2012) 'Brunei's ASEAN Chairmanship'. Foreign and Commonwealth Office. November 22. Available at: <http://blogs.fco.gov.uk/robfenn/2012/11/22/bruneis-asean-chairmanship/>.

Ferrero-Waldner, B. (2007) 'The European Union and the World: A Hard Look at Soft Power'. New York, 24 September. Available at: <http://www.eu-un.europa.eu/articles/en/article_7330_en.htm>.

Fioretos, O. (2011) 'Historical Institutionalism in International Relations'. *International Organisation,* Vol. 65, No. 2, pp. 367–399.

Forsberg, T. (2011) 'Normative Power Europe, Once Again: A Conceptual Analysis of an Ideal Type'. *Journal of Common Market Studies,* Vol. 49, No. 6, pp. 1183–1204.

Freistein, K. (2005) 'ASEAN After the Bali Summit 2003: From Paralysis to New Life?'. *European Journal of East Asian Studies,* Vol. 4, No.2, pp. 177–202.

Frost, F. (2008) 'ASEAN's Regional Cooperation and Multilateral Relations: Recent Developments and Australia's Interests'. *Research Paper. Department of Parliamentary Services, Parliament of Australia,* No. 12, 2008–9.

Gaens, B., Jokela, J. and Mattlin, M. (2012) 'The EU's Asia: Renegotiating Boundaries, Renegotiating Norms'. *Asia Europe Journal,* Vol. 10, pp. 91–97.

Galtung, J. (1973) *The European Community: A Superpower in the Making*. (London: George Allen & Unwin).

Georgieva, K. (2010) 'The Prospects for Europe-Asia Relations'. *Speech at the ASEM Conference on Europe-Asia Inter-regional Relations*. Brussels, 12 July.

Gilson, J. (2005) 'New Interregionalism? The EU and East Asia'. *European Integration,* Vol. 27, No. 3, pp. 307–326.

Ginbar, Y. (2010) 'Human Rights in ASEAN-Setting Sail or Treading Water?'. *Human Rights Law Review,* Vol. 10, No. 3, pp. 504–518.

Grant, C. (2010) 'The Strategic Consequences of the Euro Crisis'. *Europe's World*. Available at: <http://www.europesworld.org/NewEnglish/Home_old/Article/tabid/191/ArticleType/ArticleView/ArticleID/21728/ThestrategicconsequencesoftheEurocrisis.aspx>.

Grech, L. (2010) 'Delivering a Single Market to Consumers and Citizens'. *P7_TA(2010)0186 European Parliament Resolution of 20 May 2010.*

Groen, L. and Niemann, A. (2012) 'The European Union at the Copenhagen Climate Change Negotiations: A Case of Contested EU Actorness and Effectiveness'. *Mainz Papers on International and European Politics,* Paper No. 1.

Haas, E. (1958) *The Uniting of Europe: Political, Social and Economic Forces, 1950–1957*. (Stanford: Stanford University Press).

Haas, E. (1968) *The Uniting of Europe: Political, Social and Economic Forces, 1950–1957 2e*. (Stanford: Stanford University Press).

Haas, E. (2001) 'Does Constructivism Subsume Neo-functionalism?'. In Christiansen, T., Jørgensen, K. E. and Wiener, A. (eds) *The Social Construction of Europe*. (London: Sage Publications).

Hague, W. (2011) 'Looking East-UK-ASEAN Relations for the 21st Century'. *Oxford Business Group*. December.

Hall, P. A. (1986) *Governing the Economy: The Politics of State Intervention in Britain and France*. (New York: Oxford University Press).

He, K. and Feng, H. (2012) "Why Is There no NATO in Asia?' Revisited: Prospect Theory, Balance of Threat and US Alliance Strategies'. *European Journal of International Relations,* Vol. 18, No. 2, pp. 227–250.

Helmke, B. (2009) 'The Absence of ASEAN: Peacekeeping in Southeast Asia'. *Pacific News,* No. 31, pp. 4–6.

Hemmer, C. and Katzenstein, P. (2002) ''Why Is There no NATO in Asia?' Collective Identity, Regionalism, and the Origins of Multilateralism'. *International Organisation,* Vol. 56, No. 3, pp. 575–607.

Henry, L. (2007) 'The ASEAN Way and Community Integration: Two Different Models of Regionalism'. *Europe Law Journal,* Vol. 13, No. 6, pp. 857–879.

Hettne, B. (2011) 'The European Union as an Emerging Global Actor'. In Wunderlich, J.-U. and Bailey, D. J. (eds) *The European Union and Global Governance: A Handbook* (London: Routledge).

Higgott, R. (2007) 'Alternative Models of Regional Cooperation? The Limits of Regional Institutionalisation in East Asia'. In Telò, M. (ed.) *European Union and New Regionalism: Regional Actors and Global Governance in a Post-Hegemonic Era.* (Aldershot: Ashgate).

Hill, C. (1983) *National Foreign Policies and European Political Cooperation.* (London: Unwin Hyman).

Hill, C. (1990) 'European Foreign Policy: Power Bloc, Civilian Model-or Flop?'. In Reinhardt, R. (ed.) *The Evolution of the International Actor: Western Europe's New Assertiveness.* (Boulder: Westview).

Hobson, J. M. (2004) *The Eastern Origins of Western Civilisation.* (Cambridge: Cambridge University Press).

Hurrell, A. (1995) 'Regionalism in Theoretical Perspective'. In Fawcett, L. and Hurrell, A. (eds) *Regionalism in World Politics.* (Oxford: Oxford University Press).

Hyde-Price, A. (2006) 'Normative Power Europe: A Realist Critique'. *Journal of European Public Policy,* Vol. 13, No. 1, pp. 217–234.

Hyde-Price, A. (2008) 'A "Tragic Actor"? A Realist Perspective on "Ethical Power Europe"'. *International Affairs,* Vol. 84, No. 1, pp. 29–44.

Hänggi, H, Roloff, R. and J. Rüland, J. (eds) (2006) *Interregionalism and International Relations.* (London: Routledge).

Interview Respondent 1, Former Secretary General of ASEAN. (2011) (I1 AO) *In-depth Personal Interview.*

Interview Respondent 2, A Deputy Secretary General of ASEAN. (2011) (I2 AO) *In-depth Personal Interview.*

Interview Respondent 3, Academic in the Southeast Asian region. (2011) (I3 AA) *In-depth Personal Interview.*

Interview Respondent 4, Official at the EEAS in Brussels. (2011) (I4 EO) *In-depth Personal Interview.*

Interview Respondent 5, EU Academic within the EU. (2011) (I5 EA) *In-depth Personal Interview.*

Interview Respondent 6, Official at the EEAS in Brussels. (2011) (I6 EO) *In-depth Personal Interview.*

Interview Respondent 7, Official at the EEAS in Brussels. (2011) (I7 EO) *In-depth Personal Interview.*

Interview Respondent 8, EU delegation official in Southeast Asia. (2011) (I8 EOA) *In-depth Personal Interview.*

Interview Respondent 9, Official at the EEAS in Brussels. (2011) (I9 EO) *In-depth Personal Interview.*

Interview Respondent 10, EU delegation official in Southeast Asia. (2011) (I10 EOA) *In-depth Personal Interview.*

Interview Respondent 11, Official at the EEAS in Brussels. (2011) (I11 EO) *In-depth Personal Interview.*

Islam, S. (2010) 'A Fresh Start for ASEM or How to Revive Asia-Europe Relations'. Available at: <http://1226.fedimbo.belgium.be/sites/1226.fedimbo.belgium.be/files/vca_10_-_asem_a_fresh_start_for_asem_or_how_to_revive_asia-europe_relations.pdf>.

Islam, S. (2011) 'Time for a New EU-ASEAN Strategy'. *Friends of Europe Website.* 12 April. Available at: <http://www.friendsofeurope.org/Contentnavigation/Library/Libraryoverview/tabid/1186/articleType/ArticleView/articleId/2383/Time-for-a-new-EUASEAN-strategy.aspx>.

Jenkins, C. (2012) 'The Euro: A Message of Solidarity'. *OECD Observer,* No. 234. Available at: <http://www.oecdobserver.org/news/fullstory.php/aid/3884/The_euro:_A_message_of_solidarity.html>.

Jetschke, A. and Lenz, T. (2013) 'Does Regionalism Diffuse? A New Research Agenda for the Study of Regional Organisations'. *Journal of Public Policy,* Vol. 20, No. 4, pp. 626–637.

Jetschke, A. and Murray, P. (2012) 'Diffusing Regional Integration: The EU and Southeast Asia'. *West European Politics,* Vol. 35, No. 1, pp. 174–191.

Jetschke, A. and Portela, P. (2013) 'ASEAN-EU Relations: From Regional Integration Assistance to Security Significance?'. *German Institute of Global and Area Studies Focus,* No. 3.

Jokela, J. and Gaens, B. (2012) 'Interregional Relations and Legitimacy in Global Governance: The EU in ASEM'. *Asia Europe Journal,* Vol. 10, pp. 145–164.

Jupille, J. and Caporaso, J. (1998) 'States, Agency, and Rules: The European Union in Global Environmental Politics' in Rhodes, C. (ed.) *The European Union in the World Community.* (Boulder: Lynne Rienner Publishers).

Kelsall, M. S. (2009) 'The New ASEAN Intergovernmental Commission on Human Rights: Toothless Tiger or Tentative First Step?'. *East West Center,* No. 90.

King, T. (1999) 'Human Rights in European Foreign Policy: Success or Failure for Post-Modern Diplomacy?'. *European Journal of International Law,* Vol. 10, No. 2, pp. 313–337.

Kingsbury, D. (2005) *South-East Asia: A Political Profile.* (Melbourne: Oxford University Press).

Krasner, S. D. (1983) *International Regimes.* (Ithaca: Cornell University Press).

Lambrinidis, S. (2012) *Intervention at the European Parliament.* 3 September. Available at: <http://www.eu-un.europa.eu/articles/es/article_12548_es.htm>.

Landell-Mills. (2013) *Technical Assistance to Regional EU-ASEAN Dialogue Instrument (READI) Facility.* Available at: <http://www.landell-mills.com/experience/experience.asp?article=548>.

Langan, M. (2012) 'Normative Power Europe and the Moral Economy of Africa-EU Ties: A Conceptual Reorientation of "Normative Power"'. *New Political Economy,* Vol. 17, No. 3, pp. 243–270.

Langen, W. (2011) 'Speech by the Head of the European Parliament Observer Delegation, Mr Werner Langen, Chairman of the European Parliament's Delegation for Relations with ASEAN'. The ASEAN Inter-Parliamentary Assembly (AIPA) 32nd General Assembly. Available at: <http://www.aipasecretariat.org/wp-content/uploads/2011/10/Statement-of-EU.pdf>.

Leftwich, A. (1993) 'Governance, Democracy and Development in the Third World'. *Third World Quarterly,* Vol. 14, No. 3, pp. 605–624.

Lewis, J. (2000) 'The Methods of Community in EU Decision-Making and Administrative Rivalry in the Council's Infrastructure'. *Journal of European Public Policy,* Vol. 7, No. 2, pp. 261–289.

Longo, M. and Murray, P. (2011) 'No Ode to Joy? Reflections on the European Union's Legitimacy'. *International Politics,* Vol. 48, No. 6, pp. 667–690.

Lucarelli, S. (2007) 'The European Union in the Eyes of Others: Towards Filling the Gap in the Literature'. *European Foreign Affairs Review,* Vol. 12, pp. 249–270.

Lun, J. and Rogers, D. (2013) *Southeast Asia: an update.* (London: House of Commons Library).

Manners, I. (2002) 'Normative Power Europe: A Contradiction in Terms?'. *Journal of Common Market Studies,* Vol. 40, No. 2, pp. 235–258.

Manners, I. (2006a) 'Normative Power Europe Reconsidered: Beyond the Crossroads'. *Journal of European Public Policy,* Vol. 13, No. 2, pp. 182–199.

Manners, I. (2006b) 'The European Union as a Normative Power: A Response to Thomas Diez'. *Millennium-Journal of International Studies,* Vol. 35, pp. 167–180.

Manners, I. (2008) 'The Normative Ethics of the European Union'. *International Affairs,* Vol. 84, No. 1, pp. 45–60.

Manners, I. (2013) 'Assessing the Decennial, Reassessing the Global: Understanding European Union Normative Power in Global Politics'. *Cooperation and Conflict,* Vol. 48, No. 2, pp. 304–329.

March, J. and Olsen, J. (1998) *Rediscovering Institutions: The Organisation Basis of Politics.* (New York: Free Press).

Marshall, C. and Rossman, G. (1995) *Designing Qualitative Research 2e.* (California: Sage Publications).

Martin, D. (2009) 'Toes in the Water: the 'makability' of ASEAN and European Commission support to economic integration in Southeast Asia under the ASEAN-EU Programme for Regional Integration Support (APRIS)', in De Lombaerde, P. and Schulz, M. (eds) *The EU and World Regionalism: The Makability of Regions in the 21st Century.* (London: Ashgate).

Mayer, H. (2008) 'Is It Still Called "Chinese Whispers"? The EU's Rhetoric and Action as a Responsible Global Institution'. *International Affairs,* Vol. 84, No. 1, pp. 61–79.

McCarthy, S. (2009) 'Chartering a New Direction? Burma and the Evolution of Human Rights in ASEAN'. *Asian Affairs,* Vol. 36, No. 3, pp. 157–175.

Merlingen, M. (2007) 'Everything Is Dangerous: A Critique of "Normative Power Europe"'. *Security Dialogue,* Vol. 38, No. 4, pp. 435–452.

Meunier, S. and Nicolaïdis, K. (2006) 'The European Union as a Conflicted Trade Power'. *Journal of European Public Policy,* Vol. 13, No. 6, pp. 906–925.

Miller, J. L. (2011) 'A New "Democratic Life" for the European Union? Administrative Lawmaking, Democratic Legitimacy, and the Lisbon Treaty'. *Contemporary Politics,* Vol. 17, No. 3, pp. 321–334.

Monti. M. (2010) 'A New Strategy for the Single Market: At the Service of Europe's Economy and Society'. Available at: <http://ec.europa.eu/bepa/pdf/monti_report_final_10_05_2010_en.pdf>.

Morada, N. M. (2008) 'ASEAN at 40: Prospects for Community Building in Southeast Asia'. *Asia-Pacific Review,* Vol. 15, No. 1, pp. 36–55.

Moravcsik, A. (2009) 'Europe: The Quiet Superpower'. *French Politics,* Vol. 7, pp. 403–422.

Moravcsik, A. (2012) 'Europe after the Crisis: How to Sustain a Common Currency'. *Foreign Affairs,* Vol. 9, No. 3, pp. 54–68.

Murray, P. (2008) 'Europe and Asia: Two Regions in Flux?', in Murray, P. (ed.) *Europe and Asia: Regions in Flux.* (Basingstoke: Palgrave Macmillan).

Murray, P. (2009) 'A Clash of Interests? Europe's Quest for an Integrated Approach to East Asia'. In European Commission. *A Europe of Achievements in a Changing World: Visions of Leading Policymakers and Academics/L'europe des realisations dans un monde en mutation: La Vision des leader Politiques et academiques, European Commission, Directorate General Education and Culture.* (Brussels, pp. 214–236).

Murray, P. (2010) *Asia and Integration Theory*. Paper for Jean Monnet Workshop on Comparing the European Union with other Regional Organisations, United Nations University - Comparative Regional Integration Studies (UNU-CRIS), Bruges, 11–12 January 2010.

Murray, P., Berryman, A. and Matera, M. (2008) 'Coherence, Effectiveness and Recognition in EU-East Asia Relations'. Paper presented at EU-Asia Relations: A Policy Review Workshop, jointly hosted by the Contemporary Europe Research Centre, the University of Melbourne, and the European Institute of Asian Studies. Brussels, 10 July.

Murray, P. and Moxon-Browne, E. (2013) 'The European Union as a Template for Regional Integration? The Case of ASEAN and Its Committee of Permanent Representatives'. *Journal Common Market Studies,* Vol. 51, No. 3, pp. 522–537.

Murray, P. and Rich, B. (1996) *Visions of European Unity.* (Boulder: Westview Press).

Nair, D. (2011) 'ASEAN's Core Norms in the Context of the Global Financial Crisis'. *Asian Survey,* Vol. 51, No. 2, pp. 245–267.

Niemann, A. and Bretherton, C. (2013) 'EU External Policy at the Crossroads: The Challenge of Actorness and Effectiveness'. *International Relations,* Vol. 27, pp. 261–275.

Nicolaïdis, K. and Howse, R. (2002) ''This is my EUtopia…': Narrative as Power'. *Journal of Common Market Studies,* Vol. 40, No. 4, pp. 767–792.

Nye, J. S. (2009a) 'The U.S. Can Reclaim "Smart Power"'. *The LA Times*. Los Angeles.

Nye, J. S. (2009b) 'Get Smart'. *Foreign Affairs,* Vol. 88, No. 4, pp. 160–163.

Nunes, I. F. (2011) 'Civilian, Normative, and Ethical Power Europe: Role Claims and EU Discourses'. *European Foreign Affairs Review,* Vol. 16, pp. 1–20.

Oegroseno, A. H. (2012) 'Europe's Asian awakening still lacks real clout'. *Europe's World Website.* Autumn. Available at: <http://www.europesworld.org/NewEnglish/Home_old/Article/tabid/191/ArticleType/ArticleView/ArticleID/22041/language/en-US/Default.aspx>.

Olsen, J. P. (2007) *Europe in Search of Political Order: An Institutional Perspective on Unity/Diversity, Citizens/Their Helpers, Democratic Design/Historical Drift and the Co-existence of Orders.* (Oxford: Oxford University Press).

Orbie, J. (2006) 'Review Essay: Civilian Power Europe: Review of the Original and Current Debates'. *Cooperation and Conflict: Journal of the Nordic International Studies Association,* Vol. 41, No. 1, pp. 123–128.

O'Sullivan, D. (2013) *Speech at the GRIPS Forum.* Tokyo, 12 February. Available at: <http://www.eeas.europa.eu/asia/docs/20130205_grips_speech_final_en.pdf>.

Particip GmbH. (2009) *Evaluation of EC Co-operation with ASEAN: Evaluation for the European Commission.* Final Report, Volumes 1 and 2.

Patton, M. (2002) *Qualitative Research and Evaluation Methods 3e.* (California: Sage Publications).

Pelinka, A. (2011) 'The European Union as an Alternative to the Nation-State'. *International Journal of Politics, Culture and Society,* Vol. 24, pp. 21–30.

Pitsuwan, S. (2009) 'ASEAN and the Global Financial Crisis: Impact and Implications for Regional Cooperation'. *Harvard Asia Quarterly,* Vol. 12, No. 1, pp. 4–7.

Pitsuwan, S. (2010) *Press Statement at the 18th ASEAN-EU Ministerial Meeting.* Madrid, 26 May.

Poggi, G. (2001) 'Power Forms', in Poggi, G. (ed.) *Forms of Power* (Cambridge: Polity), pp. 15–28.

Poggi, G. (2006) 'Political Power Unmanned: A Defence of the Holy Trinity from Mann's Military Attack', in Hall, J. and Schroeder, R. (eds) *An Anatomy of Power: The Social Theory of Michael Mann* (Cambridge: Cambridge University Press), pp. 135–149.

Pollack, M. (2004) 'The New Institutionalisms and European Integration'. In Wiener, A. and Diez, T. (eds) *European Integration Theory.* (Oxford: Oxford University Press).

Quackenbush, S. and Rudy, M. (2009) 'Evaluating the Monadic Democratic Peace'. *Conflict Management and Peace Science,* Vol. 26, pp. 268–285.

Radaelli, C. M. (2000) *Whither Europeanization? Concept Stretching and Substantive Change,* European Integration Online Papers (EIoP), Vol. 4.

Rehn, O. (2008a) *Speech at the Centre for European Policy Studies Annual Conference 'Europe's Role in the World'.*

Rehn, O. (2008b) 'Europe's Smart Power in its Region and the World'. *Speech at The European Studies Centre, St Anthony's College.* University of Oxford, 1 May.

Reiterer, M. (2006) 'Interregionalism as a New Diplomatic Tool: The EU and East Asia'. *European Foreign Affairs Review,* Vol. 11, pp. 223–243.

Reiterer, M. (2009) 'Asia-Europe Meeting (ASEM): Fostering a Multipolar World Order though Inter-regional Cooperation'. *Asia Europe Journal,* Vol. 7, pp. 179–196.

Reuters. (2013) *EU, Singapore Finalize Details of a Far-reaching Trade Deal.* May 8.

Richardson, H. (2008) 'Smartening the EU's Soft Power'. *Speech at Waseda University.* 16 May, Tokyo.

Rillo, A. (2009) 'ASEAN Economies: Challenges and Responses Amid the Crisis'. *Southeast Asian Affairs,* pp. 17–27.

Robles Jr, A. C. (2008) *The Asia-Europe Meeting: The Theory and Practice of Interregionalism.* (New York: Routledge).

Rosamond, B. (2005) 'Conceptualizing the EU Model of Governance in World Politics'. *European Foreign Affairs Review,* Vol. 10, pp. 463–478.

Rubin, H. J. and Rubin, I. (2005) *Qualitative Research and Evaluation Methods 3e.* (California: Sage Publications).

Rössler, J. (2009) 'Eurasia: Re-emergence of Two World Regions – The Effects of Interregionalism on Regional Integration'. *Asia Europe Journal,* Vol. 7, pp. 313–326.

Rüland, J. (2002) 'The European Union as an Inter- and Transregional Actor: Lessons for Global Governance from Europe's Relations with Asia. The European Union in International Affairs'. National Europe Centre, Australian National University. *National Europe Centre Paper,* No.13.

Rüland, J. (2010) 'ASEAN and the European Union: A Bumpy Interregional Relationship'. *ZEI Discussion Paper* C 95. Bonn: Center for European Integration Studies, Rheinische Friedrich Wilhelms-Universität, Bonn.

Senior Nello, S. (2005) *The European Union: Economics, Policies and History.* (Great Britain: McGraw Hill).

Severino, R. (2006) 'Southeast Asia in Search of an ASEAN Community'. (Singapore: Institute of Southeast Asian Studies).

Severino, R. (2007a) 'ASEAN beyond Forty: Towards Political and Economic Integration'. *Contemporary South East Asia,* Vol. 29, No. 3, pp. 406–423.

Severino, R. (2007b) 'The ASEAN Developmental Divide and the Initiative for ASEAN Integration'. *ASEAN Economic Bulletin,* Vol. 24, No. 1, pp. 35–44.

Simon, S. (2008) 'ASEAN and Multilateralism: The Long, Bumpy Road to Community'. *Contemporary Southeast Asia,* Vol. 30, No. 2, pp. 264–292.

Sjursen, H. (2006a) 'The EU as a "Normative" Power: How Can This Be?'. *Journal of European Public Policy,* Vol. 13, No. 2, pp. 235–251.

Sjursen, H. (2006b) 'What Kind of Power?'. *Journal of European Public Policy,* Vol. 13, No. 2, pp. 169–181.

Sjursen, H. (2011) 'The EU's Common Foreign and Security Policy: The Quest for Democracy'. *Journal of European Public Policy,* Vol. 18, No. 8, pp. 1069–1077.

Sjöstedt, G. (1977) *The External Role of the European Community.* (London: Saxon House).

Smith, K. (2004) *The European Parliament and Human Rights: Norm Entrepreneur or Ineffective Talking Shop?* Dossier El Parlamento Europeo en la Politica Exterior. No 11/2004.

Smith, M. (2011) 'A Liberal Grand Strategy in a Realist World? Power, Purpose and the EU's Changing Global Role'. *Journal of European Public Policy,* Vol. 18, No. 2, pp. 144–163.

Smith, M. (2012) 'Still Rooted in Maastricht: EU External Relations as a "Third-generation Hybrid"'. *Journal of European Integration,* Vol. 34, No. 7, pp. 699–715.

Spaak, P. H. (1956) *Spaak Report.* Available at: <http://www.cvce.eu/content/publication/2007/2/27/4b911a0a-6bd0-4e88-bff9-4c87690aa4e8/publishable_en.pdf>.

Steinmo, S., Thelen, K. and Longstreth, F. (eds) (1992) *Structuring Politics.* (Cambridge: Cambridge University Press).

Stubbs, R. (2008) 'The ASEAN Alternative? Ideas, Institutions and the Challenge to "Global" Governance'. *The Pacific Review,* Vol. 21, No. 4, pp. 451–468.

Survey Respondent 2, Academic in the EU. (2012) (S2 EA) *The Promotion of Regional Integration by the EU to ASEAN Survey.* 12 April.

Survey Respondent 3, Academic in Southeast Asia. (2012) (S3 AA) *The Promotion of Regional Integration by the EU to ASEAN Survey.* 13 April.

Survey Respondent 5, EU delegation official in Southeast Asia. (2012) (S5 EOA) *The Promotion of Regional Integration by the EU to ASEAN Survey.* 14 April.

Survey Respondent 9, Academic in the Oceanic region. (2012) (S9 OA) *The Promotion of Regional Integration by the EU to ASEAN Survey.* 21 April.

Survey Respondent 10, Academic in the EU. (2012) (S10 EA) *The Promotion of Regional Integration by the EU to ASEAN Survey.* 23 April.

Survey Respondent 11, Academic in Southeast Asia. (2012) (S11 AA) *The Promotion of Regional Integration by the EU to ASEAN Survey.* 23 April.

Survey Respondent 13, Official at the EEAS in Brussels. (2012) (S13 EO) *The Promotion of Regional Integration by the EU to ASEAN Survey.* 6 May.

Survey Respondent 16, EU delegation official in Southeast Asia. (2012) (S16 EOA) *The Promotion of Regional Integration by the EU to ASEAN Survey.* 31 May.

Survey Respondent 19, Academic in the EU. (2012) (S19 EA) *The Promotion of Regional Integration by the EU to ASEAN Survey.* 31 May.

Survey Respondent 20, Academic in East Asia. (2012) (S20 EAA) *The Promotion of Regional Integration by the EU to ASEAN Survey*. 31 May.

Survey Respondent 28, Academic in the EU. (2012) (S28 EA) *The Promotion of Regional Integration by the EU to ASEAN Survey*. 15 June.

Survey Respondent 29, Academic in the EU. (2012) (S29 EA) *The Promotion of Regional Integration by the EU to ASEAN Survey*. 19 June.

Survey Respondent 31, Academic in the EU. (2012) (S31 EA) *The Promotion of Regional Integration by the EU to ASEAN Survey*. 23 July.

Söderbaum, F. and Hettne, B. (2005) 'Civilian Power or Soft Imperialism? The EU as a Global Actor and the Role of Interregionalism'. *European Foreign Affairs Review*, Vol. 10, pp. 535–552.

Söderbaum, F., Stålgren P. and Van Langenhove, L. (2005) 'The EU as a Global Actor: A Comparative Analysis'. *European Integration*, Vol. 27, No. 3, pp. 365–380.

Söderbaum, F. (2007) 'African Regionalism and EU-African Interregionalism'. In Telò, M. (ed.) *European Union and New Regionalism: Regional Actors and Global Governance in a Post-Hegemonic Era*. (Aldershot: Ashgate).

Tan, H. (2011) *The ASEAN Intergovernmental Commission on Human Rights: Institutionalising Human Rights in Southeast Asia*. (Cambridge: Cambridge University Press).

Tang, C. (2012) 'Southeast Asian Peace Revisited: A Capitalist Trajectory'. *International Relations of the Asia-Pacific*, Vol. 12, pp. 389–417.

Tarling, N. (2001) *Southeast Asia: A Modern History*. (Melbourne: Oxford University Press).

Tay, S. (2001) 'The Future of ASEAN: An Assessment of Democracy, Economies and Institutions in Southeast Asia'. *Southeast Asia*. Winter, 2001.

Thio, L. (1999) 'Implementing Human Rights in ASEAN Countries: "Promises to Keep and Miles to Go Before I Sleep"'. *Yale Human Rights and Development Law Journal*, Vol. 2, pp. 1–85.

Tonra, B. (2011) 'Democratic Foundations of EU Foreign Policy: Narratives and the Myth of EU Exceptionalism'. *Journal of European Public Policy*, Vol. 18, No. 8, pp. 1190–1207.

Von Hoffmann, N. (2007) 'How Do Asians Evaluate Europe's Strategic Involvement in East Asia?'. *Asia Europe Journal*, Vol. 5, pp. 187–192.

Wah, C. K. (2007) 'Introduction: ASEAN-Facing the Fifth Decade'. *Contemporary Southeast Asia*, Vol. 29, No. 3, pp. 395–405.

Wallace, H. and Young, A. (1996) 'The Single Market: A New Approach to Policy?', in Wallace, H. and Wallace, W. (eds) *Policy-Making in the European Union*. (Oxford: Oxford University Press).

Waltz, K. (1979) *Theory of International Politics*. (New York: McGraw Hill).

Webber, D. (2001) 'Two Funerals and a Wedding? The Ups and Downs of Regionalism in East Asia and Asia-Pacific after the Asian Crisis'. *The Pacific Review*, Vol. 14, No. 3, pp. 339–372.

Wendt, A. (1999) *A Social Theory of International Politics*. (Cambridge: Cambridge University Press).

Wiener, A. and Diez, T. (2009) (eds) *European Integration Theory*. (Oxford: Oxford University Press).

Wiessala, G. (2006) *Re-orienting the Fundamentals: Human Rights and New Connections in EU-Asia Relations*. (Aldershot: Ashgate).

Wood, S. (2009) 'The European Union: A Normative or Normal Power?'. *European Foreign Affairs Review*, Vol. 14, pp. 113–128.

Wong, K. S. (1991) 'Opening Statement by Wong, Kan Seng, Foreign Minister of Singapore, at the Twenty-Fourth ASEAN Ministerial Meeting, Kuala Lumpur, 19–20 July 1991'. (Singapore Government Press Release No. 38/Jul 09-01/91/07/19).

Wong, R. (2012) 'Model Power or Reference Point? The EU and the ASEAN Charter'. *Cambridge Review of International Affairs*, Vol. 25, No. 4, pp. 669–682.

Working Group for an ASEAN Human Rights Mechanism. (2012) *Working Group for an ASEAN Human Rights Mechanism Website*. Available at: <http://www.aseanhrmech.org/aboutus.html>.

Wunderlich, J.-U. (2007) *Regionalism, Globalisation and International Order: Europe and Southeast Asia*. (Aldershot: Ashgate).

Wunderlich, J.-U. (2012) 'The EU an Actor *Sui Generis*? A Comparison of EU and ASEAN Actorness'. *Journal of Common Market Studies*, Vol. 50, No. 4, pp. 653–669.

Yen, Y-M. (2011) 'The Formation of the ASEAN Intergovernmental Commission on Human Rights: A Protracted Journey'. *Journal of Human Rights*, Vol. 10, No. 3, pp. 393–413.

Youngs, R. (2004) 'Normative Dynamics and Strategic Interests in the EU's External Identity'. *Journal of Common Market Studies*, Vol. 42, No. 2, pp. 415–435.

Youngs, R. (2010) *Europe and the Euro*. Available at: <http://www.theworldtoday.org>.

Zielonka, J. (2008) 'Europe as a Global Actor: Empire by Example?'. *International Affairs*, Vol. 3, pp. 471–484.

Index

K

L

M

N

Made in the USA
Las Vegas, NV
14 November 2024

11642372R10148